APOCALYPSE AND SCIENCE FICTION

American Academy of Religion
Academy Series

Editors
Carl Raschke
William Gravely

Number 40

APOCALYPSE AND SCIENCE FICTION
A Dialectic of Religious and
Secular Soteriologies

by
Frederick A. Kreuziger

Frederick A. Kreuziger

APOCALYPSE AND SCIENCE FICTION
A Dialectic of Religious and Secular Soteriologies

Scholars Press

Published by
Scholars Press
101 Salem Street
P.O. Box 2268
Chico, CA 95927

APOCALYPSE AND SCIENCE FICTION
A Dialectic of Religious
and Secular Soteriologies

by
Frederick A. Kreuziger
Ph.D., 1979, Marquette University
Milwaukee, Wisconsin

Library of Congress Cataloging in Publication Data

Kreuziger, Frederick A.
    Apocalypse and science fiction.

    (American Academy of Religion academy series ;
no. 40)
    (ISSN 0277-1071)
    Bibliography: p.
    Includes index.
    1. Science fiction—Religious aspects—Christianity.
2. Apocalyptic literature. 3. Salvation—History of
doctrines. 4. Salvation in literature. I. Title. II. Series.
PN3433.6.K7   809.3'876   81-21482
ISBN 0-89130-562-9 (Scholars Press)   AACR2

Manufactured in the U.S.A.

TABLE OF CONTENTS

648 66

INTRODUCTION

On the margin of theology and literature there exist
bodies of writings, apocalyptic and science fiction, which
shed light on each other and, in the process, illuminate the
relationship between theology and literature.

It is easy enough to work one way in exploring the
relationship; no great leap need be taken to maintain that
apocalyptic sheds light on science fiction. James Blish,
James Gunn, Fredrick Pohl, and C. S. Lewis, for example--all
science fiction writers themselves--explicitly note the
affinity and the influence. And David Ketterer's book, used
at great length throughout this study, makes the case with
more than adequate force and clarity.

It is not quite so easy to proceed along the opposite
path--to argue that science fiction sheds light on apocalyptic.
Yet if this study is to be a dialectical comparison of
religious and secular soteriologies, precisely this is needed.
This path, then, requires the more explicit treatment and
scrutiny, and is really what the present study is all about.

Chapter One treats of the origins and early self-understanding of science fiction; presenting the case that science
fiction saw itself as the new literature for the new age. It
was consummately involved in fashioning myths situating the
"present" in the grand scheme of things and demanding of
readers a decision or choice. Chapter Two, as somewhat a
counterpoint, traces the critical understanding of science
fiction through the many attempts to appropriate this "new"
literature. Early attempts at genre criticism (science fiction
as romance, utopia, and fantasy) give way eventually to more
sophisticated appreciation of science fiction as philosophical
tale or structural fabulation. But even these, it is argued,
must give way finally to an appreciation of science fiction as
apocalyptic. Apocalyptic, in turn, becomes the genre which
opens both science fiction to a "theological" reading, and
intertestamental/biblical apocalyptic to a "popular" reading.
Chapter Three attempts the beginning of a theological reading

1

through a critique of science fiction as utopia and fantasy.
An appreciation of apocalyptic challenges the reading of
science fiction as extrapolation, the prime example of which
is utopia. Science fiction utopia as plan rather than story
issues in the post-historic era. Also challenged is the
reading of science fiction as fantasy, particularly insofar as
fantasy is characterized by a "willing suspension of disbelief."
Apocalyptic alerts us to the "willingness to believe," that is,
to desirability. Desirability, rather than possibility,
characterizes the nature of story, and finds its purest outlet
in apocalyptic, which is story about the "radically new," the
limit of desire.

The argument thus far proceeds based on assumptions
needing to be explored, both in themselves and in their oper-
ation in the dialectic. The first assumption is that both
apocalyptic and science fiction are best appreciated as popular
literature. This designation is used throughout as a critical
category, not an affirmative one. In the dialectic, then,
science fiction sheds light on apocalyptic by the simple fact
that it reveals apocalyptic as a popular literature. Why is
this important? Because, in Herbert Gans' terms, popular
literature is user-oriented rather than creator-oriented.
Apocalyptic, then, does not so much reveal the writer's
intentions (to dream, fantasize, escape, or inflict his/her
paranoia onto a hapless world) as it reveals the reader's
expectations and hopes. The question to be put to apocalyptic
is not, "What the hell was the writer really trying to say
behind and amid all that imagery and symbolism?" It is rather,
"What did the readers (the people) hope for that could only be
expressed in such outlandish use of images and symbols?" Quite
obviously this hope could not be expressed in terms of "plain
history, real politics and human instrumentality"--to use Paul
D. Hanson's formulation of the prophetic charge. The age of
the prophets in Israel's history was past. At this level
apocalyptic is already a political literature, for it was aware
of a new age already existing, a new configuration of society,
culture, politics and religion. Apocalyptic offers a critique
of prophecy, as well as an expanded horizon for political
activity.

To read apocalyptic in this new sense sheds light, in turn, on the reading of science fiction. For science fiction is also user-oriented, i.e., it reveals the hopes and expectations of the readers. Expectation, thus, is the more fruitful critical category for the study of the relationship between science fiction and apocalyptic. Extrapolation is a creator-oriented category; it focuses too much on the writer's craft. In the study of apocalyptic it issues in preoccupation with predictions about the end-time.

Now the argument proceeds apace. If expectation is the more fruitful critical category, then some serious thinking ought to be done about it. Chapter Four attempts just that. It says simply, "What you expect is mostly a matter of how you expect." This need not sound like some handy axiom to be tossed off in a panic at what advice to give a distraught client or friend. I present it as a philosophical and theological principle for the critical investigation of science fiction, apocalyptic, and indeed of the whole of a bibically grounded hope. I present it as a critical category to be used in the investigation and grounding of a political theology.

In the tension surrounding the pull between future expectation and present response it operates something like this: It is meaningless to speak of the coming of the radically new if *how* one expects it to come about is through a simple unfolding of events dependent upon "human instrumentality." The totally new can only be expected in a totally new manner. The response demanded *in the present* is a new mode of expectation, imminent expectation.

In the world of science fiction this mode of imminent expectation is portrayed in the stories grouped under the rubric of "We are not alone." What these stories tell of, what they re-present is an expectation which leaves behind all rational extrapolation, probability studies, and/or cyclical views of history--even though today rational extrapolation and scientific expertise may be considered a necessary but not sufficient condition for the expectation. *Project UFO* is the example here, along with many of the stories of Arthur C. Clarke. The point is that the expectation, "We are not alone," does not rise out of any existing or extrapolated trends; instead, it gives meaning to and grounds those trends. It is out front of them.

This can perhaps be seen more clearly in the reading of apocalyptic. Would one, for example, seriously read apocalyptic as consisting simply of a rational projection of existing trends, as consisting simply of an attempt to foretell and predict the course of future events--in terms of plain history, real politics, and human instrumentality? Even were one to substitute sacred history, celestial politics, and divine instrumentality (a là Hal Lindsay's *The Late Great Planet Earth*), I suspect the answer remains that this is not what (or even *how*) apocalyptic means.

Then what does it mean? And how does it mean? The questions, I argue, cannot be answered simply in terms of apocalyptic's telling us what to expect. This is not its meaning; for what bearing really would that meaning have on the present, except to reveal that the present is no good at all when held up to the glorious future; or, in dystopian literature, the present is all good when held up against a decadent future. The meaning of apocalyptic, rather, lies in its telling us how to expect. This does bear directly on the present and our living in the present, for it invites us to consider how we respond to moral and political choices arising from the presence of the radically new.

There is, however, a problem in all this; a problem which explains why perhaps apocalyptic is so appalling to many, why it sticks in the throat of technocratic humankind. There is no getting around the fact that apocalyptic, when it speaks of response, speaks of it in terms of a passivity, a passiveness. Waiting is the operative word here, and suffering is its memory. Our usual stories of expectation and response are invariably presented in terms of human activity: we create and are responsible for the future, for posterity. Waiting is rarely seen as being creative; it is rather a barrier, an obstacle. So also is suffering; it is to be forgotten. We have become so accustomed to reading even the Scriptures in this manner that we easily forget (or actively suppress) that the archetypal, the prototypical, "radically new" event in our Christian faith is a raising. There is a passivity, a passiveness existing at the heart of the Christian conception of history.

The typology of the modes of expectation in Chapter Four was fashioned to isolate that one particular mode, imminent, which gives meaning to and affirms the passivity characterizing so much of human life and history. Talk of fate, luck, and chance is one way to do it; but it does not ground sufficiently nor provide a meaningful interpretation of the course of historical events. Imminent expectation does, by transforming expectation and waiting into an openness to the radically new, the coming of which exceeds all hope and yet is grounded in it. The radically new, moreover, is its own control of meaning. It is not specified beforehand; nor can it be interpreted afterward by means of a conjunctive expectation modeled on before/after, so/then, cause/effect, once upon a time/happily ever after structures of narrative causality. A content analysis of the object of expectation (*what* is expected) leaves us precisely nowhere when it comes to determining the meaning of imminent expectation. That meaning begins to reveal itself, however, in the analysis of the temporal structure of narrative; for structure relates precisely to the mode of expectation rather than its content.

Temporal narrative structure now becomes the new element in the dialectic of religious and secular soteriologies. It is the focus of Chapter Five. In order to explore it the recent work of J. B. Metz is introduced. Metz has called for a revival of a "memorative-narrative" soteriology and a re-appropriation of imminent expectation as the ground for a political theology. These two elements, at first appearing disparate, are joined in the examination of how temporal narrative structure reveals the meaning of imminent expectation. In turn, the joining sheds light on the larger problematic of the relationship between emancipation and redemption, contemporary theology's formulation of the critical correlation. How the story is structured in its telling and in its reading is just as important as what the story tells. An explication of the temporal narrative structure is one way of getting at the necessary differentiation between emancipation and redemption. Emancipation is more closely linked to conjunctive modes of expectation (cause/effect, particularly), while redemption is more closely linked with disjunctive (imminent) expectation.

Passivity, particularly in its classic and literal Christian form of *passion*, is the subversive memory grounding hope for the radically new.

I found it interesting, while pursuing this topic and reflecting on my own days in the politics of confrontation in the Church and in society, that Metz links discipleship and imminent expectation. The latter, Metz writes, "does not paralyze political responsibility, but establishes its foundation." This is incredibly difficult to appreciate unless we get beyond what Metz calls the reduction of imminent expectation to constant expectation, and, what I have written of in various passages, the reduction of apocalyptic to a structural principle for action, i.e., spelling out in detail how to destroy the old in order to inaugurate the new. Apocalyptic, I argue, functions as the horizon of political theology; in the literary terms of Northrop Frye it is the "limit of desire." The question here is the relationship between apocalyptic and discipleship. Reducing apocalyptic to withdrawal, escape into infinite subjectivity, or calculated plan to bring down the old established order negates any possibility of correlating apocalyptic and discipleship.

The analysis of the temporal structure of narrative provides needed tools for that correlation. Discipleship in practice is an openness to the radically new as it comes to us in the re-telling of the Christian story. Thus the necessity of a "memorative-narrative" soteriology. Thus also the challenge; for memory undermines the cosmetic story-line of emancipatory history by re-minding us of the (hi)story of suffering told in the stories narrated by the losers, and not found in the stories which the winners tell about them. The story Metz uses for his example is Jesus' descent into hell, the subversive (underground) memory resulting in a "backward solidarity" in redemption as well as a forward one. This "solidarity," finally, is the political dimension of a soteriology which grounds the formulation of a political theology capable of critiquing the totalizing (and incipient totalitarian) emancipatory histories which abound.

Nor does the dialectic end here. The final step is to return to science fiction and read there in its stories about the tension between emancipation and redemption. The tension is symbolized roughly in the stories characterized as "future history" stories (emancipation) and the "We are not alone" stories (redemption). A content analysis alone will not suffice in defending that distinction; one must also employ here the critical categories of expectation, conjunctive and disjunctive.

This is, however, where the study ends. The real, practical critical work remains to be done. I have attempted merely to lay the foundation for that work, some of which I hope to do myself in the years to come. The larger hope is that this foundational study of the relationship between science fiction and apocalyptic will be of value to others. I have concluded the study with areas I consider to be of critical concern.

But let me conclude this introduction with notes of a more personal nature. It seems to me, following upon Moltmann's insistence that hope is the form of faith and not the act of faith, and Metz's discussion of solidarity grounding a political theology, that the critical question needs to be revised. Whereas it is most often asked, both unreflectively and in the deeper reflection of theology, "Can we believe as out brothers and sisters believed in the past and believe in the present?", the question ought to be asked, "Can we hope as they did and do?" The question, that is, concerns how we believe, not what we believe.

For me the revised question leaps out of both apocalyptic and science fiction. It always has. It is due, I think, to the fact that my first *real* acquaintance with apocalyptic and science fiction was with both as popular literature. Not surprisingly, in the case of science fiction; more so, and fortunately so, in the case of apocalyptic. Reflection on this experience more than anything else helped me see the great hope and felt immediacy informing the readers of both apocalyptic and science fiction and giving shape to the world in which they live. Everything in that world is temporally structured according to the vision of that hope. It is the form of their faith, for it structures the course of events, the unfolding of time, the fictions of history, and the immediacy of deciding in the present.

When hope is reduced to an act of faith, solidarity with past and future believers--whether early Christians, scholastic theologians, or even revisionist theologians--is ripped from the fabric of history and becomes too often, in the end, the mere intellectual juggling of concepts and ideas. But when hope is seen as the form of faith, the resulting solidarity politicizes theology because it makes the theologian responsible both to the past and to the future--to all our brothers and sisters.

THE SELF-UNDERSTANDING OF SCIENCE FICTION

> The first step in the recovery of myth is the
> transfer of the center of interest from hero to
> poet...The second, and perhaps final, stage is
> reached when the poet entrusts his work to his
> reader...(for in one sense at least) the reader
> ...is the hero of literature, or at least of
> what he has read. As we have seen, the message
> of all romance is *de te fabula*, the story is
> about you.
>
> --Northrop Frye

Introduction

In the continuing struggle to fashion a definition of
just what science fiction is, one of the more salient characteristics is often dismissed out of hand: science fiction is
a popular literature. As such it submits now to critical study
under conditions which tend to place the critic in a position
similar to that of the reader. For both critic and reader face
the same problem: until very recently, in the scheme of things,
science fiction was a literature by and large unmediated by
critical study. While the usual commentary on the plight of
current science fiction claims that fact is catching up with
fiction (the moon landing, et al.), the more telling and
immediate symptom is that criticism is catching up with writing.
As the corpus of science fiction is submitted to closer and
closer critical scrutiny, more and more is it losing the
characteristic of being a popular literature. That passing
itself must be noted by critical study, or it will fail not
only to assign the proper interpretations to the changes
currently taking place in science fiction, but it will also
fail to understand it in its origins.

In noting this passage Leslie Fiedler speaks of it as
"the breakup of the last organic literary community in the
Western world, inside of which the confrontation of reader and
writer was not mediated by critics" (22). To some older members
of the science fiction establishment that breakup seems an

"unmitigated disaster." Fiedler's characterization of science fiction's golden age and its fandom may ascribe too much to its days of glory; but the overall point is well taken: science fiction was born, grew up, and continues to thrive outside the literary mainstream. Any critical study of science fiction which changes only the writing of science fiction, without changing the reading, will result in the failure of criticism as mediator. Along with the writers who write only for other writers and/or for critics, there will exist the critics who write only for other critics.

The question facing science fiction today is not whether science fiction can become again what it was, but whether it can remain what it always was: a popular literature, read primarily for enjoyment. The further question is whether or not that enjoyment will be destroyed when the literature comes under critical scrutiny. Surely once the critical study of science fiction is undertaken the reading of it will never be the same; but it need not be less enjoyable for that reason.

There will be no attempt here to repeat the work done so thoroughly by other critics, but instead to read that body of critical work in light of the thesis of this chapter: that science fiction is secular apocalyptic literature, and that the self-understanding of early science fiction grounds that contention. The review of critical literature then will not attempt to arrive at a new consensus literary definition of science fiction, nor a consensus history of the phenomenon, but will instead attempt to come up with a consensus description of the self-understanding of early science fiction: how it viewed itself in those days when it was not mediated by critics.

It is more accurate, of course, to say that science fiction was always mediated by some critical understanding. That such critical understanding did not originate in the halls of academe leads more often than not to the dismissal of it as too subjective or simply as irrelevant. But the cost of such outright dismissal must be paid eventually; and the payment is made in the coin of the understanding of popular literature. The understanding of popular literature, in turn, produces no dividends unless investment is made in the self-understanding of popular literature.

In the case of science fiction the coin is in ready supply; for there does exist a significant body of work in the form of editorials in pulp magazines, book reviews, annotated anthologies, popular histories, and autobiographical recollections. Indeed, the writings about science fiction are as popular with the readers as are the stories themselves; and the closer the writer is associated with the science fiction world, the more weight his or her work carries.

The designation of science fiction as a popular literature does not exhaust the critics' concern, however; nor does a critical study of science fiction exhaust the understanding of popular literature. But the understanding of science fiction as a popular literature is where the critical study of science fiction must begin. Much of the following analysis is based on this starting point, particularly as it is developed in Northrop Frye's *The Secular Scripture*, a study of the popular forms of romance. In that book Frye clearly moves beyond the customary isolation of the nature of popular literature as a form of romance by describing it in functional terms: what people read "without guidance from their betters" (1976:15). Earlier Frye had characterized science fiction as "a mode of romance with a strong inherent tendency to myth" (1971:49). His study of the secular scripture builds on that movement of romance toward myth, claiming that there is "no structural principle to prevent the fables of secular literature from also forming a mythology, or even a mythological universe....a single integrated vision of the world, parallel to the Christian and biblical vision" (1976:15). The function of myth for Frye has always been social; it facilitates the entrance into and the maintenance of the social order, without which the fears and anxieties of the individual and society would predominate and overcome. Even if one dismisses popular literature as "silly" social mythology, Frye warns, "a value judgement on the social mythology is likely to be more relevant to criticism than a value judgement on the literary merit" (1976:167). Frye, of course, does not countenance the gradual withering away of judgements on literary merit; nor does this study seek to cast doubt on the validity and value of serious literary critical work.

We have attempted below not only to trace the movement
of romance to myth, but, following Frye's functional description
of popular literature (which shifts the starting point), to
trace the movement of popular literature to apocalyptic, since
apocalyptic as a popular literature is the over-arching
category which provides a needed critical tool for the continuing study of science fiction. Moreover, a critical look at the
self-understanding of early science fiction goes a long way
toward answering the perennial questions of what exactly
science fiction is, when it began, and where it will lead to--
all which necessarily concern the literary critic.

Hugo Gernsback: The Beginnings

The phenomenon we call science fiction is closely linked
with the personage and personality of one Hugo Gernsback. Most
present-day commentators shudder when mention is made of Gernsback; and they go into absolute panic when he is called the
"Father of Science Fiction." Brian Aldiss, for example, begins
his discussion of Gernsback with the statement: "It is easy to
argue that Hugo Gernsback (1884-1967) was one of the worst
disasters ever to hit the science fiction field." And he ends
his discussion with an even more iconoclastic statement: "...
it is very difficult to understand why he should ever have been
spoken of as 'The Father of Science Fiction;' but we have met
enough claimants before to realize that Gernsback was just a
midwife disguised as a Young Pretender" (1974:209-10).
What lies behind this and other very obvious dismissals
of Gernsback is the contention that it was he who tore science
fiction away from the literary mainstream and delivered it over
to the pulps, from which, only in the last decade or so, has it
been able to extricate itself. Few critics who are concerned
with the literary merits of science fiction are willing to for-
give him for that. But Gernsback was not a literary phenomenon;
he was the catalyst who touched off a chain reaction that no
doubt would have happened sooner or later at any rate. There
is a sense in which the Gernsback betrayal was a *felix culpa*;
for it was in the sub-literary world of the pulps that the
social mythology of science fiction was forged and refined,
allowing the succeeding generations of writers to build and

expand on the solid foundations of parsecs, time travel,
galactic empires, hyperspace, robotics, and all the other
consensus literary artifacts of early science fiction. James
Gunn captures some of the flavor of those times when he writes:
"*Amazing Stories* was greeted by readers as the answer to what
had been until then an unrecognized need...It was as if some
forgotten Diaspora had scattered a nation so thoroughly that
not one citizen knew another, but now...each had discovered his
Zion, and they could together in spirit in a new ghetto practice
their forbidden rites" (124).

To recast the metaphor introduced by Gunn: Gernsback
claimed he was going to lead his readers into the promised land,
whereas in reality he led them into the wilderness, where for
forty years, or thereabouts, they wandered, retelling their
stories of promise and hope. The very nature and character of
science fiction will always bear the marks of this journey
through the wilderness; it would be the height of foolishness
and critical suicide to pretend that the Gernsback turn exercised no influence over the self-understanding of science
fiction.

Gernsback, a Luxembourg emigrant, edited and published
a number of pulps before introducing *Amazing Stories* in April
of 1926, the first pulp magazine to be devoted entirely to
science fiction. And what Gernsback intended the magazine to
be is important for the subsequent course of science fiction.
In the editorial of that first issue Gernsback wrote: "*Amazing
Stories* is a *new* kind of fiction magazine. It is entirely new--
entirely different--something that has never been done before
in this country."/1/ What Gernsback states here is perhaps
the foundation of the entire subsequent self-understanding of
early science fiction: Science Fiction is a new thing; it is a
different thing. There is a deliberate invocation here of the
promise of a new age, not just a new thing. Gernsback labeled
the stories he printed "scientifiction;" by which he meant "a
charming romance intermingled with scientific fact and prophetic
vision." This understanding of science fiction as prophecy
colors all subsequent self-understanding of science fiction,
and leads to the later reflective designation of the science
fiction movement as a ghetto, as a cult or sect, as an elect

set apart from the literary, social, and cultural mainstream.
When Gunn, in his consensus history, writes of "visionaries
[dreaming] a better way" (52), and later of the "missionary
spirit" of science fiction which "demands an opportunity to
urge salvation, a change in ethics or morals or religions, a
new way of thinking or a new way of life," (225), he is harking
back to the promise as formulated by Gernsback. And the promise
is that science fiction will become the vehicle through which
humankind will be delivered from the evils of disease, poverty,
and intellectual stagnation. "Posterity," writes Gernsback,
"will point to [the great science fiction stories] as having
blazed a new trail, not only in literature and fiction, but in
progress as well."

Sam Moskowitz, the indefatigable chronicler of science
fiction, is the one who hung the label "Father of Science
Fiction" on Gernsback. It is clear from Moskowitz (if not to
him) that Gernsback was an entrepreneur; he knew what would
sell. But this does not deter Moskowitz from writing that he
was "the real father of science fiction...and no one can take
that title away from him" (1963:242). This is undoubtedly the
case for Moskowitz because, as he writes later, Gernsback
"chafed at the limitations imposed by the state of scientific
progress."

We come, therefore, to a second significant factor in
the self-understanding of early science fiction: imagination
is limitless. This, of course, has always been true of the
understanding of literature; but in a literature purporting to
be prophetic (to tell how things will be) that truth gives rise,
in the end, to the totalitarian nature of the politics of
science fiction. In our day we experience this in terms of the
technological imperative: What can be done must be done. In
the aftermath of this imperative lie the ruins of social life.
But for one who looks only to the future, and to deliverance
in the future, the sight of present evils does not deter. Brian
Ash, writing of the period in which Gernsback launched his many
publications promising the new age, says of him, "apparently he
was undeterred by any...dystopian considerations" (67). The
social problems of the day included the plight of immigrants
(Gernsback himself was one), the rise of labor unrest (which

served as the roots of socialism and militant trade unionism),
and the bloody upheaval known forever after as the Great War.
Ash might have commented, but did not (for he also touts science
fiction as prophetic literature, the readers of which alone are
competent to discuss the possibilities of the future), that for
one to be so blind to present evils suggests a blindness to
future evils.

There is one final element of the self-understanding of
early science fiction to which Gernsback was instrumental in
giving voice: although science fiction was a new thing, it was
a new old thing. In that first editorial Gernsback writes:
"By 'scientifiction' I mean the Jules Verne, H. G. Wells, and
Edgar Allan Poe type of story--a charming romance intermingled
with scientific fact and prophetic vision." Thereby Gernsback
both linked *Amazing Stories* to a past rich in literary tradition,
and proclaimed a "new kind of fiction magazine." It is obvious
that the emphasis is on the magazine; it was to become the
vehicle for progress. The past, in this understanding, becomes
the property of the present, to be used in promoting the future.
In the process, the past becomes something entirely new; its
true meaning and purpose is liberated. The procedure known as
re-interpretation leads to the inclusion of the ancients into
the fellowship of science fiction writers: Plato, Lucian, de
Bergerac, Bacon, Campanella, More, Mary Shelley,Poe, Verne, and
of course, Wells. All are now revealed to have been cryptic
science fiction writers to a greater or lesser degree; although,
as many are quick to point out, the "real" science fiction was
not written until science and technology had become a decisive
and determinative factor in Western civilization.

Finally, Gernsback linked science fiction with the
"charming romance," a liaison discussed earlier in connection
with popular literature. For Moskowitz, the coming of the
scientific romances of Burroughs and his many imitators was the
Babylonian captivity that science fiction had to endure.
"Burroughs turned the entire direction of science fiction from
prophecy and sociology to romantic adventure" (1970:291). What
Burroughs had to offer, according to Moskowitz, was story for
the sake of story; there was no attempt to educate or to preach,
as had been the case with Wells. Moskowitz is well aware of

the trade-off in this transition; and he seems willing to pay
the price. He will deny repeatedly that these stories of
Burroughs were science fiction in the accepted sense of science
fiction's self-understanding; yet he will at the same time
insist that the elements of story telling were features that
science fiction sorely needed. "Always there was a *story*, with
a beginning, a middle, and an end. There was no slice of life,
no grim realism, no character studies, no stream of consciousness, no sermons in the forms of stories or fictionalized
propaganda or promotions. But there was an enveloping human
interest, an extraordinary ingenuity of plot, far-reaching
imagination, a romantic view of life, slapstick humor, limitless variety, and true escapism" (308).

It is the escapist function of the scientific romance
that Moskowitz cannot come to grips with. Indeed, this is a
problem that continues to plague the self-understanding of
science fiction down through the years. Because of his lack of
critical tools, Moskowitz is at a loss how to incorporate the
scientific romance into the ancestry of science fiction. He
resorts to claiming that the meaning of the word "romance"
underwent a change sometime around the year 1912, which happens
to be the time at which Burroughs rose in favor. Romance was
transformed from an adventurous tale into a love story (335-36).
In other words, Moskowitz wants it both ways: Burroughs both
broadened the base of interest in science fiction (i.e., created
the audience), and at the same time changed the meaning of
term scientific romance. It was necessary, therefore, only
that Gernsback re-establish the link with the earlier form of
the scientific romances of Poe, Verne, and Wells, and move
science fiction back into the mainstream of a literature preaching the wonders of science, the unlimited nature of the imagination, and the destiny of humankind to overcome all obstacles--
all told in adventurous tales, peopled with heroes with which
the reader could identify, and distinct from other escape in
that such a tale eased "'the willing suspension of disbelief'...
by utilizing an atmosphere of scientific credibility" (1963:11).
'Scientific credibility,' in this understanding, becomes the
hallmark of true science fiction, witnessed to by Gernsback's
prerequisite for "scientific fact and prophetic vision." Thus,

the new old thing that Gernsback reincarnated in his magazine is the vision that humankind is the measure of all things, past and to come. Wherever one finds that vision, there one finds the precursors of science fiction.

In conclusion, while one may argue that Gernsback exercised little influence over the writing of science fiction, one cannot dismiss the fact that he exercised considerable influence over the self-understanding of early science fiction. Indeed, he set the parameters within which science fiction is still discussed today by those who concern themselves with more than its literary form. Gernsback stressed the prophetic and predictive nature of science fiction, and the characterization has endured to this very day, although becoming more sophisticated and nuanced in its understanding. Closely allied to this characterization of science fiction as prophetic is the claim that it is distinguished from fantasy in that it is based on "real" science, as opposed to pseudo-science.

This second claim in turn leads to a discussion of John W. Campbell, Jr., the second major influence on the self-understanding of science fiction, and a man in whom the boundaries separating real science from pseudo-science become blurred almost beyond recognition. Campbell, in short, raises the questions of what exactly is the role of imagination in real science, where does the "passive" observer end and the "passionate" believer begin, and how indeed can science fiction be reconciled with real science?

John E. Campbell, Jr. :
Full-Blown Science Fiction

John W. Campbell, Jr. is surely one of the giants of the science fiction world. Remembered mostly for his editorship of *Astounding* magazine (later known as *Analog*) from 1938 to 1971, it is often passed over that he began as a science fiction writer, first of galactic sagas rivalling the Doc Smith extravaganzas, and then of what later became known as "social science fiction," which treated more the effects of science on humankind. "Twilight" is perhaps his most often cited and anthologized story in this new vein. It tells of the twilight of the human race, when humankind courts extinction because its curiosity dies. The tale is told by a man who time-travels far into that future, and whose reminiscences conclude: "Can you appreciate the crushing hopelessness it brought to me? I, who love science, who see in it, or have seen in it, the salvation, the raising of mankind--to see those wondrous machines of man's triumphant maturity, forgotten and misunderstood. The wondrous perfect machines that tended, protected, and cared for those gentle, kindly people who had--forgotten." It is the galactic empire of the Enlightenment which has fallen here; the intellectual universe has failed, destroyed by lethargy, passiveness and acquiescence to the luxuries of the comfortable life. Campbell succeeded in transferring the battleground from the outer space of the galaxy to the inner space of the mind. His fight was ever against the accepted, the fashionable, the current, the dogmas of society, church, and the scientific establishment.

Campbell is widely acclaimed for his intellectual bent, and for the high standards he set during his editorial reign at *Astounding*. He was insistent that science fiction display good writing; the gadget era was to be left behind once and for all. James Gunn says of him that during those early years he was forming a community "that was now developing a consciousness of mission and a consensus about how to write science fiction" (60). The canon, according to which Campbell judged the worth of a story, included: scientific accuracy, logical development, askew viewpoints and novel propositions (more often these two are included under the title: thought-variant), and narrative skill.

Campbell's influence on writers was enormous. Harry Harrison, in the introduction to Campbell's *Collected Editorials from Analog*, writes: "The number of books that have been dedicated to him gives evidence of this...At a guess I would say there are at least thirty, a record that I am sure is unique in literature" (1966:vi). But his influence on the self-understanding of science fiction has been even greater. For Campbell succeeded not only in changing the writing of science fiction, he also changed the reading of it. Donald Wollheim, himself a writer and editor of science fiction, gives more credit to the Campbell editorials than to the editing. Although

Wollheim finds much to argue with in their content, still he
says they were "his workshop, his laboratory, his platform for
glory." Campbell was frustrated in his inability to participate
as a scientist in the science boom after World War II, so he
fashioned his own platform from which to work for the better-
ment of humankind (74-76). Wollheim's assessment of the
motivation of Campbell does not differ significantly from what
James Gunn sees behind the Campbell phenomenon: "He was the
prototype for the precocious youngster who turns to science
fiction to make up for his own social inadequacies, who makes
science fiction a career or a religion because reality is both
disappointing and dull" (146).

What this suggests is that Campbell was influential
because he was a man of ideas. The self-understanding of
science fiction from Campbell on was of science fiction as a
literature of ideas. Hardly a science fiction writer who re-
calls Campbell does so without mentioning the 'ideas' of
Campbell. Asimov admires this "opinionated man [for his] out-
rageous ideas" (1972:6); Aldiss says of him, "he was one of the
field's intellectuals. He had strong ideas, some of them
erroneous" (1974:225). Blish writes that Campbell saw himself
as an "educator" who selected stories often because they "act
out his editorials in story form" (86n).

When we turn to those editorials, especially those
selected by Harrison in *Collected Editorials from Analog*, we
find only one editorial that deals specifically with science
fiction. The remainder discuss the 'ideas' of Campbell about
the nature of humankind, the universe, society, science, and
various other topics of current concern. In his introduction
Harrison writes: "Campbell is always happiest when far out on
a limb, and a good number of his editorials have been prognosti-
cative. Very often the prophecy has been right" (viii). He
then cites two examples: atomic energy and the hydrogen bomb.
Neither the number nor the nature of the predictions establishes
Campbell as a prophet. What Harrison is trying to do is establish the credibility of Campbell despite Campbell's flirtations
with the pseudo-science of his day. Thus Harrison dismisses,
as belonging to another class (not prophecy), Campbell's
discussion of the Dean drive (an inertia-less device), Dianetics,

Charles Forte, and the psi-machines, saying that Campbell merely wrote about them, defending their right to be discussed.

Whether or not Campbell did in fact espouse the above mentioned pseudo-scientific theories and/or devices may be legitimately disputed. But what is beyond dispute, reading through the Harrison collection, is that Campbell was a bigot, a racist, a sexist, a person caught up in the biases and prejudices of his own time and his own mind. Harrison and others tout highly Campbell's championing of new ideas, his belief in the future and in the invincibility of humankind. All in all, Campbell is pictured as a man who stood at the height of intellectual endeavor. "The cause he supported--with blasts on the trumpet and salvos of artillery--was the right for controversial ideas to see print and be considered by authorities" (1966:viii). In short, Harrison claims, Campbell forces one to think. A closer look at the editorials, however, reveals just how 'new' Campbell's ideas are:

- Experimentation on humans cannot be legally or morally stopped because life is not sacred; it is expendable for cause. Only scientific reasons for stopping this experimentation are valid.

- Segregation according to intelligence is needed, for *de facto* whites are of superior intelligence. The *U.S. vs. Brown* decision should not be interpreted to prohibit segregation according to I.Q.

- Bleeding heart liberals would have us believe that all men are equal, when it is obvious that the poor are not equal to the rest of us in many ways.

- All that humankind ever needs in the way of cheap raw materials is available in the asteroid belt. All we need do is set up the machinery to smelt them down through the use of solar energy.

- Science and technology will make readily available all that science fiction "dreams" about.

- Capitalism by any other name is still capitalism, and the best economic system for the production of the largest amount of goods.

- Once we strictly define our terms (which will be necessary with the advent of computer translating machines)

75 percent of all human problems will be solved.

  - The only real problem for utopia is determining how the leaders are to be chosen. Since the "best" people always rise to the top of the income scale (prostitutes would be included), income alone should determine who has the right to vote.

  - Intelligence and the societal level of "natives" are what determines the type of rule imposed by colonists. That is, where tribes have been wantonly slaughtered by colonists, one can deduce that the natives were unable to assimilate or cope with the high level of civilization introduced.

  - Some races are superior. Law reduces men to equals; and so society based on a rule of law is a false goal--unless that law be scientific law, for then it is absolute.

Wollheim alone appears to be the iconoclast in his final assessment of Campbell: "What emerged from [the editorials] was a series of glib, logical sounding, very scientifically worded and able literary lectures to his readers about how there were really superior and inferior people, about the idiocy of tampering with the profit motive, of the value of greed as a driving mechanism, of the inevitability and desirability of war as a natural outlet for a naturally aggressive race, of the superiority of the U.S. over all other countries and forms of government, well--the gamut" (78). Lest one thinks that Wollheim has seen through Campbell completely however, it should be pointed out that Wollheim espouses the same beliefs in the invincibility of humankind, the inevitability of progress, and the salvific nature of science. Wollheim's quarrel with Campbell is more personal than ideological.

Ideologically, Campbell is caught up in the dialectic of Enlightenment, especially as it devolves to the structuring of society. He is both dogmatic and libertarian at the same time. He is caught in the dilemma of the need for absolutes and the necessity for change, with no adequate philosophical tools available to mediate between the two. In the matter of formulating a philosophy of science Campbell comes down heavy on the need for absolutes. He writes: "the whole progress of science has centered around the area where there are Absolutes--the areas where no man has a right to his own opinion." This accounts for the almost insignificant gains made in the social

sciences of psychology, sociology and anthropology, for example.
Campbell continues: "The progress has all been made in those
areas where dear old Mother Nature took a club to Man's thick
skull and said, in effect, '...your opinion on the matter is
completely unimportant.'" The only control of meaning and of
truth, for Campbell, in this side of his thinking, is the
objectively observable and measureable fact. "If we've got a
relativistic universe, with no absolutes in it, then I can play
deuces-wild with the units. You start being relativistic, and
I'll relativistic you right out of business. I'll make as much
a mess of your science as the humanic scientists have made out
of theirs. All I need is the right to make my choice of units
purely a matter of personal preference." These passages are
from a 1954 editorial (1966:112-114).

However, there is another side to Campbell's thinking
about science and the scientific method. In a 1964 editorial
on krebiozen (the sixties' version of laetrile and the search
for a cancer cure) Campbell is wrestling with the nature of the
scientific method and finds it, ultimately, impossible to reconcile the possession of the known facts with the innate desire
to know more--about life, the universe, humankind, whatever the
object of intellectual desire. Nor does Campbell know what to
do with the emotions, the feelings of the scientist. In writing of medicine and the doctor, for example, Campbell offers
the two usual descriptions: the doctor as trustworthy, sympathetic and concerned; and the doctor as scientifically trained,
skilled, intelligent and objective. "Look at those two ideals
carefully--and you'll see at once that they are mutually
exclusive....Strangely, a doctor could be more accurate in his
evaluation when treating a man he despised than in treating his
own wife or child" (1966:123). Still later in discussing the
relation of science and religion, the dichotomy appears from a
slightly different perspective. Science, as we know, is objective,
experimentally verifiable, cool, detached knowledge of reality.
Religion, on the other hand, concerns itself with the "non-
material side of life", it is "rooted in belief rather than
objective evidence", and "deals almost entirely with Man's
emotional and moral structure" (1966:223). Hence science not
only determines the knowledge, but also the object of knowledge.

Campbell, of course, does not know it, but his secular
religion of scientism shows through in much of his writing.
What Campbell writes about are the longings and desires which
shaped and formed his life. His ideas are scarcely more than
wishes. Because Campbell cannot reconcile in himself the
emotions and beliefs continually pushing him beyond the limits
not only of scientific fact, but also of scientific theory, he
states in many ways at many times that they are mutually
exclusive. His wishes, in turn, become the new theory; but
these theories do not explain the facts, as he insists, they
reveal the desires that lie deep in his heart. The desires
take two forms: the first is to prevent theory from fouling
up practice; evidenced by Campbell's rejection of equality,
democracy, philosopher-kings, equal opportunity--all as unwork-
able theories. The second desire is to reduce, ultimately,
even the subjective to the objective. "We must *study psi*," he
writes, "because it is the only objective, observable set of
phenomena stemming from subjective forces" (1966:225).

These dreams Campbell left to science fiction are the
controlling influences. When we consult Campbell's lengthiest
treatment of the place of science fiction in the modern world,
we find the same themes emerging and the same understanding of
science informing it. "Science should be recognized for what
it is: mankind's rebellion against the world as it is. Science
is an effort to make the world become what the idealist wishes
it were." At the same time Campbell insists that science is
value-free; its only concern is with what works. Science,
according to him, "is magic that works." And fiction, particularly science fiction, is to be at the service of science:
"Fiction is simply dreams written out; science fiction consists
of the hope and dreams and fears...of a technologically based
society." The specific function of science fiction is to be a
"means of practicing out in a no-practice area" (1953:5-17).
No matter the "desires, ardent wishes, and great human need,"
the physical scientist cannot achieve from substances results
other than what they are destined by their own nature to produce. But the science fiction writer can; he can do anything
he wants to. This is the great advantage and the destiny of
science fiction.

Science fiction, through Campbell, moves into politics and the manipulation of the masses, always imaginatively, to be sure, and through the most benign and altruistic of motives. Fed by the science boom every facet of life came under the gaze of the idealistic technologist, from love-making to language, from recreation to religion. The "willing suspension of disbelief" was made easy not by solid scientific grounding, but rather by unbounded scientific imagination and belief, in other words, by a faith that science and technology could deliver the goods, because it is a magic that works. Such is the legacy that Campbell left to the self-understanding of science fiction.

Science Fiction as Apocalyptic: The Final Phase

Campbell writes in his major essay on the place of science fiction in the modern world that at the present time it is "only about twenty-five years old as a self-aware system of literature" (1953:12). Thus he dates the self-understanding of science fiction to the early Gernsback pulp days. His own editorial on science fiction, reprinted in *Collected Editorials*, dates from 1959, while the essay in Bretnor was published in 1953. It is in this crucial 25-30 year period that the foundations of the self-understanding of science fiction were formed. Subsequent understanding and critical work goes far beyond the parameters laid down by those two figureheads, and sometimes directly controverts their claims. These later attempts to describe the nature of science fiction come down almost exclusively on the literary features of science fiction. But a look at the self-understanding of science fiction necessitates the inclusion of many other factors and dimensions into that description. Early science fiction not only cut itself off from the literary mainstream, it cut itself off from the social and cultural mainstream as well. A category which is both literary and social is needed to critique this early self-understanding of science fiction. Popular culture is simply too wide; popular literature narrows the focus, but still leaves us with no critical tools with which to confront specific themes and content of science fiction. The following synthesis will utilize apocalyptic as the type of popular literature

toward which the self-understanding of science fiction tends.
Apocalyptic allows for the study of science fiction precisely
in its wider understanding as a social movement cut off from
the mainstream, while also allowing for a literary analysis of
its works. In order for its designation as apocalyptic to hold
up under critical scrutiny, a systematic analysis of the themes,
purposes, preoccupations, and tendencies of science fiction
will be made, based on the self-understanding of science fiction
displayed by its writers, editors, readers and fans. Many of
the writings date from that critical 25-30 year period; but all
of them, to some degree or other, recall those days and use
that time period as the basis for their understanding of science
fiction.

A. Science Fiction's Ties with Romance

Gernsback's appreciation of romance is quite different
than the appreciation of romance in Frye, for example, or in
Richard Chase. Gernsback works out of the pulps where romance
is an adventurous tale, a fascinating story, a framework into
which to insert instruction and preaching. He says of the type
of story he was publishing: "They supply knowledge that we
might not otherwise obtain--and they supply it in a very palatable form."

Since science fiction needs the story, but cannot abide
by the use of story for the purposes of escape, it is caught in
a dilemma. According to Gernsback's understanding of science
fiction, therefore, there is a need to preach, a need to in-
struct; the doing of which resolves the dilemma. This internal
contradiction in the very self-understanding of science fiction
accounts for the fact that those who read it regularly and with
enjoyment defend it vigorously as a relevant, non-escape literature; and those who dabble in it infrequently look down on it
as a vehicle of escape and wish-fulfillment. Both readings are
there, however.

The early self-understanding of science fiction laid its
emphasis on the instruction and the idea presented *by means of*
the story. Gernsback and Campbell are only the initiators of a
long line of critics who point to the facts conveyed, theories
proven and predictions come true--and conclude that this is

what science fiction is really about. What few of them seem to realize, however, is that the notion of escape is inherent in the very nature and structure of romance. And that this "escape" has its positive functions, as later critics will elucidate; whether that be mythic displacement, cognitive estrangement, or the ultimate view of all life as story./2/

Early science fiction wrestled with this problem, when it called itself a literature of ideas; for then it was escape into the world of ideas. There is no referent to which the story points, other than the ideas the author has about the way he or she wishes and/or believes the world to be. This leaves science fiction wide open to the pseudo-scientific, the authoritarian bent of its politics, and the tendency toward the wholesale re-interpretation of history according to its narrow visions--past and future history. More specifically, the romance dimension of science fiction evolves into the mythopoeic endeavors, as Frye intimates happens. This is not always to its detriment. For myth is a totalizing process; it seeks to incorporate all of meaning into itself; it is a self-sufficient world. And the closer science fiction comes to that (in *Dune* and *The Left Hand of Darkness*, for example), the closer it comes to the height of literary achievement.

The early pulps, unfortunately, did not foster the creation of truly literary worlds. They had to make do with the romance of ideas, particularly of scientific ideas, and the romance of progress. The sentiments of Gunn sum up the feeling: "As the nineteenth century became the twentieth, the United States was ready for progress and the romance of progress and for the fiction that sum up those dreams as meaningful human adventures" (102). But these were also romances of the future, for the future had become the most exciting idea of all: "The delightful, thrilling future in store for us through scientific progress" (116). What British and continental writers had left behind, namely the scientific romance, the pulps had taken up, because the vehicle suited its purposes: the proselytizing of the masses.

B. The Pulp Magazines and the Hack Writers

Gernsback's claim that his magazine was a "new kind" of
magazine, "something that has never been done before in this
country," contributed to the understanding of science fiction
as a system of literature set apart from other literature. It
is prophetic, instructive, and based on real science. This
self-understanding led to the conviction that the science
fiction pulp was not like other pulps. Damon Knight, one of
the earliest critics, writes that the "science fantasy addicts
ordinarily shun other forms of pulp fiction as the plague" (37).
This ghetto mentality further encouraged the writer to produce
for the market that was there, no matter the literary quality
or style. In the pulp world the writer and reader are locked
into a relationship early writers and critics have labeled as
being unmediated by criticism. We have seen, in fact, that it
was highly mediated, by the editors of those magazines, their
choice of story, and the payment schedule. No writer of any
worth could work (for long) under such conditions. It was
necessary, therefore, to introduce a means of compensation for
the writer, that is, payment other than monetary. The solution
was the letter columns and the popularity polls conducted each
month. Some critics claim for these that they filled a highly
valuable feed-back function; but others counter that it was the
clearest example of indulging in power fantasy of science
fiction. The comments of readers and the monthly polls were
the only criticism available to the hack writer. And he or she
had to accept it, or even subsistence pay was cut off.

This type of critical mediation did little to promote
the literary worth of early science fiction. It merely reinforced the self-understanding of early science fiction as a good
story and/or an exciting idea, the most successful work being
one that combined the two. The role of the editor became even
more pronounced in this situation, for he had control not only
over the stories to be printed, but also over the letters.
Blish is particularly critical of Campbell in this regard, for
having destroyed any value of the critical feed-back function
of the letters, and appropriating them for his own uses: to
discuss his ideas (34).

Alfred Bester, one of science fiction's most notable stylists, critically assesses the plight of science fiction for having fallen into the hands of the pulp writer, claiming that with this the "great decline" set in. "Science fiction began to reflect the inwardness of the hack writer, and the essence of the hack writer is that he has no inwardness. He has no contact with reality, no sense of dramatic proportion, no principles of human behavior, no eye for truth" (82).

C. Early Science Fiction and Utopian Literature

To later critics science fiction has a peculiar and readily seen affinity to utopian literature. Such is not the case with the self-understanding of early science fiction. In fact, early science fiction is noticeable for its overt rejection of any connection, despite the fact that Gernsback's *Amazing Stories* reprinted a large number of the works of H. G. Wells, well-noted for having spawned the utopian (and dystopian) revival in British and continental writers. Even when reference is later made, by Moskowitz and others, to ancient utopian literature (Plato, More, Bacon, Campanella) as a precursor of modern science fiction, the legitimating factor is its "speculative" nature and/or its (pseudo-)scientific basis which eases the reader into a willing suspension of disbelief. Such an appropriation of utopian literature by science fiction betrays a critical lack of knowledge of the tradition in Western civilization, and further isolates science fiction from the mainstream.

But it is not only literary ignorance that contributes to this turn of events. It is the very nature of early science fiction that dictates what is to be the understanding of itself vis-a-vis the tradition of utopian literature. Utopia was traditionally too political for science fiction to appreciate and to assimilate in the beginning. The understanding of the world and society in utopia is in terms of politics and social organization. Science fiction, however, was premised on a new knowledge, a new understanding of the world and society. There was no concern, for all practical purposes, with how society was structured, nor what kind of government ruled (be it democracy, aristocracy, oligarchy, or even a totalitarian

regime). What mattered was the scientific premises on which
that government was based and through which it was legitimated.

When Campbell finally got around to discussing utopia
at length (in *Analog*, May 1961), the desirability and possibility of working toward such an "optimum culture" was a given;
the only problem was how that society was to be "engineered"
(1966:182). And the engineering problem resolved, in turn, to
selecting a "non-theoretical-rational test for selecting a
minority group of people who will be, with high reliability,
relatively wise, benevolent, and competent" (189). The test
entailed the ability to earn income, by whatever means.

One may argue the point with Campbell, but only at the
risk of granting his foundational premise: that utopia is to
be attained through engineering. Campbell bases his questioning of politics and political life on scientific principles:
"God is not democratic," which means that the scientist must be
authoritarian, since there are immutable laws which "partake,
remarkably, of the characteristics ascribed by Theology to the
will of God" (247). Another scientific principle is that
intelligence is not equally distributed, as has been determined
by scientific testing, and so it is permissible to view the
white race as superior and structure society accordingly, and so
on. Scientific knowledge, in this understanding of science
fiction, is the highest form of knowledge, and stands in judgment over any other form, be it personal, social, theological,
or political. Utopian literature, therefore, only becomes the
proper concern and matter of science fiction when one can
scientifically pronounce on structuring human society to
achieve the optimum culture.

James Gunn allows that utopias are "allied genres which
sometimes overlap science fiction." But, he continues, "They
differ from science fiction in what they are about and that
what they say about it refers to something else, usually something contemporary, that they wish to criticize or praise, and
almost always to the detriment of the story's versimilitude or
appearance of reality." For Gunn the referent of the science
fiction story is the future: "The science fiction future is
important for its own sake" (145). The future, for Gunn, is
timeless and absolute; it is as real as the absolute laws of

science are real for Campbell. Any attempt to write socially
oriented science fiction, relevant to contemporary concerns, is
an exercise in what can only be called fantasy in the derogatory
sense. Wollheim calls it exactly that, a "Pollyana Utopianism,"
which is nothing more than a "literature of heroic fantasy"
(108).

Two problems are immediately raised through such a self-
understanding of science fiction utopian literature. The first
is such an understanding reinforces the tendency of science
fiction to be concerned with the masses and not with the
individual person./3/ This concern of itself is not the grounds
for critical rejection. But when that concern for the masses
is inherently manipulative (Campbell's word is "engineering"),
then the concern is no longer really for the masses, but for
the control that one has over them. The second problem flows
from the first: When the concern for the masses reduces to
concern over how to control the masses, there is no longer any
satirical or critical function that can be exercised by that
kind of literature.

The early self-understanding of science fiction, then,
did not include at the beginning an acceptance of itself as
utopian literature, in the sense that that literature is
critical of and/or satirizes contemporary society. The prophetic visions of science fiction would not allow for such near-
sighted goals; its sights were set on the future, which alone
was real and which was possible only if humankind did not become
mired in present-day problems.

D. Science Fiction as a Literature of Ideas

At the heart of science fiction's early self-understanding was its contention that it was a literature of ideas,
including the idea of the future which it sometimes seemed to
claim to have discovered. That such a self-understanding should
lead us to the heart of our claim that science fiction is an
apocalyptic literature is evidenced by this striking passage in
Gunn:

> Earlier writers had focused on technology itself, upon
> broad social patterns, upon invention, upon adventure.
> In the Thirties main-current science fiction writers
> began to narrow their aim to a single idea and the

consequences of an idea carried out in its purest form
to its ultimate outcome. In one sense science fiction
became a Platonic fiction dealing with the ideals,
even in characterization, of which the physical representations we see around us are only imperfect copies;
in another sense [it became] eschatological fiction
dealing with the last or final things (214).

This is perhaps the clearest statement of what a literature of
ideas ultimately implies: the creation of an ideal world more
real than the one presently experienced; and the perception
that history, in the end, swallows up everything, even the
cosmos. Gunn puts his finger on a remarkable shift in the
science fiction world. For some writers the romance would be
left behind once and for all, even the romance of ideas. The
literature would become for them a philosophical meditation on
the place and role of Humankind in the universe; and for some
few, notably Olaf Stapledon and Arthur C. Clarke, a meditation
on the cosmos itself. The idea becomes the vision in which is
seen all of space and time, from primal matter to the final
extinction of the last star.

Isaac Asimov describes his early attraction to science
fiction in terms of responding more to the "ideas" than to the
"language and construction." And the idea most fascinating to
him is "the tantalizing glimpse of possible immortality and a
vision of the world's sad death" (1974:64). What both Gunn and
Asimov witness to is the fact that the "plausibility structure"
of the new apocalyptic literature is the idea (grounded in
scientific knowledge), rather than the dream or the hallucin-
atory vision. The "single idea and the consequences carried
out in its purest form to its ultimate outcome" is more believable to the modern reader than is the dream or vision of the
prophet.

Just how strongly engrained is this understanding of
science fiction as a literature of ideas is attested to by the
concern those writers who came up through the movement express
over the direction modern science fiction is taking. The com-
plaint is voiced that it is too literary. Moskowitz suggests
that science fiction has turned to the "documentary" and to
"suave writing." The latter has "rinsed out" the sense of
wonder; the former has "diluted" it. Neither gives room for
the imagination. His final plea is that science fiction

"assume the role it is best suited for: the dramatic presentation of *new* scientific concepts and the social, psychological,
and philosophical consequences of those ideas" (1963:350).
James Gunn details the concern of the modern writer with
character, language, and technique, all of which will stand
him or her in better stead with the mainstream readers and
critics. But, he warns, "Science fiction writers might be
cautioned not to sell their birthright for a mess of pottage,
not to sacrifice the concern for the idea that made science
fiction distinctive and relevant" (239).

It is the idea, then, that sets science fiction apart
from the rest of literature. But it is a particular kind of
idea. What fascinates is the scientific idea, or the idea that
can be understood scientifically. In the end, it is the very
(act of) understanding which provides the greatest sense of
wonder. Such is the lesson of Campbell's story, "Twilight,"
in which the narrator laments the loss of "curiosity" of the
human race. It is summed up quite adequately in Ben Bova's
statement: "The essence of the scientific attitude is that the
human mind can succeed in understanding the universe" (12).
There is nothing in space or in time that is beyond humankind's
grasp.

E. The Cultic/Sectarian Nature of Early Science Fiction

In light of the above self-understanding it is not
surprising that science fiction readers saw themselves as a
highly select group of individuals, set apart from the rest of
society. To the science fiction world belonged those who knew,
those who saw, those who dreamed, hoped, desired, believed in
the future with a passionate intensity which could only be
called apocalyptic. For their deep longings revealed the
future to them.

These early followers would willingly suffer the scorn
and derision of fellow humankind; and they would band together
even more tightly in the face of it. Their rejection became
the badge they wore proudly. Every scientific breakthrough in
succeeding years became another fulfillment of their prophetic
cryings in the wilderness, no matter the questions about the
humaneness, the legality, the appropriateness, or the morality

of those breakthroughs. The universally favorite example,
cited by almost every critic of the movement, is the detonation
of the atom bomb in 1945. Understood in terms of the self-
understanding of science fiction this was a sign that it was in
the know and could accurately predict the technological marvels
waiting for everyone in the glorious future. No matter that
detonating the bomb and developing nuclear energy are qualita-
tively different matters. Campbell is not dismayed that this
"practicing out" has been carried over into reality, with
effects even he could not imagine. He says simply that the
bomb proved science fiction was not "kidding" (1966:228).
Isaac Asimov writes that "the dropping of the atomic bomb in
1945 made science fiction respectable" (1969:99). Such opinions
and evaluations of one of the most inhumane, morally questionable, strategically unnecessary, and politically damaging acts
in human history could only have come from a movement with
something at stake in the outcome. In short, from a cult or
sect able to interpret events in the light of a system of
beliefs about human nature, history, and destiny. These beliefs
say in effect what Campbell writes in fact: "Human life is *not*
sacred; it is expendable for cause. The Universe doesn't hold
it sacred, quite obviously; if we do, we're unrealistic--which
means essentially, 'neurotic'" (1966:3).

The following brief compilation of what science fiction
writers and/or editors say about their association with science
fiction, and how they understood the movement, gives further
backing to the designation of this movement as a cult or sect.

Donald A. Wollheim, now one of the giants in the science
fiction publishing field, writes: "I was of that pioneering
group, the fanatical science-fiction fandom of the Thirties,
who had believed when others scoffed...in consequence a very
much beleaguered group. Our lives tended to be bent toward each
other, our world was a microcosm of our own lives, and we lived
in an atmosphere of infinite horizons that could not be commu-
nicated to most of the grim and haunted world of the Depression
around us" (2). Wollheim is one of the few critics who pays
any attention to the fact that the rise of science fiction and
the Depression were contemporaneous. Among most others it
seems to pass unnoticed.

What Wollheim says about the writer of science fiction
James Gunn says about the reader, the fan:

> At one time the alienated were a minority which turned
> to science fiction magazines in desperation to find a
> world which accepted them and a world they could accept,
> which was more exciting and more satisfying than the
> reality around them. Now the alienated are a substan-
> tial minority if not yet a majority--a subculture which
> finds in science fiction a banner to rally under...a
> missionary spirit for justice, individual merit, and
> ecology" (223).

But Gunn's assessment of the science fiction writer is much
more favorable and revealing: "Science fiction became a refuge
and a mission. Science fiction writers were the missionaries:
they worked in strange lands, they were underpaid, and they
preached salvation and a better world" (1974:188). The preaching, however, is in a language only the initiated could understand and appreciate. Yet this is necessary for the mystique
of the cult: "the possession of arcane knowledge, like that
of a secret society or lodge, which becomes reinforced by the
creation and evolution of a secret language, a jargon, a cant"
(182).

The relationship between writer and reader in this cult
took on many overtones. Moskowitz revealingly describes one of
them: "'Doc' Smith was a father image to thousands of science-
fiction readers and he regarded them with a benign paternalism
that implied he regarded them as his children" (1966:22). Such
a relationship itself comes close to bordering on the neurotic;
and in this regard Norman Spinrad speaks of the cultic intensity of the early fans (addicts, he calls them) and the
messianic fervor of some of the early writers and editors. By
the end of World War II, he writes, science fiction was "primarily being written by cult writers who led lives circumscribed
by the subculture of their own groupies. In fact, the groupies
were becoming writers. The literary world at large held science
fiction in contempt, and the feeling was quite mutual" (iii).
What Spinrad goes on to explore is how this in-breeding led
inevitably to solutions to political problems which at best
could be called questionable, at worst fascist and totalitarian.
Both writer and reader were on a power-trip, and neither in the
end were capable of standing at any critical distance from the

literary work.

Moskowitz also is unable to look critically at science
fiction. When, for example, he talks about religion and science
fiction, he is incapable of entertaining the possibility that
science fiction as a whole might be construed as a religious
literature. Thus he can write about some science fiction being
used by fringe religious groups "as a proselytizing and propa-
gandizing medium, as a means for reinforcing the will of those
of little faith or for seducing the undecided into the fold"
(1976:3). Never once does he allude to the fact that he himself, as well as countless other science fiction writers, has
used the same language to describe science fiction: it is
prophetic, instructive and the herald of the new age.

For the critic outside the fold, however, it is obvious
who comprises the fans of science fiction. W. S. Baring-Gould
quotes Thomas S. Gardner, writing in a New York fanzine:

> A great many [of the readers of *Amazing Stories*] harbor
> seriously delusions of ancient civilizations superior
> to ours, believe in pyramidology and the like...In fact,
> these groups are in a way semi-religious, since their
> members have stated that they are not interested in
> learning anything which would change their beliefs (286).

S. E. Finer, writing in the *Sociological Review*, maintains that
what sets science fiction apart is that it is made "plausible
by putting its trust in a new popular faith." He continues,
"This faith [is] as widespread and as excited as ever were the
beliefs in the supernatural or the infinite wonders of the New
World" (243). It consists, he argues, in the ability of science
and technology to deliver what it promises. Moreover, as Walter
Hirsch, another sociologist who studies the science fiction
phenomenon, points out, such a 'faith' cannot be maintained
unless there is an institutional means of instruction and
reinforcement. The editorials, the letter columns, and the
loosely organized fan organizations fill this function; and
together, Hirsch argues, they "partake of the nature of the
cult" (508).

F. Science Fiction and Authoritarian Politics

We have commented at various times above on the tendency
of science fiction to dramatize authoritarian politics. Such a
bent flows partly from the nature of the narrative structure,

that is, from science fiction's dependency on the romance and
the romantic hero. The heroic protagonist, adventurer or
scientist, discovers the secret means to deliver the world from
slavery, disease, poverty, and/or political stagnation. Partly
it originates from the shift in science fiction which makes the
idea the heroic figure. The vision of scientific understanding
and management of social and political affairs leads to the
establishment of a monolithic organization that will provide
for the needs of all for all times. And partly it is based in
the very nature of the science fiction movement as a cult or
sect, wherein writer and reader are locked in the embrace of a
power fantasy which overwhelms all rational and humane restraints.

The first two aspects of this tendency have been treated
sufficiently in literary and sociological analyses of the science
fiction phenomenon. It is to the latter we turn our attention;
for here we encounter some of the most revealing reflections of
later science fiction writers. The roots of this particular
perversion of the literary craft are found in Campbell's dictum
that "we can safely practice anything in imagination--suicide,
murder, anything whatever;" and in his contention that science
fiction is the premier means for just such an imagination. When
this is coupled with Campbell's assessment of who reads his
magazine, mostly young males between the age of twenty and
thirty-five, most of whom are trained in technology and employed
in that field, "a good one third of the young technical personnel
of the nation" (1953:24), it should become obvious that those
who are encouraged to practice out their wildest imaginings are
precisely those who have the means at their disposal to implement those imaginings on a large scale: "suicide, murder, anything whatever."

There is a certain amount of safety in such a state of
affairs; but it is the safety that the autistic child, for
example, or the blind person, or the deaf person experiences.
In similar fashion, the writer and reader, caught up in the
power fantasy, are the *least* likely to see or hear what is
really happening and/or what will be likely to happen. Moreover,
it allows the person to see only what his or her world-view deems
acceptable. Thus, when Campbell advances the position that only
the top twenty percent of income-earning power be allowed to

elect the leaders of utopia, he admits this will allow many
prostitutes to vote. What he cannot see, because his world-
view will not allow him to see it, is that while *some* prostitutes may qualify, *all* pimps will. When that obvious flaw is
grasped, it will also be understood what, in fact, Campbell is
urging is that those who are most adept at exploiting their
fellows be allowed to vote for the leaders.

Although it may be easy to discover such obvious flaws
and their ramifications from outside the movement, it is
extremely difficult to gain that perspective from within. This,
as we indicated, is due not only to the nature of the narrative
structure, nor only to the ideas which tend to become an ideology; but also to the nature of the relationship between writer
and reader. This relationship, mediated by the network of
fanzines and letter columns, far from expanding the horizons
of science fiction seems to have had the opposite effect: the
concerns became narrower and more regressive.

Moskowitz's characterization of 'Doc' Smith's relationship to fandom as "paternalistic" is a case in point. This
leaves us nowhere to go but toward an understanding of science
fiction as a literature which fills some missing childhood
needs, and/or a literature dependent on the reader as child
being kept in that state permanently. Not surprisingly some
writers see this to be exactly the case. Cyril Kornbluth writes
of the Doc Smith universe that it is one of a "nine year old,"
and consists of "boyish daydreams, the power fantasies which
compensate for the inevitable frustrations of childhood in an
adult world" (61). Kornbluth, moreover, is highly critical of
Doc Smith offering any social criticism; instead his stories
present us with a "strange blend of naive Marxism, a fascistic
leader-principle, and a despair of democracy." Some may dismiss these as "plot devices," or simply as notions current in
the era of the Depression, but the fact is these were "techniques which had not yet been revealed to the world in their
pragmatic fullness as practiced in Germany, Italy, and Russia"
(59).

What Kornbluth argues, however, is not that writer and
reader simply failed to see the connection, due to some over-
sight; but that the very "compact" between writer and reader

prevented such analysis. He describes this compact as follows:

> We are suspending reality, you and I. By the signs of
> the rocketship and the ray gun and the time machine we
> indicate that the relationship between us has nothing
> to do with the real world. By writing the stuff and
> reading it we abdicate from action; we give free play
> to our unconscious drives and symbols, we write and
> read not about the real world but about ourselves and
> the things within ourselves (55).

Kornbluth's reference to the "fascistic leader-principle
and a despair of democracy" as revealed in their "pragmatic
fullness" in Germany, Italy, and Russia, presents us with the
beginnings of a paradigm which illustrates well the authoritarian bent of science fiction politics, particularly in its
early stages. Writer, reader, and critic alike are fascinated
or horrified (as may be the case) by Hitler's rise to power.
But even the horror is tinged with awe and respect; there seems
to be an acknowledgement that here was a master "universe
maker." Brian Ash's meditations on the Hitler phenomenon
typify such horrified fascination even to this day. Ash,
writing about the mythic overtones of science fiction leads
into a discussion of Hitler and *Mein Kampf*, which could have
"readily come from the pen of a speculative writer," and "most
of which approximates to a piece of fifth rate science fantasy."
But Ash does not stop here: "Although it may seem paradoxical,
and predictably distasteful, Adolf Hitler could well emerge in
retrospect as the most 'god-like' being of the twentieth
century." As supporting evidence for this contention Ash cites
the "worship" of Hitler, his "utter contempt for human life,"
and the fact that when he fell he brought down the holocaust.
If Hitler had not happened in reality, one could dismiss him
as science fiction, Ash argues. But he is science fiction, in
a sense, because both he and *Mein Kampf* share the same hopes
and desires, "complementary views," Ash calls them. He cites
passages from Hitler's manifesto: "From the millions of men...
one man must step forward, [who will] take up the struggle for
sole correctness...At long intervals in history it may occasion-
ally happen that the politician is wedded to the theoretician"
(200). One need only substitute a term here or there to realize
that the dream is as old as Plato's philosopher-king, and as
new as Campbell's scientist-engineer. Ash, along with many

other writers and critics, is himself caught up in the understanding of science fiction as an elitist literature which need
only render an account of itself to itself. Ash writes of it
as "an enlightened stratum of society...an elitist view which
some would hold irrational--but which is not beyond humanity"
(142).

The claim is not being made here that science fiction
'caused' the Hitler phenomenon; but that they should be so often
linked in story and in criticism is indicative of something.
Brian Aldiss, speaking from the point of view of the writer,
says: "The disgrace that the science fiction community still
(perpetually?) thinks it is in, is precisely the shame it shares
with pornography, of transforming a man into an organ of conquest in a knocking-shop of wish-fulfillment" (1975:196).
Norman Spinrad concurs, when he acknowledges that science
fiction was doing "something beyond playing with words."
Spinrad talks about the manipulation of "susceptible" minds,
the playing with adolescent power fantasies, the peer-group
pressures, and the "mystic transcendence" of the works. In
this manner, science fiction writers were "drawing together
tribal cults around their works, creating pocket universes of
which they were the little gods." But Spinrad is also aware of
the social, political, and cultural milieu: "Remember that this
messianic literature was being unleashed on the adolescent mind
in an era that began with the Great Depression, produced Nazi
Germany, and climaxed in the technological Gotterdammerung of
World War II" (110).

James Blish provides the final focus for this treatment
of the authoritarian politics of early science fiction. Along
with Spinrad, Blish is not thrown off the track (as Moskowitz
would be) by the "messianic" preoccupation of science fiction.
He contends that the stories are not theological (religious)
propaganda, but rather indications of a chiliastic crisis, the
likes of which the world has not seen since 999 A.D. Science
fiction is, as Blish sees it, "the modern Apocalyptic literature" which is "overlaid with the mythologies of scientific
humanism" (54). Such has been our contention all along:
Science fiction is secular apocalyptic literature. The ease
with which it accomodates itself to authoritarian politics is

due to its messianic preoccupation, a primary feature of
apocalyptic literature throughout biblical and secular history.
The apocalyptic nature of early science fiction also accounts
for 1) the understanding of itself as a literature of ideas
(some biblical scholars locate the roots of apocalyptic in the
Wisdom literature); 2) its underlying utopian tone; 3) its
attraction to pseudo-science (again, biblical apocalyptic is
noted for its "use" of foreign cosmologies); 4) its fashioning
of future histories; and 5) its appropriation of myth. To the
latter three we now turn our attention.

G. Science Fiction's Attraction to Pseudo-Science

One person's pseudo-science is another's science; there
is no "scientific" way to determine when an understanding of
the facts is scientific or pseudo-scientific, at least not
according to what the self-understanding of early science
fiction meant by science. Gunn makes no mention of what Gernsback could have meant by the term science. Ash says of him
that his "enthusiasms were entirely rooted in the technical"
(66). Moskowitz sums up his picture of Gernsback by writing:
"Gernsback chafed at the limitations imposed by the state of
scientific progress." And later he characterizes him as a man
"of serious scientific interests" (1963:235). Campbell's own
understanding of science is readily available in his editorials;
the most illuminating description of which is: "Science is
magic that works." Campbell comes down heavy on the presence
of and the necessity for "Absolutes" in his formulation of the
philosophy of science. The case seems to be air-tight; except
that Campbell obliges by leaving a loophole through which later
he can seriously introduce the considerations of dianetics, the
Dean drive, psi-machines, metabolic slow-down, mind-reading,
telekinesis, and levitation. Campbell writes: "The system of
laws is absolutely inescapable, but...any *individual* law can be
offset by proper use of others of the total system of laws"
(1966:69). The control of meaning and knowledge is thus lacking in Campbell's understanding of what science is and how it
operates. His scientific principles do not account for it.
Some control does exist for him, however; it consists of his
hopes, desires, and beliefs. Because Campbell is so insistent

that the scientist is free from any such impulses (he writes at one point that scientists like to work with machines because machines have no beliefs, biases, or desires), he is blind to the compelling beliefs and desires which dominate his life and render him open to the most spurious of scientific endeavors.

Such is also the general problem of early science fiction; it too is peopled with writers and readers who welcome the pseudo-scientific, precisely because it fits into the vision they have of the future happiness of humankind. A description, then, of pseudo-science must include the faith-structure which underlies the willingness to accept the theory and/or working model. Campbell would have not been so enamored with dianetics had he not desired some rational, scientific means of explaining, developing, and giving meaning to human personality. He would not have so readily discussed the wonders of the Dean drive, had he not believed that humankind would indeed inhabit the stars, as was its destiny. He would not have so passionately called for the development of psi-machines, had he not desired objective proof that there was a subjective force in the universe.

All this is not to look down on pseudo-science; but only to say it must be understood in the larger context of a world-view. And a world-view is ultimately grounded in some kind of faith. The fact that the term pseudo-science is often used to make the distinction between science fiction and science fantasy only means that fantasy is not so much characterized by the willing suspension of disbelief, as it is by a willingness to believe.

The pseudo-scientific tendency of science fiction also has political overtones. Ray Bradbury, now one of the more famous and docile writers, in his youth as a science fiction fan was active in the movement known as "Technocracy, Inc." This movement believed that the American economic system was near collapse; and it, Technocracy, Inc., was ready to take over with scientists who would run the country with precision. Bradbury said at the time: "I think Technocracy combines all the hopes and dreams of science fiction. We've been dreaming about it for years--now in a short time it may become a reality" (in Moskowitz, 1966:358). Bradbury was even willing to accept

a "limited dictatorship," according to Moskowitz. The dream,
it is obvious, is what dictated the acceptance of the science
to be used in managing human society. As a postscript to the
episode, however, Bradbury disowned Technocracy, Inc., when it
endorsed Hitler and Mussolini for having put into practice what
it espoused. Bradbury was later to attack such technocratic
states in *Farenheit 451*.

A. E. van Vogt remains the science fiction writer who
jumped on the most pseudo-science bandwagons. He begins his
career espousing the idea of a "super-race" in his book *Slan*.
Spinrad says of it that it "fused Campbell's predeliction for
extrasensory perception with the Nietzschean superman and
produced one of the new archetypes of science fiction, the
human mutant, the next step after man" (39). Van Vogt moves on
next to General Semantics, a non-Aristotelian system of logic,
which he promulgated in *The World of Null-A* and *The Players of
Null-A*. General Semantics' most prominent exponent was Count
Alfred Korzybski, whose book *Science and Sanity* was premised
on the belief that scientific knowledge had reached such a
state as to surpass Aristotelian thought. General Semantics
was to usher in the New Age by enabling people to communicate
truly for the first time.

Van Vogt took his science seriously; it was not relegated
to his writings. At one time he tried the Bates' system of eye
exercise, a system which promised it could do away with the
need for glasses through visual exercises and mental condition-
ing. Van Vogt also became involved deeply in Hubbard's science
of Dianetics, himself setting up the Los Angeles headquarters.

For all his dubious scientific underpinnings (or perhaps
because of them) van Vogt remains a favorite of many science
fiction readers. Moskowitz is puzzled over the passionate
search by van Vogt for causes, and suggests the answer might
simply be that he was a "deeply religious man in the fullest
sense of that phrase." His analysis then proceeds along those
lines, describing the religious and theological themes and
symbolism of van Vogt's works. Wollheim argues that this is
the case, although he does not call the search or the beliefs
religious. Concerning van Vogt's wild image-making, Wollheim
admits it may be interpreted as "megalomania" or even "paranoia."

But the reason van Vogt has topped science fiction lists for so long is that "he has an instinctual belief in humanity, he believes in the invincibility of humanity, he refuses to accept boundaries of time and space." In this, Wollheim argues, he is speaking the dreams and beliefs of the reader (48). Van Vogt, in our estimation, stands as paradigm of the role belief plays in the willingness to accept pseudo-science. And he also stands as the prime example of the difficulty (indeed, the impossibility, some argue) in drawing any hard and fast line between science fiction and science fantasy--even at the level of so-called "hard-core" science fiction.

The linking of science fiction with the popular cults of flying saucers, scientology (what Dianetics evolved into), and the whole von Daniken phenomenon, is also evidence of the fact there is an inherent attraction of science fiction toward pseudo-science. This can be accounted for by the fact that the self-understanding of early science fiction (and later uncritical manifestations of it) is not cognizant of the role belief plays in the epistemological processes. It can thus be argued that pseudo-science is nothing other than the attempt to explain scientifically to a non-believer what one believes in; and that science is the attempt to explain scientifically to a believer what one believes in.

H. Science Fiction and Mythopoesis

There is a tendency for science romance to evolve into science myth. Such a tendency toward myth-making could only come about within the framework of pseudo-science for science of itself does not attain anywhere near the total outlook which is an essential characteristic of myth. Only a science which does not concern itself with observation of the particular and the individual (therefore not a real science at all) can formulate the hypothetical understandings broad enough to contain all of reality, while not being grounded in any particular manifestation, nor in the procedures of verification.

Science fiction in this understanding truly becomes Platonic literature, as Gunn suggests, where the "physical representations we see around us are only imperfect copies." But it also becomes mythological literature for the very same reason; for it seeks to encompass all of reality within the idea. The tension between the idea which is known intellectually in the word, and the idea which is perceived dramatically in the story, is traceable to the tension that exists between *logos* and *mythos*. The former is the word spoken by philosophy: the word which can be predicated of every individual of a class, and only about the individuals of that class. It issues, by way of the Enlightenment, in science, the systematic study and/or knowledge of an object according to verifiable hypotheses. At the other end of the spectrum is *mythos*, the idea which is not abstracted from the class, but which creates the class by creating the world within which the class exists. This, as Frye argues, is the highest goal and purpose of literature: to be mythopoeic.

The tension in early science fiction between *logos* and *mythos* arises, not because the two are mutually exclusive or contradictory, but because of the tendency, since the Enlightenment, for *logos* to assume the "totality" that rightly belongs to *mythos*, while *mythos* seeks to assume, from the same period on, the "analytic" function of *logos*. In the process of passing from logos to mythos, that is, from the "scientific analysis of the world" to the "story that creates world," science fiction repeats and recapitulates the ancient circle encompassing the two: "the myth of total reason." "Intelligibility" becomes the synthesizing agent in the science fiction story; the "unknown" becomes that which is to be overcome or transcended. *Mythos*, however, when it bases itself on a "science" that has forsaken observation and verification procedures, becomes an affirmative category, rather than a critical one. It culminates in the presentation of the future as affirming, rather than critiquing, the present order of decision-making. Martin Plattel speaks of the tension as that which exists between "scientific analysis" (what I have called *logos*) and "utopian synthesis" (what I have called *mythos*). He concludes:

> There exists a dialectical process between scientific analysis and utopian synthesis, but not one between scientific analysis and scientific synthesis. The pursuit of science with synthetical vision leads to the chaos of independently developed parts, but pursuing science in light of an assumed scientific knowledge of the totality leads to ideological dogmatism and frightful

simplifications, it results in a kind of "theology"
of society (98).

In science fiction it has resulted in the *mythos* which seeks to
present the totality of human meaning and value as it is understood presently and lived out in a future based solely on
scientific knowledge (*logos*). In short, it seeks to reduce
story to plan.

There is no clear understanding in early science fiction
of its own mythopoeic tendency, although it was there nonetheless. This is due to the commonly accepted notion of myth as a
prescientific understanding of the world, superseded by Enlightenment knowledge and the rise of the technological society.
Such an understanding is clearly evident in those stories
which seek to explain away the ancient myths by narrating how
the gods were beings from a superior world who visited earth
and possessed seemingly supernatural powers to those humans
with whom they came into contact. It still prevails in the
critical work of Brian Ash, who maintains that science can
effectively explain away any "grandiose piece of mythology"
(191). His argument is worth noting, for it betrays yet again
the uncritical nature of those commentators who, by inveighing
against all the old ways, fall into the very same trap. Ash
speaks of "an evolutionary process of growing intelligence
which functions independently of a remote creative force...
perfectly capable of assessing its own relevance in space and
time." This can be the only conclusion arrived at, Ash argues,
once you posit the preference of reason over belief (190).

But this is precisely the issue: story does not evoke
reason, it evokes belief. The arguments within story may be
logical, but the telling of the story itself is not. And the
more the story is told (particularly the story of humankind's
growing intelligence), the stronger becomes the belief, until
the myth lives again. The story does not give any new knowledge,
but it does give meaning to the search for and the possession of
knowledge. Ash acknowledges as much (without questioning his
own previous remarks) when he says that "Above reason, hope--in
the last eventuality--usually prevails." And the new mythology
he sees emerging through science fiction is that of "escape"
from the darkness of life, "the creation inside Man's head of

the counterbalance to despair" (199). Thus what science explains away, science fiction creates anew. Or in other words,
logos is transformed into *mythos*, and the cycle begins again.

The final point to be made in connection with the mythic
nature of science fiction is a reference to the distinction
Robert Philmus makes between private and public myth. Philmus
characterizes Jules Verne's work as illustrative of private,
and H. G. Wells' as illustrative of public, myth. Philmus bases
his distinction primarily on content; but it is possible to
speak also of a distinction based upon the self-understanding
of science fiction as a movement. When science fiction discovered it was no longer speaking merely to a minority group,
and when it discovered its story was the story more and more
people were telling about themselves, its myth became a public
myth and by that fact was rendered respectable. That process,
long in its coming, has reached fruition in the acceptance of
Star Wars and *Close Encounters of the Third Kind*.

I. Science Fiction and Future History

Isaac Asimov says his story "Pilgrimage" was his first
attempt to write future history. He also says it was his first
attempt to write a story on a galactic scale. While he was
working on it he felt he was working on an "epic" (1972:99).
Asimov is expressing here the understanding that one cannot
write about space without writing about time. The desire to
know eventually encompasses both; and, more importantly,
encompasses the future. But the desire to know does not auto-
matically bring about that knowledge. Just as the new worlds
and galaxies of science fiction are often models of already
known worlds and galaxies (literary ones, too), so also future
history is plainly modeled on past history. Asimov confesses
this, when he writes of a later story: "In telling future-
history I always felt it wisest to be guided by past-history"
(143). When he wrote his major future history, the *Foundation*
trilogy, he says clearly: "I intended to model [it] quite
frankly on the fall of the Roman Empire" (385).

It would be a mistake, however, to surmise that this is
all there is to the future history motif in science fiction;
that it was merely an unsophisticated retelling of humankind's

history, writ large across the galaxies. Wollheim accepts it
as such; and he further adds that the general use of such type
of future history reinforces the idea that history is cyclical,
or more precisely, spiral, since "Certain events seem to recur
predictably but always on a new and vaster scale" (38). Even
this, however, does not get at the root meaning of Asimov's
Foundation trilogy, Heinlein's *The Past Through Tomorrow*, or
Blish's *Cities in Flight*. Asimov clearly worked on the analogy
of the Roman empire, Heinlein drew his own chart, and Blish
based his story on Oswald Spengler's philosophy of history.

Robert Heinlein presents us with another facet of the
future history phenomenon; it brings us closer to discovering
its real significance. Heinlein's future history predates that
of any other science fiction writer, and differs from them in
that it consists of an actual chart detailing the technical,
sociological, cultural, and political history of humankind,
from 1951 to 2600 A.D. Into this history Heinlein inserted his
individual stories. The chart was a necessity, Heinlein writes,
"to keep me from stumbling as I added new stories." Heinlein
calls it a pseudo-history; and says he was not attempting
prophecy. When he concludes later that for stories he was
writing now he no longer needed the chart, for "the fictional
history embodied in it is at least as real to me as Plymouth
Rock" (1951:v), Heinlein unwittingly reveals the significance
of the future history theme. It is to give meaning to the
structuring of time, known and unknown. Future history is
symbolic in nature; symbolic not of the extrapolations of
scientific people, but instead of the expectations of believers.
Some room must be created in time as well as in space into
which people can move. And that room must be imagined as inhabitable. The future histories of early science fiction are
just such examples of inhabitable room. They do not predict
what is going to happen; but they do give meaning to the expectations of technically and scientifically imaginative people.

Damon Knight's dismissal of Asimov's trilogy on the
grounds that history does not repeat itself is beside the point.
Asimov's story is not about the extrapolation of the Roman
Empire into the galaxy (even though Asimov says it is); it is
about the expectations Asimov's readers have for the future.

Chief among those expectations is that humankind will be able to direct, predict, and shape history to bring about the least amount of suffering. This task will be accomplished through "psychohistory," the mathematical and statistical manipulation of large masses of people.

Future history is also a prime feature of apocalyptic literature. Thus the identification of science fiction as secular apocalyptic is strengthened at another critical point. When one reads widely in apocalyptic, both biblical and secular, the most evident characteristic is that of a literature of hope, that is, of expectation. The so-called determinism which many critics ascribe to apocalyptic in general can be understood not as an imposition of some extraneous philosophy of history upon the course of future events, but rather as the need to give shape to otherwise formless expectations of people. The world must be made inhabitable before people can live in (and into) it. When Wollheim claims that Asimov's trilogy was "pivotal" in early science fiction, he is saying that Asimov's work crystallized the expectations of readers (37). Now their hopes and dreams about space travel, conquest, galactic empires, explorations, and struggle against the unknown could be fitted into some larger framework which give them meaning. The whole story had to be told for any of the parts to have meaning.

Apocalyptic literature does exactly this. It says the expectations of a people that all will eventually work out for the best are meaningful expectations, because when the whole story is told people will see where the trials fit in. So apocalyptic develops a future history. Wollheim's reading of the consensus "Cosmogony of the Future" is a prime example of science fiction's view. The premise on which it is based betrays the limited nature of its expectations: "There is only a limited number of general possibilities open to human conjecture ...This [cosmogony] does seem to be what all our mental computers state as the shape of the future." His consensus cosmogony: 1) the initial voyages to the moons and the planets; 2) the first flights to the stars and contact with extraterrestrials; 3) the rise of the galactic empire; 4) the full bloom of the empire; 5) the decline and fall of the empire; 6) the Interregnum; 7) the rise of a permanent galactic civilization; and 8) the challenge to God, with "the end of the universe, the end of time, and the beginning of a new universe or a new time-space continuum" (42-44). The closed, cyclic nature of this consensus future history reveals ultimately the limits of the science fiction imagination: God is merely another stage in cosmic evolution, transcendence another goal to be achieved. Olaf Stapledon and Arthur C. Clarke are the foremost examples here.

Conclusions

Thus briefly the opening arguments in the case that science fiction is to be considered as apocalyptic literature, albeit of a secular variety, is presented. For apocalyptic is a literature involving an intense longing for a new age and a new world. As such, apocalyptic views the present-time as a time of crisis, and concurrently a time of great expectation, indeed imminent expectation. The use of apocalyptic language and symbols gives voice to this feeling of crisis and expecta- tion, mediating the tension which exists between the two. It judges and it consoles; it also guides a community through the dark times, telling in symbol and story of the end of the old and the coming of the new. Apocalyptic is a literature of hope; it grows out of a common, shared vision of the meaning of life, of the world, of the universe, and of history.

Such is the literature of science fiction, particularly according to its self-understanding in the early days of the pulps. We have pointed out how that self-understanding is grounded in the understanding given it by the two great found- ing figure-heads, Hugo Gernsback and John W. Campbell, Jr. All the remaining characteristics discussed above (science fiction and romance, the pulps and hack writers, utopian facets, science fiction as cult or sect, authoritarian politics, pseudo-science, its mythic pretensions and its fashioning of future history) flow in some way from the understanding given to it by Gerns- back and Campbell. In turn, these characteristics are the basis for our contention that science fiction is a secular apocalyptic literature.

The claim is not new. Blish, from within the circle of writers, Finer, from outside as a sociologist, and Ketterer, as

a literary critic--all designate science fiction as apocalyptic.
What has been done here, briefly, is to further substantiate
the claim; and to lay the groundwork for its fuller exploration
in the succeeding chapters. For this, it is necessary not only
to accept science fiction as apocalyptic, but also to accept
apocalyptic as a legitimate mode of symbolizing, and indeed of
understanding the world, cosmos, and history.

As apocalyptic literature, science fiction is a literature of hope; its understanding is grounded in a trusting faith
that the salvation of humankind will be achieved through the
miracle of science and technology. This is the common shared
vision informing early science fiction and its self-understanding. Insofar as one uses the referent of a shared faith in
salvation, one can more easily correlate science fiction and
apocalypse, for science fiction as secular apocalyptic parallels
biblical apocalyptic insofar as 1) it purports to be revelation
of things to come; 2) it is built upon a body of (secret) knowledge and tends towards gnosticism; 3) it re-appropriates the
myths of the beginnings and the ends; 4) it at the same time
re-writes past history according to its beliefs; 5) it arises
in similar social and political settings (that is, its understanding of itself and its role in the social and political
life of the nation is similar); 6) it becomes the gathering
point of the strange, the occult, the para-normal (that is,
pseudo-scientific) understanding of life; and 7) it looks for
salvation and deliverance from something or someone beyond
present reality (of which it despairs), whether in terms simply
of the future (through chance), or in terms of extra-terrestrial
life. The "We are not alone!" referent of the current movie,
Close Encounters of the Third Kind, is an example of how the
last characteristic mentioned (salvation from beyond) sheds
light on all the others. Salvation is what religion is all
about.

All the above themes will be taken up at further length
in the succeeding chapters, with a view toward illustrating
that in understanding itself as apocalyptic science fiction has
been correct in the understanding of its enduring appeal.

THE CRITICAL UNDERSTANDING OF SCIENCE FICTION

> Eschatology is that form of myth which accounts
> for the unknown future. Men walk in a here and
> now whose extent varies somewhat with their
> historical and geographical observation. Beyond
> the limited bounds of that here and now, in any
> stage of culture, they must fall back on an
> imaginative picture of what preceded the known
> and what is to follow it. They usually fore-
> shorten the disappearing continuity of past and
> future, and construct in either case a mythical
> beginning and a mythical end which serve to
> focus in themselves all the past and all the
> future, and which become the termini of temporal
> experience.
>
> --Amos N. Wilder

Introduction

The claim that science fiction is the last popular
literature unmediated by criticism is a claim which itself must
be critically looked at. The editorial practices and the editorial columns filled a highly critical function. Likewise,
the popularity polls, letter columns, fanzines, and science
fiction conventions all can be understood as being critical in
the final analysis, if not in their primary intent. The claim
thus means that the literature may have been unmediated by
criticism from outside but the self-understanding was highly
mediated from within. Any subsequent critical work which remains entirely bounded by literary critical categories will
inevitably fail to come to grips with the totality of the
science fiction movement, and the inner mediation of its self-
understanding. The "confusion of forms" which characterizes so
much of contemporary science fiction criticism can be traced
back to that failure. The narrow categories of romance and
myth, interpreted narrowly, cannot encompass the scope of
science fiction pulp fiction, the proliferation of fanzines,
the dogmatic pronouncements of editors and writers, or the
passionate claims that science fiction be judged according to
its own standards. On the other hand, the wide categories of

popular literature and apocalyptic, interpreted widely, can
embrace the whole phenomenon. The confusion of forms results
from the practice of passing uncritically between these two
characterizations. It is evident in the first serious academic
critical study, Bailey's *Pilgrims through Space and Time*; and
it also underlies the latest offering in the field, Scholes'
and Rabkin's *Science Fiction: History, Science, Vision*.

The present chapter will attempt to assess some of the
major critical studies of science fiction in light of the claim
that the self-understanding of early science fiction demands it
be read as a popular literature tending toward apocalyptic, and
that to refuse to do so results inevitably in a confusion of
forms. It will then be argued that David Ketterer's *New Worlds
for Old* comes closest to providing the categories necessary for
a critical understanding and interpretation of science fiction
in all its dimensions.

J. O. Bailey: The Critical
Pilgrimage Begins

In his forward to the re-issue of J. O. Bailey's *Pilgrims
through Space and Time* Thomas D. Clareson hails it as "*The*
intellectual and literary history of the development of science
fiction," at the present time (viii). Clareson writes in 1972;
the book was originally published in 1947. It was written
largely, however, in the years immediately preceeding World War
II, having been offered to a publisher first in 1939. Bailey
himself calls it a "pioneering presentation" (187); and it
certainly was that. Until the appearance of Amis' *New Maps of
Hell* in 1960, no other work appeared which dealt seriously with
science fiction in its popular forms. And in 1972, according
to Clareson, Bailey's study was still the "indispensable" handbook for the teacher and student of science fiction.

It can be argued, moreover, so pioneering was this work
it would have passed completely unnoticed had it been published
in 1939, as Bailey originally wanted. The intervention of
World War II not only delayed publication; it also forced
Bailey to re-work material introducing and concluding his study.
What results are actually two separate treatments of science
fiction: 1) the original study of scientific romances, from

their origins in stories about marvelous inventions and trips
to other worlds to their final form as cosmic romances; and
2) the framework, consisting of the reflections of Bailey about
the meaning and purpose of scientific romances in the context
of the atomic age, which had dawned at the conclusion of World
War II. The consequent critical focus of the book is blurred;
and Bailey is never quite able to link his critical study of
the scientific romance with his plea for the compelling relevance of such literature. In his opening remarks it is the end
of the war, the state of international affairs, and the introduction of atomic power which Bailey cites as justifying his
study. Yet when one reflects on the fact that Bailey undertook
the study when none of these factors was present (at least in
the scope later apparent), it becomes necessary to look elsewhere for an understanding of science fiction which compelled
Bailey to his task.

Using the guideline that any discussion of the atomic
age indicates material written after World War II, the original
study can be said to begin in Chapter Two, "Scientific Fiction
Before 1817." It is in the opening passages of that chapter
that we find the understanding which guides Bailey in his study
of scientific fiction, explaining why it is popular in the
first place and what constitutes its areas of concern for the
critic. Bailey writes: "As science has developed, on the one
hand it has replaced belief in magic with belief in law, but
on the other hand it has seemed to the popular imagination a
modern kind of magic" (13). Thus the categories that Bailey
uses throughout: 'marvelous' journeys, and 'wonderful' machines,
inventions, and discoveries. For Bailey the genre is early on
shaped by its themes; but it is also shaped by an understanding
of science almost identical with that advanced by Campbell:
Science is magic that works. That is, while the genre may be
shaped by its themes, the themes are themselves shaped by a
popular understanding of science. This forces one to make a
critical evaluation of that understanding, or else all subsequent categorization fails.

Bailey, to his credit, does take up the task of evaluation near the end of his study, when he lists and describes the
"creeds" which shape humankind's attitudes toward science and

scientific progress. These creeds are what inform scientific
fiction, the multiplication of which Bailey sees as a "mass
phenomenon" and the attempt by humankind to adjust to an ever-
changing, growing, and evolving consciousness brought on by the
machine age. For Bailey, then, the problem is described in
mechanical terms; for "Every adjustment has been disturbed into
maladjustment, until finally, as evolution and relativity have
influenced thought, the theory has been widely stated that life
is dynamic, never adjusted, but always in the process of becoming adjusted" (293).

In the course of his discussion Bailey alternately uses
the terms theory and creed to describe the framework according
to which science is to be understood and interpreted, and
according to which science understands and interprets the
world. At one point, however, he writes that the "masses who
read fiction for entertainment are inclined to be impatient of
theory; the generalization, heavy with meaning for the philos-
opher, has little weight for people--certainly most people of
the world--who do not think abstractly" (294). Yet, Bailey
argues, humankind needs theory; and they have it in the form of
creeds. Thus, in effect, he is arguing that a theory which is
not understood nevertheless is accepted in the form of a creed.
This fits in well with his initial critical insight that science
to the popular imagination seems to be "a modern kind of magic."
Yet Bailey does not elucidate further the critical role "belief"
plays in his understanding of scientific fiction. The central
issue to be addressed in this regard is the theological maxim:
Credo ut intelligam, I believe that I may understand. The
maxim is not only theological, in that narrow sense; it is
epistemological, in the sense that the line between scientific
theory and scientific creed is exceedingly fine. This failure
on the part of Bailey (to carry over his analysis of what
characterizes past scientific fiction into his analysis of
current scientific fiction) leads to the oft repeated formula
that what differentiates modern from ancient science fiction is
the former is based on real science.

Such a formula depends on a complete disassociation of
matter from form, harmful enough in theological thought, but
utterly fatal in literary criticism. Bailey, nonetheless,

claims exactly that: "Since scientific fiction tells the story
of an imaginary invention or discovery, and the adventures that
follow, naturally it differs from other fiction chiefly in substance, that is, in what the story tells" (216). The form,
thus, can easily be disposed of through a discussion of the
"scaffolding:" the structure, narrative method, and characterization. Exactly what their function is is hard to say. Bailey
writes: "Because scientific romances treat inventions and
discoveries that are imaginary, they have the task not imposed
upon other fiction of making the improbable seem true" (191).
The scaffolding, therefore, seems merely, as the term implies,
something external to the real 'message' of the scientific
romance; it is there only to establish the veracity of the
scientific claims. Such deficiencies in the critical method of
Bailey--namely, his thematic treatment of the precursors of
science fiction, his refusal to treat seriously his own insights
concerning the faith-character of scientific romances as still
operative in current science fiction, and his almost complete
neglect of the form of science fiction in favor of its sub-
stance--all these lead to a grand confusion of forms, the first
of many which still plague the critical study of science fiction.

In summary, because Bailey does not discriminate sufficiently in his treatment of the form of scientific fiction,
refuge is sought in thematic categorization. The danger in
this is it reinforces the treatment of science fiction as a
literature of ideas. This is precisely the trap into which
Bailey falls. Moreover, dismissal of form fosters a confusion
of forms. This confusion characterizes much of later science
fiction criticism, especially with regard to fantasy and utopia.

In his preface and in various passages added after World
War II, Bailey's understanding of science fiction becomes much
more radical and politicized. No longer is Bailey concerned
with the scientific romance in terms of the wonderful discovery
and the adventurous tale, and how, at root, science is a modern
kind of magic. The times have forced science fiction to be
read much more seriously. This high seriousness extends even
beyond reading it in terms of the creeds which help humankind
adjust to change. World War II and the coming of atomic power
have ushered in the new age. The problems and complexities of

this new age are beyond anything humankind experienced before.
Bailey writes:

> The tangled path before statesmen today would, I think
> seem an open road in comparison with the leavings of
> atomic terror...to avoid this World War III and at the
> same time to establish Permanent Peace I, the states-
> men of the world need wisdom of a deep, new texture,
> broadly based on the understanding of all human prob-
> lems. They need wisdom such as the world has never
> yet observed in the councils of state (2).

Bailey does not argue that science fiction will provide all the
wisdom needed; yet it may be a prime source, for it has always
dealt with the impact of science upon humankind.

Of particular importance to Bailey is the suggestion for
a "University of the World...a permanent brain-trust for mankind." This idea was first suggested by Francis Bacon in *The
New Atlantis,* and modified and built upon by numerous science
fiction writers since. It would learn of the wisdom of the
past to be used in the light of the future; its members could
work without interference from private industry; it would be
international in composition, taking the best from each culture;
it would educate the best from each country to return them to
fill the influential roles of professors, statesmen, researchers,
lecturers--in short, "sowers of the seed of a new wisdom necessary for a new age" (3). Thus for the first time humankind
would be educating its cream for the awesome responsibility of
making the future. Piecemeal treaties, hegemony and spheres of
influence, technical-warfare espionage, the maintenance of
peace-time armies--all could be done away with, and for a
nominal cost.

Such a high-minded reading of science fiction necessarily
influences how Bailey will conclude his treatment of the genre.
The task is addressed by him in the final chapter, "Journey's
End." Bailey notes that while most "serious" fiction of the
twentieth century is realistic in mood, the popular books read
for pastime are by and large romances. Since romance is generally equated with escape (and Bailey accepts that equation),
the literary value and meaning is not to be found there. Instead, any claim science fiction has to literary value is to be
ascribed to its esthetic value as myth. Second, science fiction
opens a wide area of the imagination; for "a widening knowledge

of science in the nineteenth century and a deepening faith in
it as wonder workers have prepared men's minds to include these
realms [distant worlds and distant futures] within the area of
imaginative art" (318).

At this point, however, Bailey retreats; he throws out
all literary critical methods and says the esthetic judgment
finally rests on what one means by art, and on which romances
are to be judged. What he is leading up to is the favorite
ploy of science fiction critics: science fiction has to be
judged by different standards. It has to be accepted as valuable (read: of literary merit) because it treats seriously of
serious concerns. Or, as Bailey puts it: "Concern with civilization in a changing time gives these stories some importance
as vehicles for conveying ideas to a wide audience" (319). One
can readily see how this final esthetic evaluation fits in with
Bailey's guiding description of the parameters of the science
fiction genre:

> A piece of scientific fiction is a narrative of an
> imaginary invention or discovery in the natural sciences
> and consequent adventures and experiences. The invention
> must be imaginary at the time the romance is written...
> it must be a scientific discovery--something that the
> author at least rationalizes as possible to science...
> The romance is an attempt to anticipate this discovery
> and its impact upon society, and to foresee how mankind
> may adjust to the new condition (10-11).

What finally can be said of Bailey's proto-critical study
of science fiction? First of all, it must be said that in the
end Bailey fails to come up with any truly literary description
of the genre of scientific fiction. Although he explores its
roots, beginning in the wondrous tales of marvelous inventions
and journeys, traces it through the historical romances of the
future, and concludes with cosmic romances (tending toward
myth), Bailey is never quite able to explore the inner connection between form and substance. This leads to his final
analysis and evaluation of science fiction as a literature of
ideas, valuable for its predictive and prophetic qualities.
Science fiction is not romance; nor does Bailey subscribe to
the equation of science fiction with utopian literature on any
grand scale, for utopia is too static a concept for the
dynamic aims of science fiction's vision of the future. Satiric

fiction also does not encompass the field of science fiction, for again satire is too concerned with reflection upon present practice, while science fiction is concerned with future predictions and consequences.

The retreat Bailey makes is into his own version of the self-understanding of science fiction discussed above. Although science fiction according to Bailey may not be an entirely new thing, humankind is living in a new age and therefore science fiction must be read in a new way: not as an escape, but as a literature which seriously discusses serious problems. The basis for the serious discussion is, of course, the scientific principles on which it is grounded. "Where the science in a romance is science and the author is intellectually honest and informed...the recommendations are more to be trusted than most of the political-isms characteristic of our age. The basis is sounder: scientific principle. The leverage is longer: the point of view of biology or geology" (320). Such sentiments are virtually indistinguishable from those expressed by Gernsback and/or Campbell.

Finally, what figures most prominently in Bailey's ultimate failure to evaluate science fiction critically is his dismissal of the pulps. Their "hey-day" was in the thirties, he writes. And, upon reading the latest issues, he says: "I seemed to be reading something I had read several times before" (187). This dismissal of the pulps, and the self-understanding of science fiction contained and nourished in and through them, results in a similar critical judgment being brought down upon Bailey. In reading through his understanding of what science fiction is, why it is popular, and why it is of vital importance for our age, we seem to be reading something we have read several times before.

All this is said not by way of dismissing the "pioneering" work of Bailey. For what Bailey does in his work is point to exactly the same understanding of science fiction as was seen to characterize that of early science fiction. But this conclusion must be drawn: as long as a critic of science fiction does not come to grips with the self-understanding of early science fiction, his critical work will further the "confusion of forms" so prevalent today. Bailey is merely the first in a

long line of critics who have used narrowly the narrow categories of romance-tending-toward-myth; and once having made
that designation, have not known how to proceed from there, or
where to proceed, and have subsequently retreated into the
treatment of science fiction as a literature of ideas with a
tendency toward practical application. Similar fates have be-
fallen those critics who have used narrowly the narrow categories of fantasy-tending-toward-escape, utopia-tending-toward-
escape, and utopia-tending-toward-satire. The end product is
all too often a virtuoso performance which has little or no
basis in any critical reading of the texts or other critical
works.

Kingsley Amis: Mapping Hell and Other Places

        In 1959 Kingsley Amis, noted British author and some-
times science fiction writer and editor, gave a series of
lectures on science fiction at Princeton University. They were
subsequently published in 1960 in book form, under the title of
New Maps of Hell: A Survey of Science Fiction. It is almost
universally hailed as being the first widely read, critically
respectable examination of the genre, in addition to setting
the parameters for much of the critical discussion of science
fiction in following years./1/ The respect Amis shares among
his peers in the literary field certainly has much to do with
the influence of his work; but the book commands respect in
itself. It is on the whole a balanced, literate, and highly
thought-provoking analysis of what science fiction is and how
it ought to be criticized from a literary point of view.

        Amis is a writer of science fiction himself; yet he al-
ways keeps his critical distance. He has his likes and dis-
likes in the field of science fiction and adjacent fields; yet
he always makes it clear what those are. He rarely slants a
treatment without the reader's knowing about that slant, and
seeing the reasons for it. Still there are some presuppositions
Amis has that even he is not aware of; and so his work too must
be put to the test.

        Central among the critical positions affecting Amis'
survey of science fiction is his dismissal of the fantasy

dimension of science fiction. To fantasy is attributed nearly
all excesses of imagination, flagrant disregard for scientific
fact, and even "express or tacit approval of authoritarianism"
(101). This dismissal of fantasy is consequent upon Amis' bias
for the realistic mode of the novel. This bias, in turn, leads
Amis to read science fiction as a literature concerned primarily
with social criticism, the "admonitory utopia." His definition
of science fiction gives expression to that bent:

> Science fiction is that class of prose narrative treat-
> ing of a situation that could not arise in the world we
> know, but which is hypothesised on the basis of some
> innovation in science or technology, or pseudo-science
> or pseudo-technology, whether human or extra-terrestrial
> in origin (18).

According to Amis the science fiction writer is primarily
concerned with verisimilitude, even in his/her extrapolations
into the future. Even should the writer be forced to resort to
science or technology of the flagrantly pseudo variety, a con-
certed effort is made to minimize what is self-contradictory.
Amis continues: "A difference which makes all the difference
between abandoning verisimilitude and trying to preserve it
seems to me to make all the difference, and in practice the
arbitrary and whimsical development of nearly every story of
fantasy soon puts it beyond recovery" (23).

Thus the critical point has been raised and the issue
joined. For the question is precisely that: Is the development
in fantasy "arbitrary and whimsical?" And, further, is it
"beyond recovery?" Amis himself lays the groundwork for making
sense out of the "arbitrary and whimsical" developments in
fantasy, and, indeed, for its recovery through critical tools.
In his opening chapter, "Starting Points," Amis begins by discussing the "addiction" of the science fiction reader, pointing
out that this reader will experience another dimension, related
to but distinct from what the ordinary reader will experience
in terms of literary interest. He continues: "The point about
addiction is the one where investigation should start." For to
the addict entertainment is not incidental, but essential.
Amis, however, does not go on to discuss exactly what this
addiction consists of (other than comparing it to the addiction
to jazz); but instead describes how it manifested itself in the

science fiction phenomenon. His description of science fiction
is quite similar to that presented above. Science fiction:
1) emerged as a "self-contained entity" in the twenties or
thirties; 2) is characteristically American (i.e., Western);
3) has a "noticeably radical tinge;" 4) has "arrived at a state
of anxious and largely naive self-consciousness;" and 5) has for
almost half a century separated itself from the literary mainstream (16-17).

The point to be raised here is whether or not one can
understand that addiction, and the forms in which it manifested
itself, without averting to the fantasy dimension of science
fiction. The two are so closely linked as to be virtually in-
separable. To try to force a separation arbitrarily leads only
to a misunderstanding of science fiction, both as a movement
and as a literature. The fantasy dimension figures prominently
in an understanding of the "romance" ancestry of science fiction, the authoritarian bent of its politics (as Amis does
acknowledge), the attraction toward pseudo-science, and the
tendency toward myth. It can also be said to have influenced
science fiction's self-understanding as a self-contained entity,
possessing an "anxious and largely naive self-consciousness."

What Amis does not address at length in his book is a
working critical distinction between fantasy and realism. Such
a critical distinction will accord to fantasy its own role and
its own place in the literary world. It will also recognize
that there is a structure and a logic to fantasy. Finally, it
will demand tools for the critical recovery of the meaning of
fantasy, not being thrown off by its arbitrary and whimsical
nature.

In one sense Amis does foreshadow much of this discussion,
when he touches on the role of fantasy in his chapter, "New
Light on the Unconscious." Amis begins by citing a passage
from H. L. Gold, editor of the science fiction magazine *Galaxy*:
"Few things reveal so sharply as science fiction the wishes,
hopes, fears, inner stresses and tensions of an era, or define
its limitations with such exactness" (64). Thus Amis, in
following Gold, establishes what is the real referent of science
fiction: the expectations of a people, not the extrapolations
of a few of its members. This is an immensely important

critical tool, the use of which demands the inclusion of fantasy
within its search. Amis himself acknowledges this demand, saying that he will treat equally of science fiction and fantasy,
"in the belief that the latter sometimes offers materials
which no wielder of the probe can afford to miss." Amis' referent in this particular chapter is going to be the "wishes,
hopes, and fears as they reveal themselves in contemporary
science fiction" (64). We have argued above that a wider term,
encompassing all these, is the expectations of a people. Understood socially and culturally, as these expectations manifest
themselves in the stories and myths by which the people live,
they constitute the basis for a religion, albeit a secular
religion. This, it seems, is the necessary corollary to Frye's
positing a secular scripture. Exactly what Amis is lacking is
Frye's sense of myth as social, indeed, of literature as social.
This lack is evident in Amis' title for this chapter, with its
referent of the "unconscious." There is no sense here that the
unconscious is ever anything other than something highly personalized, individualized, and privatized.

Nonetheless, Amis does single out fantasy, along with
science fiction, as a vehicle for the expression of the hope,
wishes and desires of people (if not a people). It will be
argued below that it is the fantasy dimension of all science
fiction which is the vehicle. That is, unless all science
fiction were fantastic to some degree or other, it could not
adequately deal with those expectations, and consequently could
not induce a kind of addiction. There is a need to have
expectations transcending those created by simple extrapolation
of known facts and accepted theory. There is a logic to the
miraculous, a sense of wonder which necessitates the introduction of the unknown, the transcendent.

That this is a central concern of science fiction is
witnessed to by the conscious debunking of religion that goes
on in its stories. What it speaks out most strongly against is
that which it is most susceptible. Amis' discussion of this
concern is similar to that of other critics: religion is merely
another theme of science fiction, another subject matter, though
for some of its more exceptional stories. Conversely, religion
is reduced to feelings of "humility and reverence," and is

almost always individualized and privatized. Amis cites a
story by Clifford Simak, "Contraption," in which a small boy,
from a home lacking affection, encounters alien beings who are
warm and loving.

> Johnny went down on his knees without knowing it and
> held out his arms to the things that lay there among
> the broken bushes and cried out to them, as if there
> was something there that he might grasp and hold--
> some comfort that he had always missed and longed for
> and now had finally found (quoted on 84).

The only step that need be taken is to read this story as
referring to the expectations of a people, thus making of
religion something public and political, instead of privatized
and individualized. The consequence is that science fiction
is to be read as the literature of this religion; and further,
that it is apocalyptic literature, since it treats explicitly
of what is to be revealed in the new age which gives meaning
to the present expectations. Thus, what science fiction kicks
out the front door enters by the back; and what Amis dismisses
pre-emptorily (i.e., fantasy) is welcomed back surreptitiously
by way of being a source of needed evidence. The similar
process in both cases suggests that they are linked: namely,
that fantasy is a vehicle for the dissemination and practicing
out of expectations; that chief among a people's expectations
are those things they trustingly believe in; and that consequently fantasy is the vehicle for nourishing the "faith"--even
a secular faith.

Amis began his study by maintaining that the "addiction"
of the science fiction reader is where the study of science
fiction must begin. In the end he is at a loss how to explain
that addiction. Our contention is that through an analysis of
the fantasy dimension of science fiction one can begin to
appreciate the addiction, and see in it the positive grounding:
the need for a faith-world. Amis' dismissal of fantasy does
not invalidate the bulk of sound critical analysis contained in
his book, however. His first chapter, "Starting Points," is
one of the more often printed essays in collections of science
fiction criticism, as well it might be. In addition to situating science fiction in relation to other literature, Amis
critically assesses the attempts to include every historical

work of imaginative literature in the science fiction canon,
dismissing most of them as having simply "accidental similarities" (29). Amis' description of what happened to science
fiction in the twenties and thirties contraverts the self-
understanding of science fiction. While the latter saw it as
the coming into the promised land, the emancipation of itself
from the narrow concerns of realism (descriptive simply of the
way things are); Amis sees in that period the eclipse of the
"admonitory utopia," the original intent and purpose of science
fiction. Fantasy is to be blamed for that state of affairs,
the flight from utopia. Science fiction, on the other hand,
is not to be considered "educational" or "prophetic." "Its
most important use, I submit, is a means of dramatizing social
inquiry, as providing a fictional mode in which cultural
tendencies can be isolated and judged" (63). In his concluding
chapter Amis takes up this point again; he praises science
fiction for being a "forum" for the discussion of serious problems facing humankind. In this regard he treats of the *Idea as
Hero*, the use of which accounts for the well sounding para-
phrases of science fiction stories, and the tendency to allow
stylistic concerns to fall by the way.

The Interregnum

It is said of Kingsley Amis that he was the first to
lecture publicly at a university on science fiction as literature. The distinction of inaugurating the first recognized
course treating exclusively of science fiction belongs to Mark
Hillegas, who introduced such a course at Colgate in the Fall
of 1962. In an article in the science fiction journal, *Extrapolation*, in 1967, Hillegas relates his difficulties in attempting to reconcile science fiction and serious literary criticism
in the face of disparaging comments from his faculty colleagues.
In 1975 Hillegas' doubts are even more far-reaching, extending
not only to whether science fiction is a "viable" term, and
whether there are any science fiction works that rank with the
great literary masterpieces, but also to the institution of
English departments themselves, as conservative, high-browed,
and hostile to science as they are.

Hillegas' doubts, however, have done nothing to halt the proliferation of science fiction courses, estimated in 1975 to number in the 500s in colleges, and in the thousands in high schools. It is this "academic awakening," along with the institution of the *MLA* ongoing seminar on science fiction, and the publication of the science fiction journals, *Extrapolation*, *Science Fiction Studies*, and *Reiverside Quarterly*, which created the climate within which the serious study of science fiction could flourish and grow. In the second half of the sixties, and the early part of the seventies, it began to bear fruit and the books began to appear, signaling a sustained effort to critically evaluate the science fiction phenomenon and its literary worth.

The first efforts were halting: Mark Hillegas' *The Future as Nightmare: H. G. Wells and the Anti-Utopians*, and H. Bruce Franklin's *Future Perfect: American Science Fiction of the Nineteenth Century*. Both are literary historical studies, necessary as a prolegomenon to serious study of science fiction, but unconcerned ultimately with the "entirely new thing" modern science fiction considered itself to be. Thomas D. Clareson, editor of *Extrapolation* since its start, edited a volume of critical essays, *SF: The Other Side of Realism*, in 1971. It set out to establish once and for all that science fiction is a form of fantasy. In this it largely succeeds; and it sets the stage for the subsequent attempts at science fiction and genre criticism. Finally, Robert Philmus, in 1971, published a study called *Into the Unknown: Ehe Evolution of Science Fiction from Francis Godwin to H. G. Wells*. The title is deceptive, however, for it is less an historical study than an attempt to apply contemporary literary critical tools to the reading of past and contemporary science fiction. Specifically, Philmus uses Wayne Booth's tool of "rhetorical strategy" as the criteria by which he differentiates science fiction from other categories of narrative, particularly fantasy. This rhetorical strategy involves "employing a more or less scientific rationale to get the reader to suspend disbelief in a fantastic state of affairs" (vii). The purpose of the strategy is "mythic displacement," through which present reality is seen anew, for the first time, as it were, and can be interpreted in a new manner.

In the context of the development of science fiction criticism Philmus's study represents what I consider to be the first sustained use of a literary critical tool in the study of science fiction, other than, that is, the use of the categories of fantasy and utopia, which even Campbell and Moskowitz make allusion to. From Philmus on, the study of science fiction must necessarily proceed from within "the order of words" Frye discusses: Literature building on literature, and criticism on criticism. Philmus's work, therefore, sets the stage for the two studies occupying our attention in the next portion of this chapter: Robert Scholes' *Structural Fabulation*, and David Ketterer's *New Worlds for Old: The Apocalyptic Imagination, Science Fiction, and American Literature*. These works were chosen for further consideration because they represent the clearest examples of what happens when a critic transposes the self-understanding of science fiction into predominantly literary categories (Scholes); and what happens when a critic applies a wide new category widely to science fiction and opens up its literature to a new reading (Ketterer).

Structural Fabulation:
Science Fiction as Cognition

As with Amis' study of science fiction, Robert Scholes' book on *Structural Fabulation* grew out of a series of lectures at a university. Given at Notre Dame in 1974, it was published by their press in 1975. Robert Scholes is an accomplished and prolific literary critic, treating in his work mostly with critical theory. It is no surprise then that Scholes uses science fiction for the purpose of extending and modifying and giving concrete foundation to his ever-developing theory of literature, especially as seen in and through narrative forms. It is also no surprise why this book is of interest to this study. But what is of special interest is how the concluding opinions of Scholes about science fiction repeat in his literary critical categories what was expressed so uncritically, so boastfully, in the self-understanding of early science fiction. Let us try to detail that claim.

Structural Fabulation is a polemical book. It argues to its point out of a "structural" view of literature, with its sweeping statements, light fantastic excursions into history, sociology, scientific thought, and polemical criticism. It argues to its audience, presumably literate in all of the above fields, as well as knowledgeable in science fiction, out of a moral passion for the continued welfare and survival of human-kind.

Scholes readily acknowledges the polemical nature of his study, but defends it on the grounds that literature (especially the "fiction of the future") must serve a grander moral purpose: not only sublimation, but also cognition. "How can fiction be most useful to mankind in the present and in the future?" (1975:11). This is the question Scholes pursues in the four brief lectures which constitute the book. The answer is not long in coming: "I am asserting that the most appropriate kind of fiction that can be written in the present and in the imme-diate future is fiction that takes place in the future" (17). Later on he argues that "to live well in the present, *we must see into the future*" (75, author's emphasis). The structural fabulists, those story-tellers who extrapolate into the future the systems and the structures (i.e., the paradigmatic in-sights) of the past century of science and scientific thought, allow us to see cognitively into the future, and therefore help us to live well in the present. The model for this is the feed-back system; for by their fabulations about what present structural understandings imply, the structural fabulists help us to assume responsibility for the present.

In Chapter Two, "The Roots of Science Fiction," we dis-cover the ancestry of structural fabulation, and, consequently, where science fiction fits into the grand scheme of literature. Since the eighteenth century, Scholes writes, criticism has broken fiction down into two great streams: novels and romances, also designated as realism and fantasy. The novel, or realism, is posited on the basis of a radical continuity with the world; the romance, or fantasy, on the other hand, on a radical dis-continuity. The question he specifically addresses in this chapter is how this radical discontinuity is symbolized. Ancient fantasy symbolized it through heaven, hell, fairyland, utopia, Atlantis, etc. As the symbols lose their power, discontinuity is achieved through a suspension of the laws of nature; and

further down the line it is achieved through the development of
the laws of narrative. The end result, however, is that discontinuity is achieved through sublimation: writer and reader
know that the world of the story is there for purposes of
escape.

There is another way, however, a radical discontinuity
which emphasizes cognition. "When romance returns deliberately
to confront reality it produces the various forms of didactic
romance or fabulation we usually call allegory, satire, fable,
parable" (29). Although the world created is discontinuous,
the didactic romance returns to confront it in a cognitive way.
What didactic romance says, therefore, is that there is more to
the world than meets the eye. Traditionally this has been
religion's major theme. But now science has taken up the theme;
it trades dogmas for speculation and field theory. Thus, from
didactic fabulation two new forms emerge: dogmatic fabulation
and speculative fabulation. The latter, in turn, bifurcates,
resulting in pseudo-scientific fabulation and structural fabulation. The former speaks for itself; the latter is based upon
the conception of man which has replaced the religious world-
view. Scholes cites stages in the development of this conception: Darwin's theory of evolution, Einstein's theory of
relativity, the developments in the study of the human systems
of perception, organization, and communication, the linguistic
philosophy of Wittgenstein, the gestalt psychology of Kohler,
the structural anthropology of Levi-Strauss, and the cybernetics
of Wiener. These developments have turned humankind's self-
understanding around. Scholes concludes: "In its broadest
sense, this revolution has replaced Historical Man with
Structural Man" (35).

In an "Afterword" Scholes graphs the development of the
romance as follows:

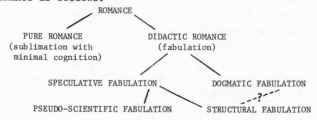

That he placed a dotted line, with a question mark, between
dogmatic and structural fabulation is Scholes' way of acknowl-
edging that in a sense he is "preaching" a "new dogma called
structuralism," and that structural fabulation (his understanding of science fiction) receives a "kind of religious sanction
based on science" (103).

This exercise in genre criticism, therefore, ends up at
the same point at which the self-understanding of early science
fiction did: science fiction is ultimately to be understood in
religious terms, albeit secular religious terms. The route to
that understanding lies along the same paths: through an analysis of science fiction's roots in fantasy, and through an insistence that science fiction is the most relevant literature
being written.

Thus far noted Scholes' argument could be presented,
understood, and defended as literary criticism. One could
maintain the legitimacy of studying science fiction as a psycho-
sociological phenomenon with "religious" pretensions, even
fitting it into the larger framework of Frye's study of the
secular scripture. But Scholes will not let his case rest. He
not only argues for the legitimacy of this approach, he argues
for its exclusivity in understanding science fiction. And his
argument on behalf of science fiction is based on that most
specious and tantalizing of all philosophical dilemmas: Which
comes first, the word or the idea?

Having posed the dilemma, Scholes argues that science
fiction saw no choice but to opt for the idea: the idea is
more important than the word because it lends itself more easily
to the categories of structuralism. The fiction of today (the
best-seller realism), according to science fiction, is useless
because writers and critics alike accept the fact that language
is no longer an adequate system of notation; it can no longer
"represent" reality. Thus the morass in which the literary
world finds itself, the naive realism of the current best-
sellers, and the solipsistic dead-ends of Beckett and others.
Scholes says that science fiction accepts the diagnosis pronounced on language, and finds the way out through being a
literature of ideas, that is, structural fabulation.

Structuralism, the theory which lies at the heart of
Scholes' book and its title, is much wider in its scope than
literary criticism. Its roots trace back to Russian formalism,
the linguistics of Saussure, and gestalt psychologies. But its
most notable works, perhaps, have been in the structural anthropology of Levi-Strauss and the linguistics of Noam Chomsky.
Scholes elsewhere refers to it as an activity and a method,
rather than as an ideology. But he does acknowledge that perhaps today we do need structuralism precisely as an ideology
(1974:197). Put simply, structuralism is the response to the
need for a coherent system of meaning in the face of the demise
of all the classical systems of meaning. That structuralism is
gradually being transformed into a "new system of belief" is
but an acknowledgement that only as "belief" can an ideology
justify its continued existence (2-3). Structuralism is not
only the activity of trying to unify all the sciences, it is
the belief that it can be done under some one unifying principle.
In structuralist thought "the universal and the systematic [are
emphasized] at the expense of the individual and the idiosyncratic" (190). In literary criticism, for example, structuralism first formulates a model of the system of literature itself;
this serves "as the external reference for the individual works
it considers" (10). The referent, then, of all literature is
this conceptual model.

This understanding of structuralism is central to Scholes'
argument that structural fabulation is the most appropriate form
of fiction, now and in the future. With the intensity of a
believer (reminiscent of early science fiction), he argues that
structural fabulation fills the need for the structuring of our
lives, our society, and our history, by providing us with imaginative accounts, drawing its ideas from the social sciences
mainly (sociology, economics, anthropology, history, behavioral
psychology). "It is the new *idea* that shocks us into perception,
rather than the new *language* of the poetic text" (1975:47,
emphasis added). The shift away from idiosyncratic language to
the systematizing idea is critical to Scholes' argument that for
science fiction language is no longer an adequate system of
notation. Language of itself is useless, except that it does
communicate ideas; and ideas are the stuff of speculation, our

dreamings about the future. At the present, Scholes says, no
other representational media can match the "speculative agility
and imaginative freedom of words." Thus we still need words to
communicate ideas. "Until the mind can speak in its own tongue-
less images, the word will be its fleetest and most delicate
instrument of communication" (38).

David Ketterer: New Worlds
for Old (Beliefs)

There is a sense in which Ketterer's study, *New Worlds
for Old*, begins where Scholes' leaves off; for Ketterer's presupposition is that science fiction is apocalyptic literature,
and thus can be considered a secular scripture. But, whereas
Ketterer's analysis does open up the possibility of reading
science fiction in an entirely new way, by failing to follow
through radically in his understanding of apocalyptic, Ketterer
in the end does not exhaust the possibilities he creates. In
brief, his treatment of the secularization of apocalyptic,
involving as it does a transformation of expectation into
extrapolation, and of Biblical apocalyptic into philosophical
apocalyptic, prevents him from reading science fiction as a
social and socializing literature, and from exploring the roots
of science fiction in fantasy. Both of these figure prominently
in any identification of science fiction as apocalyptic; and
they are linked by an understanding of fantasy as a literature
of expectations.

The subtitle of Ketterer's book, "The Apocalyptic Imagination, Science Fiction, and American Literature," sets the
boundaries for his study. Ketterer argues that science fiction
is the purest outlet for the apocalyptic imagination which
characterizes much of mainstream American literature. Ketterer
bases his treatment of apocalyptic imagination on an extensive
re-working of Northrop Frye's discussion of apocalyptic myth in
Anatomy of Criticism. The main revision consists in the expan-
sion of Frye's categories to include not only the world human
desire creates, but also the one human desire rejects; that is,
the demonic is subsumed into the apocalyptic, the latter having
now both a positive and a negative charge. In science fiction
imagery the positive charge is realized in the description of

the new heavens and the new earths--the world freed from disease, corruption, poverty, and even death; the negative charge
is seen in the descriptions of the holocaust and doomsday, the
passing away of the old. What Ketterer has done is link the
two in an act of the imagination; this type of imagination he
calls apocalyptic.

Ketterer is intent on formulating a critical tool which
he can employ in categorizing and criticizing major American
writers for expressions of the apocalyptic imagination, and
selected major works of science fiction writers for evidence of
the same. In the final formulation of what he calls the apocalyptic imagination, or "philosophical apocalypse," he finds
such a tool.

> Apocalyptic literature is concerned with the creation of
> other worlds which exist, on the literal level, in a
> credible relationship (whether on the basis of rational
> extrapolation and analogy or on religious belief) with
> the 'real' world, thereby causing a metaphorical destruc-
> tion of that 'real' world in the reader's head (13).

Philosophical apocalypse, then, is the exchange of new worlds
for old, however brief that exchange may be. That the apocalypse is philosophical only underlines the fact that science
fiction cannot shake the label of an "idea" literature.

The literary-philosophical creation of other worlds,
according to Ketterer, is accomplished either by means of
extrapolating from the present world, or by means of introducing a startling new *donnè* which offers a reader a radically
new perspective on the present 'real' world. Extrapolation
from the present world, however, can be of two kinds; it can
rise out of present circumstances, ("Other Worlds in Space and
Time"); or it can rise out of a modification of present circumstances ("Other Worlds out of Time and Space"). The introduction of the startling new *donnè* creates the story which is
about "The Present World in Other Terms."

To his credit, however, Ketterer does not take his categories too seriously; he realizes no work of science fiction
can be fitted neatly into one category. Ketterer apparently
fashions the categories simply to allow for a critical study of
the third thematic mode: the present world in other terms.
For he finds "the third type to be the most significant as an

expression of the philosophical sense of the apocalyptic imagination...this category has not previously been isolated by critics of the genre" (19). It is here that Ketterer makes a significant contribution to the critical study of science fiction, and to the exploration of the apocalyptic imagination in American literature. For not only does he provide extremely detailed analyses of such science fiction writers as Stanislaw Lem (*Solaris*), Kurt Vonnegut, Jr. (*Sirens of Titan*), and Philip K. Dick (*The Man in the High Castle*); he also brings the tool of philosophical apocalypse to bear on Melville's *The Confidence Man* and Twain's *A Connecticut Yankee in King Arthur's Court*.

In speaking of "the present world in other terms" Ketterer is obviously formulating a practical application of Frye's anagogic phase of symbolism. In this category Ketterer searches out the still center of the literary universe, the literary work as the mediator of all meaning. All literature, he argues, presents us with a startling new perspective; what emerges out of our reading is not a new world, but a new old world. Philosophical apocalypse occurs in the reading of any literary work: "I am concerned here...with profound redefinitions of man leading to the conception of a new man whether in quasi-spiritual, mechanistic, evolutionary, or philosophical terms" (64). Or, as Frye would have it, "This is not reality, but it is the conceivable or imaginative limit of desire, which is infinite, eternal, and hence apocalyptic" (1971a:119). What Ketterer does, then, is go beyond the 'reality' to the heart of literature, the creation of entirely new worlds, the by-product of which, not its aim, is the destruction of the old world. In this he not only isolates the third mode, and does the work of practical criticism; but he also lays the groundwork for a re-reading of all science fiction as something more than simple extrapolation. For the latter view of science fiction is all too readily appropriated by the preachers of doom and the tellers of glory, by the social analyzers and the social technicians.

Although Ketterer's definition of philosophical apocalypse may be an adequate tool for the critical reading and categorizing of science fiction, there is some question whether it can function on any other level. Part of the problem is

that Ketterer is too deeply caught up in the secularization of
the apocalyptic imagination. This leads him early on in his
summary treatment of the religious apocalyptic imagination to
discuss exclusively the *Apocalypse* of John the Apostle, and in
his discussion to characterize John as suffering from paranoia.
It would seem, to the contrary, John had some legitimate reasons
for railing against the Roman empire: he was living in exile
and his fellow Christians were being persecuted and systematically executed for their beliefs. It is noteworthy not that
some bitterness and paranoia show through in the *Apocalypse*,
but that there is so little of it, and that it is not the over-
riding concern of the book. The same, however, cannot be said
for the other apocalyptic literature of that era. That is the
further point: apocalyptic literature is a genre much wider in
scope than the *Apocalypse* of John. A study of the genre in
itself and in its history might have acted as a critical counter
to the tendency of Ketterer to take too seriously the paranoic
characterization of John, with the attendant conclusion that
Biblical apocalypse calls for the destruction of the old so that
the new may come. Ketterer claims that philosophical apocalypse
reverses the order, in that in it "the evocation of the new precedes the destruction of the old world" (34). This is simply
a misreading of the *Apocalypse* of John; it happens because
Ketterer fails to take seriously his own notation that apocalypse functions as a "recapitulative coda" of the whole Biblical
story. In that story Jesus is the new world which precedes the
destruction of the old./2/

Ketterer further compounds the secularistic reading of
apocalyptic literature by shying away from its mystical dimensions. After having modified Frye's treatment of apocalyptic
so as to include the demonic, Ketterer traces the demonic facet,
displayed in paranoia, through satire and ultimately to the
literature of silence. He then follows its polar opposite,
apocalyptic, the visionary theme, through wonder, utopia, and
the literature of fantasy. But just as Ketterer failed to see
the hope behind the paranoia and bitterness, so he fails to see
the mystical faith behind the wondrous visions. Revelation, in
the secular apocalypse of Ketterer, becomes the mere transfer
of information, or the logical process of rational extrapolation.

What was hidden is now revealed through the instrumentality of
human knowledge. When that happens the unknown becomes the
known, and no longer exists in a credible relationship with the
'real' world.

Ketterer's analysis of apocalyptic literature is dependent on a criticism more concerned with the writer's craft than
it is with the readers'(36) and consequently more concerned
with an understanding of the constitutive act of the apocalyptic
imagination as extrapolation rather than as expectation. This
is the basis for his formulation of the "philosophical apocalypse," which is inherently privatized and individualized. But
apocalyptic is a public and political literature, expressive of
the hopes and beliefs that a people share. It is the expectations of a people, in the end, which are destructive of the
'old' world, and not the extrapolations of some few of its
writers.

Ketterer does raise the question of the nature of apocalyptic literature and its relation to the matter of religious
belief. But Ketterer's secularization of apocalypse has muted
that question for him, reducing the nature of belief to its
secular counterpart of human desire, and the expression of it
to the three forms of extrapolation he describes: the new world
created by simple extrapolation from the present world, the new
world created by extrapolation from a modification of the
present world, and the new world created by the introduction of
a wholly new given which provides a radically new perspective.
Other critics have taken him to task for precisely the opposite
reason--for not having made that reduction, but rather for
allowing the inclusion of religious belief into critical discourse. The passage in Ketterer to which they refer reads:

> While mimetic literature addresses itself to reproduc-
> tions of the 'real' world, fantastic literature involves
> the creation of escapist worlds that, existing in an
> incredible relationship to the 'real' world, do not
> impinge destructively on that world (13).

Ketterer than goes on to formulate his definition of apocalyptic
literature (given above), of which the key element is that the
relationship of the created world to the real world be a 'credible' one. The weight of Ketterer's argument, as Robert Canary
points out, comes down upon the word "credible," for it is the

only word which "imposes any limits" (131).

The parenthetical remarks of Ketterer within his definition, concerning the basis for credibility, are of critical
importance. They become the battleground, not over the question
of whether science fiction is apocalyptic literature, but over
the question of whether the credibility of its claims rests on
rational extrapolation or on religious belief (or quasi-religious
belief). Ketterer argues for the inclusion of both; Canary says
that to include the latter is to "water down" the definition.

The usual compromise between the two positions takes the
form of suggesting that rational extrapolation has acquired the
status of quasi-religious belief among science fiction writers
and fans. But extrapolation is ultimately a rational process,
unable to transcend its own sources. Although it may account
for the creation of new worlds, it alone cannot account for
their credibility. Ketterer insists that extrapolation can
account for credibility: "The mysticism [which science fiction
brushes against] must never exceed the bounds of plausibility
...the technique of extrapolation demands a commitment to logic"
(18). The point here is not that Ketterer and Canary agree in
the end (which they do, for both place the basis for credibility
in rational and logical extrapolation), but that the critical
viewpoint is based on an analysis of the writer's craft, not
the reader's. Yet the destruction of the 'real' world is to
take place in the reader's head. It becomes ever more difficult
to see how, barring a theory of reading, that destruction is to
be mediated. Certainly the text is critical in any theory of
reading; but the function of the text will vary, based on the
expectations brought to it. These expectations, ultimately,
are what determine the credibility of the text and the world it
creates through extrapolation or through 'religious' belief.
The expectations of readers cannot be explicated by a theory of
writing, such as Ketterer offers in his book. Expectations are
notorious for being neither rational nor logical; they are of
another order. Extrapolations indeed may tell us what the
future will be like in the future; but expectations tell what
role the future plays now. The latter is of much more vital
importance. To read science fiction merely as a literature of
extrapolation is to reduce it, not fantasy, to escapist literature.

Finally, there arises the problem of what to do with
that science fiction whose "rational extrapolation" is no longer
credible, having been superseded by theoretical or technological
developments. Much of that literature is still "credible" to
the science fiction addict. The reprint business is in full
bloom: 'Doc' Smith, Edgar Rice Burroughs, the anthologies of
early science fiction. This suggests that its credibility cannot rest on rational extrapolation, but rather must rest on a
world-view informed by a faith in science and technology. The
most criticism can do in this matter is explicate the meaning
of rational extrapolation as that which delivers one to the
threshhold of belief. In other words, reason does not destroy
faith, but grounds it. The readers of science fiction have
always realized this (whether or not they could articulate it);
and it is to this that critics must begin to pay attention.
This is why a theory of reading is so critically important.

Ketterer is not only correct, then, in his designation
of science fiction as apocalyptic literature, but also in allowing for the inclusion of 'religious beliefs' into critical
discourse, even though they may be secular religious beliefs;
for these latter are what ground and establish credibility, and
according to them even rational extrapolations are judged.
Rational extrapolation is the tool this secular religious belief
uses, not to make the story or the new world believable, but to
make itself believable in an age which demands new forms of
belief. It is in this sense, as Philmus argues, a "rhetorical
strategy." Finally, it is not the rational extrapolation which
creates the new world, nor even the story; it is rather the
belief itself which creates. For of these three, belief is the
only one which has the power to create--although that creation
must take place through the medium of the word (story) and in
the language of the times (rational extrapolation). Thus
Ketterer is really talking about "new beliefs for old beliefs,"
not "new worlds for old worlds."

The Critical Reading of Apocalyptic:
An Introduction

There remains the task of introducing some critical
theory on apocalyptic literature, particularly as it bears on

reading of science fiction. Ketterer's treatment begins with a discussion of apocalyptic in its biblical roots. But, as mentioned above, it is limited by his selection of only the *Apocalypse* of John the Apostle. Nevertheless, Ketterer derives four considerations from a close look at that work: 1) apocalypse has both a negative and a positive charge, i.e., there is a necessary correlation between the destruction of the old world and the creation of the new; 2) the prophetic dimension of apocalypse is compromised by the fact of persecution, for Ketterer this means John possibly suffered from paranoia; 3) apocalypse functions as a recapitulative coda of the entire Bible, i.e., the 'end' gives meaning to all that has gone before; and 4) the scope and grandeur of times, places, and events leads to a diminished status for the individual, and even for humankind itself (7). When looked at more closely, one dynamic is seen operating in all four. Ketterer maintains that "apocalypse allows for a dialectic, conflict, or tension of opposites;" and that is the stuff of literature (8).

In tracing the form and function of apocalyptic down to contemporary times, Ketterer describes the current transformations of those four considerations: 1) the destruction of the old world and the creation of the new is a process which happens in the mind of the writer; 2) satire confronts prophetic mysticism to provide a form of judgment; 3) the creation of purpose and meaning collides with the possibility of non-meaning and chaos; and 4) apocalypse involves a breadth of vision which generally precludes an interest in detailed characterization (13). Before developing Ketterer's argument, we must again point out that it is difficult to see how 'apocalypse' which happens in the mind of the writer can cause a "metaphorical destruction...in the reader's head," without some theory of reading, which Ketterer does not provide for us.

When Ketterer says apocalyptic allows for dialectic and tension he approaches the critical appreciation of apocalyptic. But he does not succeed in going the whole way. The ultimate dialectic, in terms of which apocalyptic resolves all the other conflicts and tensions, is the dialectic of promise and fulfillment. The core of apocalyptic is thus: How can the present be the fulfillment of the promise? For Ketterer the dialectic is spoken of as one between the pragmatic and the speculative, between the material and the transcendental, between an ethic of violence and a hallucinogenic ethic. These might better be understood as the dialectic between the "is" and the "ought to be," between, that is, the descriptive and the normative. Transposed into the categories of promise and fulfillment, the question is thus raised: Which is more normative, promise or fulfillment? Apocalyptic, both biblical and secular, opts for the promise.

The charge always leveled at apocalyptic is that it is escapist, that it has opted out of the struggle for meaning and purpose by forsaking the public forum and the political arena. The question put to it is this: What good is a promise if it can never be fulfilled? But the question apocalyptic puts in return parallels it: What good is a promise if it can be fulfilled? Particularly if the fulfillment alone never causes us to look critically at the present. Only the dialectic between promise and fulfillment does that; and it is apocalyptic literature which keeps that dialectic before us in the purest form.

Ketterer, to categorize his examples of the dialectic in terms of promise and fulfillment, places at the promise pole speculation, transcendentalism, and a hallucinogenic ethic-- all of which can be understood as promising salvation through knowledge, the latter, the hallucinogenic ethic (or, the drug culture), being only the latest instance of it. At the fulfillment pole is the reality (Ketterer's 'real' world) of pragmatism, material gain, and violence. The latter three are the way it is; the former the way it ought to be. The tension exists within the literary work, not in some mental exercise which compares the literary world with the 'real' world.

The best of science fiction never allows promise or fulfillment to exist without its dialectical partner. In a wider sense, however, all literature exists in that tension. It seeks, as Frye maintains, to encompass all reality within the world it has created. This means the reader happens *into* apocalypse, rather than apocalypse happening inside the reader's head. Apocalypse is literary in this radical sense, rather than philosophical in the sense of being a head trip. The story is not about revelation; the story is the revelation, which not only gives knowledge, but also meaning.

This latter distinction (between knowledge and meaning) is critical to the discussion of science fiction as a 'religious' literature. For the transformation of the *logos* of science into the *mythos* of science fiction constitutes the passage from salvation through knowledge to salvation through meaning, and opens science fiction to the field of theological inquiry. Science fiction as *mythos* not only contains the tension Ketterer designates as apocalyptic (that between the descriptive and the normative), but also the tension existing between itself and *logos*, the origin of the promise it mediates. The promise reveals itself not only as giving knowledge, but also meaning—and in science fiction it is the latter which ultimately saves, as it is in all religion.

Science fiction itself, however, gives no clear indication how it should be read—although as we have seen the self-understanding of early science fiction clearly came down on the *logos* content of science fiction: science fiction possessed the 'secret knowledge' through which order would be brought out of chaos. Yet, as we have also seen, it is the *mythos* dimension of science fiction which clearly sets it apart from the rest of literature, and its readers apart from the social, cultural, and political mainstream. It literally fashions a world in which the hopes and dreams of its followers have meaning, and thereby gives them an identity through which one is able to survive whatever evils may come. Part of the confusion of forms characterizing science fiction criticism evolves from this failure critically to distinguish between salvation through knowledge and salvation through meaning. To read science fiction as 'promising' knowledge leads to highlighting the utopian features and functions; to read it as promising meaning leads to emphasizing solely its fantasy nature.

It remains now to discuss how and why the *logos* of science had to become the *mythos* of science fiction. Briefly, since science is a body of knowledge which seeks to be superseded by its very nature, and story is not, the promise had to be carried by a vehicle that itself could not be superseded./3/ Such precisely is *mythos*, or story. It is the nature of story, moreover, to promise rather than to fulfill; and in apocalyptic, as we

have seen, promise is more normative than fulfillment. Science
fiction holds to the promise in the face of any fulfillment
which might surpass or negate that promise.

The promise as received and preached by science fiction
is that "science saves." But the roots of that promise, and
the transformations it undergoes, from *logos* to *mythos*, are of
more interest and pertinence to our study than repeating what
by now is a commonplace, that science is a deity. The promise
of science is long in its formulation and incredibly tenacious
in its history. For the purposes of our study it is helpful to
treat of it under the form of one of its earliest appearances:
the myth of salvation through knowledge. For this highlights
the passage from *mythos* to *logos* and back again. What is at
issue here is not what the stories of science fiction are about
--that is, the referent (science) which exists outside the
story and which does work wonder after miraculous wonder--it is
rather what the stories present: science saves. It is a world
of meaning and value which is presented; not a collection of
data and information about reality.

Both the relationship between *mythos* and *logos*, and the
resulting tension which arises when the differentiation is made,
are contained within an early "story" which promises salvation
through knowledge. But it is noteworthy to highlight what
happens to the story when it is interpreted in light of the
logos of Enlightenment philosophy. According to Paul Ricoeur,
in his treatment of the "myth of the exiled soul," the evil
from which one is to be saved is the present condition, that is,
from "the alteration of life and death," which is symbolized by
the body (the other) and the soul (the same). Ricoeur concludes
how this salvation is to be achieved according to the "myth of
the exiled soul":

> Now the act in which man perceives himself as soul, or,
> better, makes himself the same as his soul and other
> than his body--other than the alteration of life and
> death--this purifying act *par excellence* is knowledge (300).

The story (*mythos*) of the soul/body distinction not only
develops at the same time as the discovery of *logos*, it is in
fact the story of that discovery. The story and its symbols
tell of what is happening (in the process of differentiation of

consciousness) when no discursive account exists to tell of it,
and when *logos* itself cannot. The story does not create the
absolute dichotomy, nor does it argue that knowledge (*logos*)
depends upon a clear and radical divorce of soul from body--or,
in more philosophical terms, of subject from object. It merely
tells of the unity (the unifying act which is salvation) of
identity and non-identity which transpires in the process of
knowing. In the differentiation there is a joining. What is
being dramatized, therefore, is the struggle to maintain this
unity in differentiation which was susceptible to being absorbed
into the object of knowledge, i.e., back into the chaos of the
undifferentiated. It is through the story about knowing (not
through knowing per se) that there is appropriated a unity in
differentiation. This is salvation.

Contemporary philosophy speaks of this unity from the
perspective of the subject, arguing that in consciousness, in
lived inner experience, identity (subject-as-subject) and non-
identity (subject-as-object) are grounded. But it is only
mythos which is able to convey the insight, and keep the unity
before us; for inner experience ("interiority") is the lived
unity of identity and non-identity; it is never susceptible to
total objectification./4/ Only relatively recently in Western
thought, with Descartes particularly, does the differentiation
between subject-as-subject and subject-as-object (presented as
a unity in differentiation in the early myth) become "objectified" and result in a radical split between subject and object
--or, in the story's terms, between soul and body.

Given this "objectification," story (*mythos*) is no longer
able to mediate the unity in differentiation; for subject and
object (soul and body) become radically separate entities. It
is conceptual knowledge (*logos*) which must bear the burden; and
it does so by speaking of the "identity" between knower and
known, between subject and object, one of which imposes its form
upon the other. "Control" becomes the metaphor of mediating
identity. It makes little difference, in the end, whether soul
(subject) controls body (object), or the reverse: both models
forsake story and opt for the conceptual content. Story remains; but now it is knowing (rather than story about knowing)
which delivers identity. *Logos* has been ripped from *mythos*; it

becomes the former rather than the latter which saves.

Knowledge, the act by which a person "makes himself the same as his soul," that is, keeps his identity, is control over the body through a conscious differentiation and distancing of self from it. Thus it is also control over the object of knowledge through the naming of it as other. The soul/body dichotomy, according to the interpretation given to it by the Cartesian *logos*, is symbolic of the radical split taking place in human consciousness, between self and other, subject and object. Salvation through knowledge, in this framework, is no longer cosmic and/or collective, but rather personal and individual. Salvation is the process of achieving identity; that is, knowledge saves because it gives an identity which transcends the dichotomy. But the price *logos* pays in engendering the split is that the gulf between subject and object is complete. Some kind of control over the object is necessary; and knowledge offers this control: the identity is an identity of mind. That which is controlled and that through which one controls, is the idea, which has become in the Cartesian formulation the "clear and distinct idea," the eminently manipulative reality. The pathos of the Enlightenment, of course, is that it works the other way also.

The pathos of the Enlightenment is also that the movement between *mythos* and *logos* can work both ways. *Logos*, ripped from the *mythos* of Greek culture by the Enlightenment philosophers, becomes in turn a *mythos* itself. It is the story science fiction tells over and over again. The story is not about the process of transformation; the story is about itself. It could hardly be otherwise; for the unity of lived experience (which only *mythos* can present in its narrative drive without reducing it to total objectification) seeks constantly to re-assert itself over the conceptual and the abstract. We see the movement perhaps most clearly in what transpires at the time during and succeeding the Enlightenment, the immediate precursor of the promise that is constitutive of science fiction.

In his provocative study of the origins and "doctrines" of the Enlightenment philosophers, *The Heavenly City of the 18th Century Philosophers*, Carl Becker traces the soteriological implications which their philosophy necessarily had to bear.

The "climate of opinion" prevailing in that century was one in which history replaced theology, science replaced philosophy, and the scientific method replaced logic. Although God was not replaced straightway, he now revealed himself through nature, not the church. Natural law, moreover, was transformed into the "laws of nature;" and harmony, not final wisdom, was the goal of rational methodology. History, having now assumed the mantle theology once wore, was understood as a collection of truths. Facts gleaned from the past as examples were illustrative of the doctrine these philosophers held about "man in general": 1) man is not natively deprived; 2) the end of life is life itself; 3) reason and experience are the guides to this end; and 4) the essential condition of progress is freedom from ignorance (102).

Thus the *logos* of the Enlightenment philosophers. But what they had yet to contend with was the *mythos* of Christianity, the story it told, the drama which unfolded in its liturgies and in its liturgical year. Christianity saved, according to Becker, because it gave meaning to the natural life of man in terms of an archetypal drama, a drama which unfolded from the past, through the present, and into the future. The *mythos* was a narrative in three phases: 1) life is good; 2) it has regressed to where it is at the present time (sin); and 3) it will be redeemed. In the cosmic drama of salvation, the three phases are creation, the fall, and redemption; in the personal drama of each Christian, they are innocence, sin, and justification. Becker writes in this regard:

> The importance of the Christian story was that it announced with authority...that the life of man has significance, a universal significance transcending the temporal experience of the individual (128).

The Enlightenment philosophers, however, also convinced that life is good, since man is not natively deprived, and that the present time is a regression from the past "golden age," accounted for by the fact of human ignorance, needed an ending to the story they were telling, an ending which would fill the role of justification/redemption. In Becker's imagery this is the role played by the heavenly city. Moreover, since they were convinced that the end of life was life itself, they had

to locate their heavenly city within the confines of human life
and history. That they needed a "heavenly city" is evident,
Becker argues, else "the religion of humanity would appeal in
vain to the common run of man" (129). The *logos* of the Enlightenment philosophers became, in effect, the *mythos* which informs
much of science fiction today: 1) Eden is transformed into the
golden age; 2) the fall is brought about by ignorance, not sin;
and 3) posterity becomes the "judge and justifier" of human
actions (142). The heavenly city is to be built in history by
the efforts of humankind; the meaning (and therefore the salvation) of human action depends on its completion.

In a talk given to a gathering of Nobel laureates in
1975, Langdon Gilkey ascribes the soteriological force of science
to the (relatively) newly acquired "certainty in the knowing
process, a new freedom from tradition...and a new confidence in
the power of our freedom to control the future." He compares
the status and role science now possesses to that once possessed
by theology, as the Queen of all the sciences: to know the
ultimate meaning and purpose of life, and so be able to exert
control over the evils that might destroy humankind. "Sacred
knowledge," Gilkey says, "establishes and guarantees the power
to control what menaces us." Both Becker and Gilkey, then,
argue that science had to assume a soteriological role, once it
claimed to be the one, true method of knowledge. But salvation,
if it is to be a shared, collective experience (that is, if it
is to truly save us), must be mediated in a form which allows
for it. *Mythos* does, *logos* does not. The *mythos* of science
fiction is needed, if the *logos* of science is to be salvific;
the meaning is what ultimately allows the knowledge to save.

The biblical story in Genesis, long read as a story about
creation, is now read as a story which creates. And the stories
of science fiction, often read as stories about promise (that
science will save), will have to from how on, in this understanding, be read as stories which promise meaning now, not
knowledge in the future. For the knowledge they contain is
already dated by the time the ink dries; while the meaning is
always new and always reassuring: the efforts to know, to do,
to build, to forge, to fashion, to live--all are worthwhile,
for that is the destiny of humankind, to which there is no limit.

Yet the science fiction story once told (not what the story is about, but the story itself) is the negation of the promise. For the story promises the unlimited, and delivers only the limited: human knowledge, the knowledge of science. This ambiguity is what a critical reading of science fiction as apocalyptic literature yields. It is illustrated in Campbell's story, "Twilight," cited in the first chapter. The tale ends with the lament of the time-traveler:

> Can you appreciate the crushing hopelessness it brought to me? I, who love science, who see in it, or have seen in it, the salvation, the raising of mankind—to see those wondrous machines of man's triumphant maturity, forgotten and misunderstood. The wondrous perfect machines that tended, protected, and cared for those gentle, kindly people who had—forgotten.

The fundamental ambiguity as to what exactly the time-traveler laments, the loss of wonder or the loss of knowledge (science), can only be resolved by a theory of reading. The reader who listens to the preaching will, along with Campbell, lament the loss of scientific knowledge. But the reader who listens to the story will, also along with Campbell, lament the loss of wonder and curiosity. The science fiction insider, the fan, the member of the cult or sect, is no longer in need of preaching; he or she already believes. The insider listens to the story, not to the messages which are preached. But the two exist in a dialectical tension; and the story, taken in a wider sense (which the self-understanding of early science fiction never appropriated), contains that tension—if it truly be literature, and not thinly disguised discursive reasoning.

Whatever Ketterer's analysis of science fiction as apocalyptic literature does in the end, it forces us to read it as story, and not as a collection of themes, symbols and images, plausibility devices or futuristic visions, ideas, concepts, or model world cities. The same can be said of biblical apocalyptic; it is inextricably linked to *mythos*, which resolves ultimately to the dialectic of promise and fulfillment. We will treat this more fully in Chapters Four and Five. In science fiction, which is our primary concern here, when promise is reduced to human expectation and based only on rational extrapolation, fulfillment inevitably means negation of the promise,

for the expectations have been met and are no longer the driving force. It is only when science fiction as true apocalyptic
literature moves beyond excessive concern with fulfillment
that it allows promise to exercise its critical role: to provide a critique of all final solutions.

What Ketterer's analysis also does is force us to read
apocalyptic science fiction as a body of literature which,
taken together, is one story. The reader who picks up Asimov's
Foundation, for example, but who fails to follow through with
Foundation and Empire and *Second Foundation* very obviously has
failed to read the whole story. But even the reader who fin-
ishes the *Foundation* trilogy, and then never reads another
science fiction work, also fails to read the whole story. The
whole story, when it is finally told, will have to be a story
which always promises; that is, at the end the promise will
still remain. It will thus somehow have to exceed human expectations, or transcend rational extrapolation--else the promise
will have been fulfilled and will no longer be normative. In
biblical apocalyptic this role is played by God, who in himself
and in his promises is transcendent. When the whole story is
told in biblical (and apocryphal) apocalyptic, there remains
God and his promise; they are not surpassed.

In science fiction there are two symbolic modes for this
transcendence, that is, for promise which extends beyond rational
extrapolation. On the one hand, as seen in Wollheim's construct
of the consensus future history, the end is even beyond God,
located in the end of history and the cosmos, and the beginning
all over again of the cycle. What is symbolized therein is the
fundamental inability of the human desire to transcend itself;
an inability which is witnessed to in all the final solutions
that have wracked the world from Babel to Dachau. On the other
hand there is the promise that "We are not alone!" Whereas the
consensus future history portrays the future rising out of the
present, this symbolization presents a future breaking into the
present, that is, into history. We will see later that these
correspond roughly to prophetic and to apocalyptic eschatology,
respectively. The theme of "We are not alone" (currently popularized by *Close Encounters of the Third Kind*, just as *Star Wars*
popularized future history) has a long and tenacious history in

science fiction. But its most profound treatment is to be
found in the relatively recent works of Arthur C. Clarke,
particularly *Childhood's End*, *2001: A Space Odyssey*, *Rendevous
with Rama*, and *Imperial Earth*. In the latter work, it should
be noted Clarke desists from describing the actual encounter,
but concentrates merely on the promise: There must be (other)
intelligent life in the universe, else all meaning vanishes.
This corroborates our contention that it is the promise, rather
than the fulfillment, which is normative.

Documentation supporting this "promise" in early science
fiction is found in a story by the sociologist Walter Hirsch,
"The Image of the Scientist in Science Fiction: A Content
Analysis." Hirsch does a random sampling of the science fiction
pulps from 1926 to 1950. In them he finds scientists to be the
central figures, sometimes villains, sometimes heroes. By and
large the analysis fits in with the first set of symbols:
science saves. But at a certain point after World War II,
faith in science and the scientist subsides, and the "alien"
more and more intervenes to solve human problems. Hirsch
writes: "It seems...possible that there has occurred a more
radical disillusionment with any sort of rational scientific
means and hence a recourse to 'magical' solutions." He declines,
however, to call this a pessimistic outlook; nor does he ascribe
to it any "return to religion." "If the 'aliens' represent any
sort of principle or power, it would seem to be 'chance' rather
than some anthropomorphic deity" (511).

The promise that "we are not alone," moreover, is increasingly becoming the promise of the scientific establishment.
The search for extra-terrestrial intelligent life was recently
the subject of an article in *The New York Times Magazine*, "Seeking an End to Cosmic Loneliness." The article recounts the
serious, systematic scientific search for extraterrestrial
intelligence. One of the more ambitious efforts along these
lines is *Project Cyclops: A Design Study of a System for De-
tecting Extraterrestrial Intelligent Life*. A passage from
Intelligent Life in Space by Frank D. Drake, a pioneer in radio
astronomy, is cited on the dedicatory page:

> At this very minute, with almost absolute certainty,
> radio waves set forth by other intelligent civiliza-
> tions are falling on the earth. A telescope can be
> built that, pointed in the right place, and tuned to
> the right frequency, could discover these waves.
> Someday, from somewhere out among the stars, will come
> the answers to many of the oldest, most important, and
> most exciting questions mankind has asked (iii).

Finally, Alvin Toffler, in a forward to *Cultures Beyond the
Earth*, writes: "If life in outer space does not exist, we are
justified in inventing it" (vii).

It is clear from the titles and the contents of these
and other works that although the search for extra-terrestrial
intelligent life is neither a return to religion nor to an
anthropomorphic deity, nonetheless it represents much more than
the power or principle of chance. It is a search for meaning--
for "answers to many of the oldest, the most important, and the
most exciting questions mankind has ever asked." Moreover, it
is science which conducts the search, does the listening and
watching, and will be the means through which humankind will
discover that it is not alone. This again is the normative
promise.

As we will see later, both these symbolizations, future
history and "We are not alone," treat of the dialectic of
destiny and freedom--and ultimately of the spectre of fate
hanging over humankind due to the limited nature of their views
of the future. The meaning of history is what is at stake here;
and the "flawed transcendence" of science fiction can revert
only to the cycle of history on the one hand, or the luck of
chance on the other. Both are attempts to establish the
normativity of the promise, it is true; but both empty it in
the end of any meaning. Yet the science fiction story continues
to be told, because it does hang together, it does make sense,
and it does establish a meaning which people find comfortable,
and into which they can live. The secular apocalypse of science
fiction, taken as a whole, is a fiction whose "ends are consonant with [its] origins, and in concord, however unexpected,
with their precedents" (Kermode:5).

The passage is cited from Frank Kermode's penetrating
study of narrative structuring in literature, life, and history,
The Sense of an Ending. Kermode bases his study on the model

of apocalypse, for it is a "radical instance of such fictions
and a source of others" (6). He is concerned with understanding the End in terms of the fullness it gives to each lived
moment. More particularly he is concerned with what he considers to be the passage from a naive imminent expectation to a
more sophisticated understanding of the end as immanent. Apocalypse is an example of the former (a "radical instance"), and
fiction, including the fiction of history, an example of the
latter. The occasion for the "imaging of the end" is our "living in the middest," or in more contemporary terms, living in
"ceaseless transition." We need to project ourselves past the
end "so as to see the structure whole, a thing we cannot do
from our spot of time in the middle" (8). This gives a meaning
to the transition period, a period which belongs neither to the
end, nor to the age which precedes it. It becomes a special
time, having special characteristics, and calling for a special
ethic.

When Kermode goes on to list the doctrines of apocalypse,
he cites crisis, decadence and empire, and the divisions of
history into mutually significant phases and transitions. All
these give meaning to the time of transition in which the
apocalyptic writer and reader feel they are living. But Kermode's major concern is with "disconfirmation," which he maintains is the inevitable fate of a detailed eschatology.

Kermode argues that people living in transition make
"considerable imaginative investments" in patterns which co-
herently tie together the origins and the ends and render the
whole story (of life) satisfying. He concludes: "That is why
the image of the end can never be *permanently* falsified." But
because people have to take account of what is happening now,
"there is a recurring need for adjustments in the interest of
reality as well as of control" (17). Thus there arises an
"indifference to disconfirmation;" and a further insistence
that what happened was supposed to have happened; that is, it
was consonant with the end. Although there may be falsifica-
tions of expectations, there can be no real falsification of
the end. However, when the experience of disconfirmation is
repeated over and over again (or experienced once in a most
profound way), then the end is no longer experienced as imminent.

Rather the image of the end becomes immanent and is happening at every moment. Humankind, in this understanding, lives in a state of perpetual crisis. For Kermode our experience of history as crisis is dominated by this understanding. An age of perpetual transition is always read as an age of perpetual crisis by an apocalyptic imagination.

The remaining portions of Kermode's study attempt to see the world as structured in time, rather than in space. History is the "imposition of a plot on time," and fictions are "models of the temporal world." This central concern with time flows from naming apocalypse as the paradigmatic and radical instance and source of our fictions; for fictions, as he writes else- where, are "our ways of finding out about the world" (54). Fictions are also described as personalized myths, what happens to apocalypse when it becomes demythologized. Fictions are temporal, not spatial art forms. It is the end (even when per- ceived as immanent) which makes of the interval between it and the beginning a significant and meaningful duration. The example Kermode uses is the tick/tock of a timepiece. The sound is exactly the same, physically; yet we need to designate one as the beginning (birth) and one as end (death), else the interval is indeterminate, and efforts to live according to its rhythm are reduced to chaos and absurdity. We also need the rhythm of tick/tock in the fictions that we read, else the "slice of life realism" degenerates into mere chronological succession. The tick/tock in fiction "is a way of speaking in temporal terms of literary form. One thinks again of the Bible: of a beginning and an end, denied by the physicist Aristotle to the world, but humanly acceptable and allowed by him to plots" (58).

Even more, we would argue, it is necessary to plots, especially since the personalization of myth and the rendering of the end as immanent no longer allow apocalypse to function publicly and politically as a "concord fiction." It is not only the triple-decker world which has succumbed to modern phenomenological and existential thought, it is also the temporal world which has collapsed. The collapse of the latter is much more significant; and consequently it is the recovery of apocalyptic that is critical to a renewal of theology, as evidenced by the work of Moltmann and Metz.

This is precisely the point at which science fiction enters, however; for it is a re-mythologization of apocalypse, a making public and political of the concord fictions, and a restructuring of the temporal world. The transition to the new world and the new age is no longer an indeterminate and meaningless period, for the end is again imminent. Time is no longer measured by clocks and digital computers; it is measured by inventions, discoveries, space-flights, and encounters (of the third kind)--all of which are only tomorrow away. Science fiction is certain of our origins, and certain of our end; and thus it is certain that tomorrow will bring a new age. Science fiction is about the expectations of a people, rather than the extrapolations of a few of its writers. This is precisely where that insight fits into the reading of apocalyptic, to use the categories of Kermode. For the self-understanding of early science fiction is filled with the themes of imminent expectation. For all the careful, measured, logical and chronological plotting, the editorial blurbs and jacket covers told the real story: "This is about a world only tomorrow away!"

That science fiction is a-political is due to the fact that politics participates in the world of duration: it takes an indeterminate amount of time to bring about change politically. That science fiction leans toward authoritarian politics, on the other hand, is due to the fact that the *fiat* of a ruler brings about change instantaneously, or at least by that 'tomorrow'. The impatience of the believer is expressed in the fictions that do away with graduated change and the possibility of reversal. The same dynamic, it seems, is to be found in biblical (and apocryphal) apocalyptic, where God has determined the course of events from before all time. In this regard the editorial of Campbell, "God Isn't Democratic," sheds some interesting light on the issue of determinism as it crops up in biblical and secular apocalyptic. Campbell argues that because we have forsaken "Absolutes," God is no longer relevant. "The revolt is not against God--but against the concepts of discipline, of forces in the Universe greater than human will..." Later in the same editorial Campbell admits that "Perhaps there is no God after all." He continues, however, with a statement

which clearly grounds his understanding of science fiction in
a determinism every bit as rigid as that which we encounter in
biblical apocalyptic: "But there is One Universe, and its laws
are absolute, unswerving, unyielding, and enforced on us without argument" (1966:247-48). Obviously the "One Universe"
Campbell talks about refers more to the one universe of the
whole story of science fiction than it does to the physical
universe. Unity is much more necessary for a story's meaning
than it is for scientific understanding. Kermode writes in
this regard: "The events [of apocalypse] derive their significance from a unitary system..." (5). The point here is that
determinism and absolutes function in a time-frame which differs
fundamentally from an evolutionary time-frame according to which
we live. Absolutes, we say, are time-less; that is, they belong
to that temporal world which has collapsed. To re-introduce
them is to re-introduce that temporal world, and to make both
yesterday and tomorrow imminent once again. This all happens,
moreover, in the only universe in which we live: the one universe of story. For only story is expansive enough to contain
all the longings of humankind; and only story can satisfy the
most fundamental of all longings: the longing for meaning.

We have in the course of this chapter travelled through
a critical understanding of science fiction and arrived at the
point where the critical understanding of science fiction is
grounded in and builds on the self-understanding of science
fiction as apocalyptic literature. In the course of this
journey we have seen that the characterization of science fiction as romance tending toward myth leads inevitably to a confusion of forms; but that a characterization of it as popular
literature tending toward apocalyptic aids in clearing up that
confusion. Moreover, we have gained an insight into why this
is so: the linking romance with popular literature and myth
with apocalyptic allows us to include elements of the self-
understanding of science fiction--elements which are important
if the later critical understanding of science fiction is to be
grounded in reality.

UTOPIA AND FANTASY:
THE LIMITS OF THE UNDERSTANDING OF SCIENCE FICTION

> Without stepping beyond the analogy of that which
> is known, it is easy to people the cosmos with
> entities, in ascending scale, until we reach some-
> thing practically indistinguishable from omnipotence,
> omnipresence, and omniscience. If evidence that a
> thing may be, were equivalent to proof that it is,
> analogy might justify the construction of a natural-
> istic theology and demonology not less wonderful
> than the current supernatural; just as it might
> justify the peopling of Mars, or of Jupiter, with
> living forms to which terrestrial biology offers no
> parallel.
> —Thomas H. Huxley

Introduction

The characterization of science fiction as a popular literature tending toward apocalyptic allows for a critical appropriation of science fiction's own self-understanding as a literature set apart, i.e., distinctive because it is "some-thing entirely new" and ushers in a new age. At the heart of this self-understanding is the category of trusting faith whose objects are: 1) science as the form of knowledge which will allow for the creation of the new world; 2) human destiny which calls for the implementation of this new world; and 3) the future which is the condition of its possibility and the pledge of its achievement. There is no way to approach the self-under-standing of early science fiction nor to comprehend its inev-itable tendency toward apocalyptic, without an explication of that faith, not only as it informs the readership, but also as it informs the literary productions of science fiction. Such an explication will be one of the tasks of this chapter, inso-far as we treat of the fantasy roots of science fiction; for fantasy is intimately tied up with belief.

We have seen also that the critical understanding of science fiction has reinforced our initial characterization of science fiction as a popular literature tending toward apocalyptic. It has given us the tools necessary for a critical reading of it and other forms of apocalyptic. Most importantly it has shown that to read apocalyptic as literature one must read it as story. For Ketterer this means reading it as "dialectic, conflict, or tension of opposites." For Kermode apocalyptic is the radical instance of "concord fictions," those stories in which the origins and ends are tied together so as to render the whole meaningful, and, more particularly, to give a meaning to the period of transition in which people find themselves. The result is that apocalyptic is to be read as temporal art form which is about (or better, presents) a temporal world in which the origins, the present meaning of, and the ends of life are patently clear.

At the heart of the critical understanding of science fiction as apocalyptic literature, then, are the categories of time, change, development, and history, seen from a perspective which allows for a view of the "whole story." But because science fiction is tied so closely to an understanding of these categories (of time, change, development, and history) in terms of rational extrapolation, both in its self-understanding and in some of its critical understanding, the literary form that it has chosen to be the vehicle is utopia, the rational projection of an idea of society into the future. And the stories it has told are about the creation, existence, and/or demise of such future utopias. Thus our treatment of science fiction as apocalyptic literature must also include a discussion of the utopian dimension of science fiction, for utopia is intimately tied up with history and its negation.

In keeping with our presupposition that for apocalyptic promise is more normative than fulfillment, we concluded the preceding chapter with a brief analysis of how the rational extrapolations of science fiction are pushed to the limits in order to hold onto the normativity of the promise. For promise to remain normative it must somehow exceed human expectations. In this regard we isolated two symbolic representations of the transcendence of promise: 1) future history, culminating in the end of the cosmos, time, history, humankind, and meaning (all of which will eventually be exhausted), and the beginning all over again of the cycle; and 2) the promise that "we are

not alone," that some other intelligence exists in the universe,
contact with which will give a fullness to human life and history they now lack.

Roughly, the two genres in science fiction which are the
vehicles for these symbolic representations are utopia and fantasy. Utopia in science fiction is at root a rational extrapolation which, in the course of its fulfillment, ushers in the
new age, and which, pushed to its limits, eventuates in the
post-historic era. This is exactly what is symbolized in the
future history utopias of science fiction. The flaw is not in
the craft or the vision of the creators of this utopian future
history, however, but in its very structure. For utopia is
about the limits of rational extrapolation. Fantasy, on the
other hand, seeks the radically new perspective which will
foster a new understanding, yet not exhaust the possibilities
of future understanding. Still, the promise that we are not
alone, the ultimate fantasy of science fiction, is so indeterminate in its forms and empty in its content that its normativity suffers as a result. Non-fulfillment becomes the condition
of its possibility, assuming a greater normativity than the
promise itself. But any ordinary appreciation of fantasy will
realize that this is looking at the whole problem backwards;
the promise that we are not alone is the story, not what the
story is about. "We are not alone" is a negation of negation,
not simply a negation. Science fiction fantasy is about the
limits of disbelief.

Finally, in our introductory remarks, we would be remiss
if we did not point out that the temptation to combine these
two symbolic representations in one grand linear model is a
temptation to be avoided. What we have here are two radically
different configurations of the meaning of human life and history. Rational extrapolation does not issue logically in the
expectation of something which (or someone who) exceeds radically those expectations. Thus, for example, the existence of
aliens within the future history model does not mean the same
thing as the introduction of extra-terrestrial beings within
the "we are not alone" model. "Bug-eyed monsters" are simply
rational extrapolations of what is already known about the fears
of humankind, and as such almost always appear within the future

history type of story. They are merely displacements of the
savage, the redskin, the underside of human experience. The
aliens within the "we are not alone" story serve another function altogether. They symbolize the unknown, the existence of
that which we have no logical reason to expect, yet which we
need if our world is to be complete. The trusting faith in
the existence of other intelligences in the universe is not
merely another stage tacked onto the consensus future history
of science fiction; it constitutes a wholly separate formal
mode of relating the promise which exceeds all expectations.

In terms of expectations we could roughly equate these
two modes with prophetic and apocalyptic eschatology. The
future history mode, in this equation, is the secularized
transformation of prophetic eschatology; while the "we are not
alone" mode is the secularized transformation of apocalyptic
eschatology. Whereas the former conceives of the future rising
out of history, the latter sees it as breaking into history.
In keeping with our analysis of apocalyptic as a literature
incorporating the dialectic between promise and fulfillment,
and as being a literature which seeks to restructure the temporal world (much more so than the spatial), it is precisely
under the aspect of "future expectation" that we will treat of
utopia and fantasy.

Utopia and the Limits of Extrapolation

The fundamental ambiguity of the word utopia, meaning as
it does both "no place" and "good place," is compounded in our
day by the fact that the "place" of utopia is more temporal
than geographical. The deeper ambiguity, however, allows for a
deeper understanding of utopia and the limits of utopia. For
utopia in contemporary terms means both "no future" and "good
future." And according to this understanding we are forced to
consider what exactly is the role of a perfect society, and, in
the end, what price does it exact?

Our answer to that question will be that the price utopia
pays (when yoked rigidly to rational extrapolation) is the
denial of history; for the utopia which science fiction en-
visions, the linear extrapolation from present circumstances

and/or their modification, results in a good future which is in
the end no future at all, but merely the continuation of the
present "in other terms." Utopia in science fiction, for all
the technological predictions, rarely rises above the present,
nor does it allow for the introduction of the radically new.
It is static, one-dimensional, and monolithic in its structure
and in its conception of change, time, and history.

It should be noted, however, in saying this we are arguing that the utopia of science fiction is a corruption of the
literary form; for the transformation of the utopia of literature and literary art into temporal art form need not, as has
been largely the situation in science fiction, result in the
creation of future societies which exist in no critical relationship with the present. It is possible to understand the ambiguity of utopia temporally as meaning "no present" and "good
present." This forces us to read utopia as a commentary on the
present, more so than on the future; that is, the future expectation will offer a critique of the present understanding. In
this sense the "good present" of the utopian world stands in a
critical relationship to the "no present" of the reader, saying
that his/her present is not the summation of all that is good
and to be desired.

Our discussion of utopia will treat transformations of
future expectation effected in the different modes of the
utopian mentality. We seek to discover what happens to the
understanding of time, change, development, and history when an
"idea" assumes the dominating position and becomes the structuring principle.

Utopia was at first rejected by science fiction as a
literary form because it was too political; it dealt with the
present in terms of a critique of it and in terms of some
realizable political goals. The utopias of science fiction, as
Frye argues, trace their lineage to Bacon's *New Atlantis* rather
than to More's *Utopia* (1970:112). Their main concern is with
the technological configurations of society, rather than with
legal and political configurations. The adoption of utopia by
science fiction occurred only when it learned to write its
history in scientific and technological terms, that is, when it
became supra-political. Its conception of history, therefore,

is radically different from that of other utopian manifestations.
It does not read history in legal, political, or even rational
terms, such as critical theory does; nor does it read history
in theological terms, as we will attempt to do in the final
chapter. Science fiction has its own politics and its own
theology.

In effect, what science fiction has done is to translate
literally the utopia isolated in space into the utopia isolated
in time. Just as in the typical literary utopia there is no
way to get there, except by accidental discovery, so in the
science fiction utopia there is no way to get there from here--
except by catastrophe, or some intervening disruption of normal
time. And the more technological and scientific the society
extrapolated, the less political and historical the transition
becomes, until, in the end, there is no description of the
passage (unless in mythical history) and even, in the most
extreme cases, overt rejection of the study of history. All
the roots have been chopped away. Thus H. G. Wells, in narrating how his great utopias came into existence, begins with the
prediction of the collapse of the present world order, due to
the fact that this order remains based on nation-states' auton-
omy long after scientific and technological revolution has
rendered that political structure obsolete. In the wake of the
inevitable collapse, a world-state utopia is established. This
story is told in his *War in the Air*, *The World Set Free*, and
The Shape of Things to Come. In a later Wells' work, *A Modern
Utopia*, whose business at hand is the actual description of
utopia, there is no recounting of the passage from "present"
state to "future" state. Utopia is presented as an accomplished
fact, already existing in a parallel world.

It is no great step from this refusal to recount the
history of utopia to the refusal of history itself as offering
anything of value to human understanding. Perhaps the most
explicit example of this step is found in B. F. Skinner's
Walden Two, with its undisguised disdain for history. "History
is honored in Walden Two only as an entertainment," says Frazier
to his guests (115). Later on, in discussing the educational
system, Frazier comments:

We don't regard it [history] as essential in their
education...Nothing confuses our evaluation of the
present more than a sense of history...None of your
myths, none of your heroes--no history, no destiny--
simply the *Now*! The present is the thing. It's the
only thing we can deal with anyway in a scientific
manner (238-39).

Walden Two, it comes as no surprise, itself has no history; and
if Frazier will have his way, it will never have one.

The founding of Walden Two is never recalled publicly
by anyone who took part in it...All personal contribu-
tions are either suppressed altogether or made anonymous. A simple historical log of the community is kept
by the Legal Manager, but it is not consulted by anyone
except Planners and Managers who need information (235).

What is obviously happening in *Walden Two*, and in many
science fiction utopias, is a simple refusal of history, in that
it presents a future society, but does not reveal to us how that
community came to be. Utopia in this understanding is a simple
indulgence in the desire to transcend the processes of human
history and arrive immediately at the perfect state. There is
here a perversion of the literary form of utopia, especially as
Northrop Frye outlines the *mythos* of utopia, and the literary
varieties of its forms. Frye writes of the two conceptions of
society which can only be told in the form of a story: 1) the
social contract, which tells the story of the origins of society;
and 2) utopia, "which presents an imaginative vision of the
telos or end at which social life aims" (1970:110). The science
fiction utopia, the victim partly of wish-fulfillment and partly
of the technological imperative (which epistemologically is the
process of rational linear extrapolation), has seized upon the
telos or goal to be achieved, but has forgotten the more basic
premise of utopia: that it is grounded in an analysis of the
present and must return to it. Frye sees this cognitive return
to the present society in terms of two invariable features of
the literary utopia: 1) the behavior of the utopian society is
always described ritually; and 2) the rituals, which appear
irrational, become rational when their significance is made
clear (110). Frye, however, does not detail at any length the
different configurations of future expectation which result
from a refusal to begin in an analysis of the present and to
return to it. In explicating the relation of the model of

utopia to the present existing society, Frye resorts to the
tension between the normative and the descriptive, what is and
what ought to be. His only references to the temporal symbolizations are to Christian myth (which he argues, is not utopian
in a strict sense because it relies on divine intervention),
and the reappropriation of the pastoral myth by William Morris
and his followers: utopia is the projection of a simplified
past into the future.

   Frye's analysis as always is incisive and to the point.
But we want to move the discussion in another direction. Even
in Frye utopia is so much more plan than story that in its writing, and in the critical analysis of it, time, change, development, and history are foreign elements, for all practical purposes. Yet when it is remembered that utopia is a story that
"presents the imaginative vision of the *telos* or end at which
social life aims," then some analysis of the varying forms of
future expectation must be made, insofar as future expectations
determine one's conception of history and the dynamics of
historical development. The aiming is as critical as the goal.

A. The Utopian Dialectic

   Critics of utopia and utopian literature generally agree
that the term utopia has undergone changes since its introduction into our intellectual heritage by Thomas More, though each
analysis will place its emphasis differently. Moreover, all
will generally concur that the changes in its understanding and
its function refer to the changes which take place in society
and its structure, and to the restructuring of society along
different class lines. Thus Karl Mannheim's *Ideology and Utopia*
assumes an important place in any discussion of utopian literature.

   Mannheim too seeks to understand utopia in terms of the
relation the model has to present existing society. But unlike
Frye he will not reduce it to the tension between the "is" and
the "ought to be." He speaks, on the contrary, of the actual
and the possible. Further, his goal is not to explicate utopian
literature per se, but rather the utopian mentality. We are
dealing with two different levels of criticism; but to draw the
hard and fast line between social commentary and literary

criticism is an difficult here as anywhere. By using the critical tools of a sociology of knowledge, Mannheim refuses to be trapped into discussing utopia as a normative idea which existed in an embryonic state at the beginning of historical consciousness and developed logically and rationally through time. He argues instead that utopia is a dialectic. Mannheim begins his discussion of the utopian mentality with the succinct statement: "A state of mind is utopian when it is incongruous with the state of reality within which it occurs" (192). He ends his discussion of the utopian mentality with the argument that "the only form in which the future presents itself to us is that of possibility" (260). In between, Mannheim discusses the role of situational transcendence, wish-fulfillment, and the stages of the utopian mentality in "modern" times. The imperative enters only after all the possibilities have been noted and a choice must be made. For in this choice history is fashioned and the interpretation of history can be undertaken.

What is of special interest to us is Mannheim's treatment of the stages of the utopian mentality in modern times, and, more particularly, his comments on the relation of each mentality to future expectations and the experience of time. This experience of time and its possibilities Mannheim relates to the wish-fulfillment roots of utopia, saying, in effect, that utopia is a people's dominant social wish. Mannheim concludes:

> The innermost structure of the mentality of a group can never be as clearly grasped as when we attempt to understand its conception of time in the light of its hopes, expectations, and purposes (209).

In history, that is, the whole comes before the parts and includes not only the past but the future also.

Utopia arose in the modern consciousness when the "apocalyptic" conception of the millennium was joined to the active demands of the oppressed strata of society; that is, when it became a wish for a certain select group. This is the first form of the utopian mentality, with its roots clearly sunk in eschatological terminology and revolutionary rhetoric. As for the experience of time that characterizes this "orgiastic chiliasm," Mannheim describes it as "absolute presentness" (215). The here and now, the immediate, the present was the only point

in time which mattered; for all that was going to happen was
going to take place now. This immediacy and urgency is so over-
riding that there is really no expectation of the future as
rising out of the present. The future is the radically new.
In the second form of the utopian mentality, the liberal-
humanitarian, utopia is an idea whose projection into an
infinite future serves as a goal regulating the course of
society's life. A linear conception of time predominates; and
utopianism is concerned more with "becoming" than with the
sudden intervention of the new. Directly opposite this utopian
mentality is the third form, the conservative, which is actually
a counter-utopia. It is not concerned with some future fulfillment of an absolute idea; but, reflecting on the praxis of
existing society, locates utopia in the institutions as they
exist at present. Time is seen as duration; and that which
endures is de facto the good society. The future is seen as
the continuation of the present--only more so, for there is no
becoming, and there is no need for change. The fourth form of
the utopian mentality, the socialist-communist, seeks to steer
a clear path among the other three. It rejects: 1) the anar-
chist and/or sublimation tendencies of the chiliastic mentality,
while holding to its call for revolution; 2) the indeterminate,
slow evolutionism of the liberal-humanitarian, while keeping
the function of the idea as goal; and 3) the vested-interest
analysis of the conservative mentality, while maintaining that
present conditions do determine the theorizing of reflective
analysis, the goal of history, the idea of the future, and the
course of action to be taken. "Time" in the socialist-communist
mentality "is experienced here as a series of strategical points"
(244), with the goal being constantly clarified, refined, and
re-interpreted as each new "strategical point" is assimilated
into the analysis. The dialectic is always central and on-going.
"Historical experience becomes thereby a truly strategic plan.
Everything in history may now be experienced as an intellectually and volitionally controllable phenomenon" (247). It is in
this context that Mannheim speaks of "possibility" being the
only form in which we know the future; and of "choice" being
that which constitutes history and allows for its study. Utopia,
then, becomes central to any study of history, for it, as story

and symbol, exists as a pre-thematic re-presentation of the
dialectic of future expectations which constitutes historical
consciousness. For the critical choice the utopian mentality
must make is to keep the possibilities open in any configuration
of a future society.

The critical problem in the science fiction utopia is
whether science (understood in its technological manifestations
as manipulative of human behavior) can be part of the "strategic
plan" under which all of human life and history is "experienced
as an intellectually and volitionally controllable phenomenon."
The rise of dystopian science fiction, from E. M. Forster on
through Huxley and Orwell, to the nightmarish vision of the
future city in, for example, Roger Elwood's anthology of the
same name, seems to suggest that a significant number of science
fiction writers themselves reject the science fiction utopia.
But the flaw of the science fiction utopia, generally, may not
be so much the particular vision it espouses, but rather the
conception of time, change, development, and history which
underlies its structure. For, by and large, the science fiction
utopia is structured along the lines of a simple rational extrapolation of existing or highly desired trends--a structuring
which parallels its conception of time and history. In this
process choice is all but ignored as constituting any real
determining role in the formation of utopia. There is no choice
in the face of facts and technological expertise; "If it can be
done, it must be done"--so dictates the technological imperative.
What happens then in the experience of time according to the
rational extrapolative technological imperative mentality is
that choice is obliterated and "becoming" is ignored. The fact
of a future perfect society is as real as the fact of a present
perfect technique. This is what accounts for the total disregard for the "history" of utopia, and in its extreme cases
the actual disdain for history. There is in the science fiction
utopia no need to be concerned with the "coming to be" of the
perfect society; for, as the technological imperative dictates,
there is no choice, it simply must be done. The coming to be
is disposed of through oblique references to a catastrophe or
to a revolution suddenly reversing the existing order.

Science fiction utopian literature, then, is radically non-dialectic, exhibiting a static view of time and history. It is not science fiction's future vision which is incongruous with present existing order, but its view of time, change, development, and history. Utopia in science fiction is not escape from the present, nor is it escape into the future; instead, it is escape from the terrible process of becoming and the choices involved in it. It issues in what has come to be known as post-historic humankind.

From another perspective, however, the central flaw of the science fiction utopia is that it cannot account for the limits of rational extrapolation. The supreme symbolic manifestation of this flaw is its inability to confront the fact of death. The preoccupation with personal immortality (particularly in Heinlein) is an undisguised example of this. But the more profound symbolic representations consist of the limitless idea of progress, the invincibility of human destiny, the almost timeless duration of galactic empires, and, in its extreme forms, the transition of humankind to a higher order of existence (as in *Childhood's End* and *Last and First Men*), the state of pure thought in which there is no change or corruption. Death does not figure into the projections of rational extrapolation because death is seen, ironically, as the end, pure and simple. It is the end of the story, but is not a part of the story (because, as we have suggested, utopia is not story as much as it is plan). The science fiction imagination, for all its power and insight, cannot extrapolate beyond its own non-existence; and thus seeks to disguise this lack in the true fantasies of immortality, personal, racial, or cosmic. Pushed to its limits, most noticeably in Wollheim's consensus future history, rational extrapolation does admit to some notion of death as a passage. But even here it is merely the passage from one cycle to another--in the end there is no end. There cannot be, for the end signifies the negation of all there is.

In the Christian configuration of time, change, development, and history, however, death is the negation of negation, the true transformation, the passage to new life--a life existing in continuity with this life. Thus the resurrection of Jesus (not the resurrection of a *new* Jesus) assumes such a

critical role in the eschatological theologies of Moltmann and
Metz, both in terms of subversive memory and future promise.

Death is also a central theme of apocalyptic literature;
in fact, according to one critic it is the core theme and symbol
of all biblical apocalyptic (Collins, 1974). Surely in the
secularization of apocalyptic, of which utopia is a prime example, the triad of beginning, middle and end (creation, fall
and redemption; thesis, antithesis, synthesis) suffers from the
secular horizon's denial of death, especially in its refusal to
treat of death as passage, as symbolic of the continuities of
life and history. On the other hand, the pseudo-Christian
conception of apocalyptic as promising a life after death, instead of life over death, amounts to the same thing in the end.
Both issue in a denial of history, because both see death merely
as a negation, not the negation of negation. In effect, both
deny the end, and thus their story (and their history) is flawed
radically in its structure. It is for this reason that Ketterer,
for example, denies that there can be any true science fiction
utopia as story, for there exists no tension, which only an
acceptance of an end can provide. And for this reason also many
reject (rightfully) the Christian notion of apocalyptic as
speaking merely of life after death; for again, this is no story
(or history) of the faith-life of a people.

B. Utopia and Apocalyptic

Mannheim sees the rise of the utopian mentality occurring
at that point in history when the chiliastic hopes of apocalyptic
became identified with the oppressed peoples of society; that is,
when somehow the millennium became not only desirable but
achievable through human effort. Norman Cohn, in his definitive
study, *The Pursuit of the Millennium*, argues that the politiciz-
ing of eschatology (actually a re-politicizing, since it was
demythologized and personalized when Christianity became the
state religion of the Roman Empire) occurs when the millennial
hopes of Christianity are seized by the "marginal" groups of
society. Cohn, in a historical postscript, traces the sectarian
nature of Nazism and Communism to the chiliastic rhetoric and
fantasies of 15th to 17th century northern Europe, saying in
effect they are modern manifestations of a dream which refuses

to die. Mannheim, in his discussion of the four stages of the
utopian mentality, takes the longer route through the dialectical development of that mentality; but he clearly links its
rise to the "secularizing" of apocalyptic. The distinguishing
secular characteristic is that the millennium is terrestrial
in nature, and achievable through human effort--even if the
human effort demanded is only to destroy the old world so that
God can establish the new.

It should also be noted that Northrop Frye, in his discussion of the varieties of literary utopias, singles out
utopia's achievability as the distinguishing characteristic.
This, he argues, is precisely what allows utopia to function as
a critique of the present society (1970:120). Frye also singles
out the "conscious, rational plan" of utopia as a distinguishing
mark, arguing that utopia arose in opposition to the disintegra-
tion of Christian feudal society, and the anarchy threatening to
overwhelm all of Europe. His reading of utopia, of course, is
from a literary point of view, while Mannheim's issues from his
sociology of knowledge. The differences are resolved only when
it is understood that utopia and apocalyptic exist in a dialectical tension, not that one causes the other to come into
being, nor that there is a simple succession of forms. The
opposite of utopia is not dystopia, but apocalyptic. The
opposite of apocalyptic is not providence, but the secular
nature of the utopian mentality.

The themes of utopia and apocalyptic are interwoven all
through the literature of each form, suggesting that a thematic
analysis alone will not result in a description of what separates the two. When, for example, Cohn writes of the "egalitarian
state of nature" taken over from the Greek and Roman tradition
and fused with the millennialist rhetoric, it is difficult to
see how the themes of that state differ in any essential manner
from those contained in More's *Utopia*. Cohn's list includes:
1) a society in which all men were equal in status; 2) and in
wealth; 3) in which there was no exploitation of one by another;
4) in which all relationships were characterized by "universal
good faith;" 5) by brotherly love; and 6) by a total sharing of
property, extending even to wives (195). More's *Utopia* is
similarly constructed. The differences between the two must be

traced to the differences in future expectation, resulting in
divergent views of time, change, development, and history.
For this it is necessary to explore the relationship between
utopia and apocalyptic from another perspective: not apocalyptic tending toward utopia (as Mannheim argues), but utopia
tending toward apocalyptic, as Melvin Lasky in his mammouth
study, *Utopia and Revolution*, seeks to chronicle.

At issue here is not only the attraction between utopia
and revolution, but also the contention that the limits of
utopia inevitably seek to be overcome, not by a dismissal or a
revision of the end goal, but by the introduction of a new
sense of time and a new language of future expectation. It is
not that utopia looks for perfection in spatial metaphors, and
chiliasm looks for it in temporal metaphors. Utopia, as Mannheim argues, implies a definite experience of time. Lasky's
central argument is that the millenialists' dream of a terrestrial paradise cannot be transformed into its secular counter-
part, utopia, without the necessary means to achieve that
paradise: revolution. That is, the longing for perfection
will inevitably produce the means to achieve it. And central
to the means is an experience of time which is, at heart, apocalyptic, in which the experience of time is as "imminent expectation." Lasky writes:

> As the millennium lost its transcendence and became part
> of this world [Cohn's and Mannheim's analysis], the far-
> away utopian refuge (which from its inception was always
> somehow, somewhere part of this world) lost its escapist
> character and became the whole of this world (419).

When utopia (the desired human state of perfection) does
become the whole of this world, it adopts according to Lasky
(citing Eliade) the "whole magico-religious paraphernalia." It
becomes a secular ideology tending toward belief; its messianic
pretensions come to the fore; it singles out a chosen class to
be the bearers of this hope for a new age; and it fabricates a
"great chain of human hope" which consists of the story of
crisis, vengence, catastrophe, promise, climax, and dawn. This
is precisely the apocalyptic world-view in temporal story terms.
Thus the fears of Thomas More are realized; for More was ready
to burn his books, especially *Utopia*, lest they become the cause

for inciting revolution, fomented by those who were impatient
with the usual course of events. Lasky concludes, writing of
the "recurrent elements of utopian and revolutionary militance:"

> We have here another full turn of the ideological cycle
> as the archetypes return: the high-minded quest for an
> ideal social order; an angry commitment to radical
> social change; an impatience with moderation and melior-
> ism; a predisposition to violence as the morality and
> strategy of deep and genuine social reconstruction; a
> burning longing for the fires of redemption. And so the
> chain holds fast. One is tempted to think of it as a
> kind of *politica perennis* (149).

What emerges from this very brief juxtaposition of utopia
and apocalyptic? Certainly that it is extremely difficult to
speak of the future merely in terms of "possibility." One must
also wrestle with the future in terms of desirability. Utopia,
when it is extrapolated solely as a possibility, falls into the
same trap as does the conception of science as value-free. The
writings of the contemporary school of "critical theory" take
issue with such a conception of science, and dismiss it as being
radically uncritical. At the heart of critical theory's understanding and position is the argument that science (particularly
the human sciences) may be considered value-free only if value
is understood in terms of an "authoritarian, transcendent world-
image." Such an image implies a pre-critical understanding of
history as determined beforehand by divine or human interests.
Value in critical theory is associated with the *humanum*,
threatened as it always is by rationalistic, manipulative, and
exploitative concerns. Critical theory, then, maintains that
there is a "critical core to science" (it must concern itself
with critiquing the forces that threaten the *humanum*), and that
there is a "scientific core to critique" (scientific criteria
must be used in the analysis of praxis).

In a study of "utopian and critical thinking," Martin
Plattel argues that when we speak of the future only in terms
of possibility we are touching on the "exploratory value" of
utopia (77-82). He goes on to argue that in critical theory
there is also a "normative value" of utopia; for utopia cannot
remain a "neutral instrument." The fundamental utopian dialectic
operates in this manner: utopia places itself at a distance
(negation) from the present now (affirmation), and seeks to

create a better future (negation of the negation)(45-49).
Utopia, in this understanding is a "present absence," the
desired horizon projected not for the purposes of escape, but
to stand as a critique of the absent present. Central to
Plattel's argument, however, is his contention that utopia
helps to fashion means as well as ends. It does this by reliev-
ing technology and science of the task of constructing a synthesis of all of life and history. For what technology and science
have done (contrary to their own self-understanding) is to
formulate the vision of totality of the future as an affirmative,
rather than a critical category. Thus, in their synthesis,
"the increasing rationality of means [technique] to guide [human
history] is put into the service of the irrationality of goals"
and the irrationality increases exponentially (94). A utopian
synthesis, however, standing as a critical, not an affirmative
category, unburdens scientific analysis of that task, and so
frustrates its tendencies toward positivism, fragmentation,
and over-specialization.

Surely one could argue this is the meaning and purpose
of utopia in science fiction; but it remains to be seen whether
science fiction's utopian writings benefit from this analysis
of the future as coming to us not only in our rational projections, but also in our desires. The over-whelming critical
acceptance of rational extrapolation as the differentiating
factor which constitutes science fiction as a genre capable of
separate critical scrutiny, coupled with a similar critical
acceptance of the dystopian visions of science fiction as constituting the more literate and literary examples of the technique of rational extrapolation, seems to indicate that science
fiction writers and critics somehow acknowledge that desirability (or undesirability) does in some critical manner have
to be linked to possibility, else the resulting work may succeed
as plan, but fail as story. Another reason utopia in science
fiction fails as story is, as argued above, that it has no real
beginning; it cannot (and does not) explain its own coming into
being. But the reverse side of the same coin accounts for its
failure as plan: utopia in science fiction (that is, utopia
based on scientific, rational extrapolation) cannot explain its
inevitable succession by new forms. The science fiction utopia

is thus a denial of the science on which it is constructed. For science is by its very nature a body of knowledge that seeks to be surpassed.

The science fiction utopia is ultimately about the limit of theory. Theory can only function undisguised in a world that is post-historical, a world that is not concerned with the "awful rowing toward God," the suffering and crucifixions of the oppressed and the outcast and their longings for deliverance. The post-catastrophe utopias function as the secular equivalent to the "life after death" theologies of a Christianity which have forsaken the cross for the empty tomb. In the more radical understanding of Christianity, on the contrary, it is the "empty God" who stands as the symbol of hope and the future of life.

What the science fiction utopia needs now, as it has always needed and sometimes shown, is a reassessment of its relationship with apocalyptic. Such a reassessment would clarify the role of expectations of the future, insofar as expectations are plurisignificative: they create not only possibilities, they also create desires. One cannot extrapolate the future in terms of Wollheim's consensus future history, for example, and decline to state unambiguously whether it is projected merely as a possible future, or also a desirable future. Wollheim, as many other science fiction writers, cloaks his desires in the scientific jargon of probability structures. The same can be said for John W. Campbell; as noted in Chapter One, his desires are thinly disguised in the language of scientism.

The point here is that utopia does not so much need an end, as it does "the sense of an ending;" and this sense can only come through a clarification of its desires, and a purging of its fears. Both its desires and its fears, moreover, are intimately joined with the concept of limit, the unlimited desire of its goals being the transmutation of the fear of the limit of death.

Utopia also needs to be in dialectic with apocalyptic for another reason: so that the relationship between the model world and the present existing social order can be seen not merely as the relationship between the actual and the possible,

the descriptive and the normative, but also as that between the
promise and the fulfillment. For only this dialectic is able
to explicate fully, in terms of possibility and normativity,
the function of the future, without falling prey to that most
common of traps: reducing promise to its fulfillment, desire
to what is possible, and normativity to what is actual.

We will treat of all these relationships in more detail
in Chapter Four when we survey the critical understanding of
apocalyptic and seek to construct a typology of the language
and the forms of future expectation. For new we will take up
a discussion of the fantasy roots and dimension of science fiction wherein, as Tolkien argues, desirability is more constitutive of the literary form than is possibility.

Fantasy and the Worlds of Belief

In fantasy the possibility/desirability tension is faced
head on, insofar as fantasy refuses to reduce expectations to
the possibilities emerging from a simple linear extrapolation,
but reminds us that all expectations engage us on the level of
what is humanly desirable. In this it will open the literature
of science fiction to analysis in terms of the promise/fulfill-
ment dialectic. For when we designate fantasy as that which
concerns itself with what is humanly desirable, we are making
explicit the connection between fantasy and apocalyptic.
Northrop Frye, in discussing his "theory of myths," designates
apocalyptic imagery as that which symbolized the limits of
human desire, and demonic imagery as symbolizing that which
human desire totally rejects. Ketterer, as noted above in
Chapter Two, combines the two, speaking of the positive and
the negative charge of apocalyptic. What is at stake here is
precisely the question of the role of the promise of a new
world and a new age, whether one can dream of the new world/age
without implying the destruction of the old, and, in terms of
our present concern, whether wish-fulfillment can exist without
its negative counter-part. In more specific Christian symbolism
we are concerned here with the central mystery of human existence:
whether life comes after death, or whether life rises out of
death and is affirmed through death. The destruction of the

old (death) is not something simply to be undergone so that the new (life) can flourish; it is not merely an obstacle that stands in the way, to be surpassed in the quickest way possible so that the real goal can be achieved.

It is the negative charge of apocalyptic which has stood out as constituting the genre and been seized on by critics to discredit its value./1/ But a failure to hold critically the negative and the positive in balance, or to deny the negative, results in a soft, evolutionary liberal theology which agonizes over evil, but can do little more. The negative charge of apocalyptic is not some morbid desire for wholesale destruction and catastrophe, some fantasy escape from the harsh realities of life into the realms of heavenly reward, some longing for the deserved come-uppance of those who have plundered, pillaged, and raped the earth and its people. The negative charge of apocalyptic is a stark facing up to and an affirmation of the fact of human limitations--and, in our perspective here, of the ambiguity and limitations of human desire. The promise, in the Christian apocalypse, is that life comes out of or through death; fulfillment, therefore, is never a simple matter of granting human desires, but a terrible tearing apart and tran- scending of those desires, so that a radically new life can flourish in its stead.

The science fiction utopia, as noted above, in its failure to confront death and the limitations of human desire, symbolized the longing for a fulfillment without the terrible passage of history. And thus it forsakes the re-counting of the story of its own coming into being, and in extreme cases, denies history itself. It stands, in this regard, as the polar opposite of apocalyptic, for it has no beginning and no end. Furthermore, by reducing desirability to possibility, it cannot mediate the passage of the future, for it subordinates ends to means. It either leaves its followers caught in the paralysis of indecision, or it delivers them over to the bondage of the technological imperative. When possibility functions as the condition of possibility we are trapped in the sophistry of the technological milieu and subjected to the tyranny of means through the technological imperative. In the end to choose to be guided only by the possible is to choose only to be subservient to opting for the best possible means. This is to go nowhere; and in science fiction this is what utopia means precisely. Nowhere becomes the end of possibility--in both senses of the term.

It is in this regard that dystopia assumes such a critical role in science fiction, and in literature as a whole. For dystopia is not merely a story about the impossibility of extrapolated worlds; it is a clear statement about their undesirability. What we have in dystopia, moreover, is not just a negation of the extrapolated world, but a negation of the extrapolation itself. Dystopia is a realization that to be guided only by the possible, and to be subservient only to means, leads in the end nowhere but to a destruction of the *humanum*. In a negative way, then, dystopia affirms that desirability, more than possibility, is what characterizes human value and serves as the object of human hope. Expectations cannot be grounded in possibility alone; they must be informed by and witness to what is humanly desirable.

In an essay on the future of prediction John P. Sisk argues that nightmare visions of the future act as a counter to the complacent daydreams of utopian science fiction. They are meant to shock us out of the inattentiveness which is the result of unrestrained daydreaming. "Daydreams," Sisk writes, "have exponential growth patterns as against the logistic patterns of actual experience" (328). Sisk's argument is incisive and relevant; yet it is precisely the exponential growth patterns of technology which have become the reality, along with the catastrophic consequences which have accompanied it. Mass starvations in Bangladesh and in the Sahel, power outages, the energy crisis, the technological sophistication of terrorists and the police states--all have been realized in the same daydream state as have been the technical marvels which have become the hallmark of Western dominance, and the source of its pride. What has happened, in brief, is that desirability has succumbed to possibility; and the latter has become the measure of the desirable.

A. Fantasy: Undisplaced Belief

What fantasy does is bring us face to face with the
desirable in an undisplaced form. If the favorite phrase of
almost all critical writing on fantasy and science fiction
(that fantasy is dependent on a willing suspension of disbelief)
is to mean anything, it should mean that in fantasy we willingly
acknowledge, give voice to, and affirm our desires. In science
fiction it means that we accept future expectations as desirable.
In the Christian constellation of virtues belief has always contained the dimension of desire and desirability, under the name
of hope. In *Hebrews*, we read: "To have faith is to be sure of
the things we hope for, to be certain of the things we cannot
see" (11:1).

In fantasy, then, we enter the world of desire and we
enter the world of belief. To characterize fantasy as that form
of narrative which depends on a willing suspension of disbelief
is to tell only half the story. The other half is to characterize fantasy as narrative which depends on a willingness to believe; which, in the context of our discussion here, also means
an affirmation of our desires. In nightmare fantasy, of course,
it means the confirmation of our (worst) fears. Our subsequent
treatment of this theme will speak primarily of the positive
side: the belief which affirms desire, rather than the belief
which confirms fear. For it is the former which underlies the
fantasy dimensions of science fiction; the latter issues mainly
in the supernatural horror story.

What has characterized most critical work concerning
science fiction and fantasy is that it has confused the displacement of the literary world (the world created which stands
as critical counter to the existing order of things) with the
displacement of desire and belief. The willing suspension of
disbelief, or as we would rather state, the willingness to
believe, is what exists in fantasy in an undisplaced form or
manner. It is only because of this that there can exist a
credible relationship between the displaced world of the literary work and the existing world of the reader.

Robert Philmus argues this point at length in *Into the
Unknown*. Philmus begins with the task of differentiating

science fiction from other forms of fantasy. The differentiating feature consists of a "rhetorical strategy of employing a
more or less scientific rationale to get the reader to suspend
disbelief in a fantastic state of affairs" (vii). It is this
strategy, rather than the subject matter, which defines science
fiction as a genre. The science in science fiction is there
for strategy's sake, to induce belief in a fantastic state of
affairs. In the literary work the fantastic state of affairs
is believed in, not the strategy. The latter is simply a means
to an end; it is not concerned with belief or disbelief. Philmus goes on to argue, however, that too often the strategy of
employing a more or less scientific rationale becomes the locus
of credibility, instead of the whole fictive situation and its
signification. It is the latter, however, that must bear the
burden, for

> The truth, and hence the credibility (in a meaningful
> sense), of the fantastic state of affairs can be said
> to pertain ultimately to the perception in the fantasy
> of the reality that it displaces, and thereby inter-
> prets, rather than to the scientific rationale or the
> anticipations of the future in that fantasy per se (20).

Only when displacement is seen in this perspective (Philmus
calls it "mythic displacement") can one speak in any meaningful
way about the content of science fiction and fantasy.

The confusion science fiction criticism fosters much too
often is traceable to a refusal to make the critical distinctions Philmus makes between credibility resting on a simple
acceptance of the scientific rationale (and its extrapolated
future), and the perception of the real world standing in
relation to the displaced world in the work of fantasy itself.
To base credibility on the scientific rationale is to displace
desire and belief, and to generate a work which does not stand
in a credible relationship with the existing order of things,
for that world of fantasy is accepted as undisplaced. It is
accepted simply as a model of reality.

This confusion can be traced to two factors, one existing
in the scientific rationale itself, and the other existing in
the body of literary critical theory on which all science fiction criticism is based. The scientific rationale, from
Descartes on, is based on systematic doubt; it accepts nothing

"on faith," but only admits of what can be verified by direct
sensory observation. In its theoretical formulations it goes
further; it admits not only of what can only be verified, but
also of what can only be falsified. That is, if one cannot
through direct sensory observation prove or disprove a hypothetical model, then it cannot be accepted as a working model
which explains reality, or upon which further systematic study
can be fruitfully based. The intense battle between science
and religion has been waged predominantly on these grounds.
For any systematic body of knowledge will seek inevitably to
encompass all of reality within its purview. Ever since God
was declared an "unnecessary hypothesis," the issue has been
clear. But what has been unclear is the resolution of that
issue. While most studies of religion's reaction to the
skepticism of modern consciousness have focused on religion's
retreating defense of God and the stop-gap uses to which he
was (is) constantly being put, the more fruitful study may lie
in the area of explicating the wholesale displacement of belief
that occurred among the ranks of the doubters. We have been
arguing throughout this study, particularly in Chapter One,
that so thorough has been the displacement of belief that in
the end it is undisplaced; it has created the objects which it
must have to satisfy its desires. If anyone has fashioned the
myths which told the stories of the gods and literally gave
them life, it was the writers of science fiction--even more so
than the tellers of the ancient stories. And if we are to
accept the arguments of the structuralists that myths are not
created, but are stories which write themselves, then the willingness to believe is what accounts for the fantasies of science
fiction being transformed into modern myths. Critics, such as
Scholes, are correct when they argue no one can set out consciously and deliberately to fashion a modern myth (1975:20).
This is true for the same reason that the ancient myths have
long defied any debunking: there are no real tellers of myths,
there are only listeners. The theory of reading, cited above
as what is lacking in Ketterer and many other critics of science
fiction , is of critical importance in the study of fantasy and
in the study of apocalyptic.

In a theory of reading one is able to make critical distinctions among systematic doubt, skepticism, unbelief, and disbelief. It is the uncritical mixing together of these four which is the prime cause of the confusion surrounding the criticism of fantasy, particularly when it comes down to a treatment of the phrase: the willing suspension of disbelief. That phrase above all has misled many a critic into thinking that the reader who picks up a copy of *Slan*, for example, is the same reader who picks up a copy of *Scientific American*; that suspending disbelief is the same thing as suspending systematic doubt or unbelief. Disbelief is not a method, as systematic doubt is; nor is it a stance toward an organized body of beliefs, as unbelief is. Finally, it is not a habitual state of mind, as skepticism is. All three of these may be brought to a text as prior mental attitudes. Disbelief, on the other hand, rises out of the reading of the story, and lasts only for the duration of that reading./2/ Disbelief consists essentially of the hesitation to believe, when the wanting not to believe exists along side the wanting to believe. As Julius Kagarlitski writes: "When disbelief arises side by side with belief, fantasy comes into being" (29). Both belief and disbelief are fostered by a reading of the story; and the disbelief suspended willingly is done because of the belief affirmed willingly, not because the reader beforehand decides to suspend it for the sake of enjoying the work. The scientific rationale, which should elicit a displaced form of belief (whose object is the credible relationship of the world of fantasy and the existing order of things), all too often exhibits the character- istics of an undisplaced belief, because of the failure to accept it as a strategy whose aim is precisely to place that literary world in a critical relationship with the existing order of things. In science fiction fantasy, for example, all too often the literary world of the fantastic future is taken for the whole of reality, for the way things really are (or will be); and no thought is given to the fact that such an acceptance is only accomplished through an act of faith, not through a rational, intellectual act. The fantasy in science fiction has become, in the end, the reality; and the reality is appropriated in the same manner any reality is--through an act

of faith, undisplaced here because to the unbeliever faith is
not a critical category.

When the critical tension between the literary world of
the fantastic state of affairs and the world of the existing
order of things is denied, the whole tension between belief and
disbelief breaks down, and all critical distance is lost. The
description of the future world becomes the norm; the actual
future world become the possible, uncritically; and the promise
of the new world/age only has to await its fulfillment, inevitably. In the end, the confusion does not result from the
fact that the future world is undisplaced, but rather from the
fact that the belief (existing within and alongside systematic
doubt, unbelief, and skepticism) is undisplaced. That is,
because the reader refuses to take the text literally (i.e., as
a work of literature), belief is seen as a polar opposite to
unbelief, systematic doubt, and/or skepticism; and the resulting
tension can only be resolved by believing in the actual future
world instead of the literary future world. Thus the science
fiction reader will often dismiss the specific literary world
of Heinlein's future history, for example, yet believe something like it will indeed be the future reality. Faith as a
process is actually undisplaced; the object has merely been
changed. For the reader will create through a separate act of
faith a future into which he or she can live. Instead of believing in the present (and its pluri-dimensionality, including
past and future, personal and collective), the believer has
faith merely in the future.

The second factor that contributes to this confusion is
one which exists in the body of literary critical theory all
science fiction criticism, no matter how uncritical its pretensions, rests on. I. A. Richards, in his *Principles of
Literary Criticism*, draws the line hard and fast between scientific and emotive language, and between scientific and emotive
belief. The former distinction Richards states very succinctly
in a passage often quoted:

> A statement may be used for the sake of *reference*, true
> or false, which it causes. This is the *scientific* use
> of language. But it may also be used for the effects
> in emotion and attitudes produced by the reference it
> occasions. This is the *emotive* use of language (267).

The truth or falsity of language can only be spoken of when referring to the scientific use of language, that is, in its referential usage. Emotive language can neither be true nor false, since what it refers to cannot be verified. When attempts are made to verify the referent of emotive language, the reference is always to another, wholly separate framework: pantheism, inspiration, revelation, and so forth. As for the different forms of belief, scientific belief implies an unconditional acceptance, as though in all circumstances the statement were true. Emotive belief, on the other hand, is limited and provisional; it is entered into for the sake of the "imaginative experience which it makes possible" (277).

Poetry, for Richards, is the highest form of emotive language, and it induces the purest form of emotive belief. Emotive belief cannot in any way be supported scientifically; but it can be justified if it succeeds in filling the "needs of the being" (281). And the needs of the being are precisely those attitudes, feelings, and beliefs produced; for they clarify things, they let us see into the heart of things, they are visionary and revelational. Richards concludes that they do not really give us any new knowledge, but they are in fact "the conscious accompaniment of our successful adjustment to life" (284).

While Richards does not treat explicitly of fantasy, nor of Coleridge's phrase: "a willing suspension of disbelief," his literary theory has been the foundation for the wholesale acceptance of the phrase into the critical study of fantasy. But precisely because Richards drove the wedge between scientific and emotive language, the willing suspension of disbelief has been shifted from an intra-literary framework to an extra-literary one. Once outside the world of story, the suspension of disbelief takes on all the connotations associated with the scientific usage of language: one disbelieves because this is not really the way things are, or because the statement does not really refer to the existing order of things. And if it is this disbelief which is suspended, willingly to boot, then the belief which is willingly entered into does not in fact deal only with attitudes and feelings; it deals also with new knowledge, but a knowledge of reality through belief. This is precisely what we argued in Chapter One, especially in the

discussion of the "philosophy" of John W. Campbell. The wanting
to believe which characterizes the reading of science fiction
has very little to do with the structure of the story, its
credibility and its critical relationship to the present; but
it has everything to do with the desire for a new (and secret)
knowledge of the universe.

To treat of fantasy, then, merely in terms of a literature whose nature it is to induce a willing suspension of disbelief is to enter on dangerous ground. For the temptation is
to focus exclusively on the disbelief, and to miss the belief
which is also induced. More importantly, it is to miss the
tension which exists within the work, between belief and disbelief, and thus to miss what the form and the function of
fantasy really is.

Fantasy, as noted above, exists to bring us face to face
with our beliefs and with our desires, insofar as they flow
from those beliefs. One does not fantasize the possible, one
fantasizes the desirable. That is the form of fantasy. But
the function is closely associated with it. Fantasy brings us
face to face with those desires for the purpose of mediating our
passage through them. That is, it returns us to the existing
order of things. This is to recall once again Philmus' argument, but this time to take up explicitly what he labels "mythic
displacement." For Philmus this occurs when fantasy becomes
myth, that is, when the metaphor is dramatized and becomes a
model of reality (20-22). A failure to note this mythic displacement results in situating credibility solely in the scientific rationale. What concerns us here is the fact that another
result of this same failure is the inability of fantasy which
does not undergo the transformation to mythic displacement to
mediate the reader through the gates of desire (and fear).
Joseph Campbell's work in comparative mythology, and more
particularly in creative mythology, is relevant to our discussion at this point./3/ Campbell argues that the ancient archetypal and mythological symbols and images no longer induce the
experience of awe, wonder, sympathetic union, etc.; but rather
once the experience is had, the symbols and images are used by
the artist for interpretation and communication. With that
distinction in mind one can reappropriate the myth, insofar as

it once again functions to mediate the reader/listener past the gates of desire and fear; that is, myth enables us to see more clearly. Campbell takes as his model the work and the literary theory of James Joyce, who derives a "psychology of aesthetic arrest," based on wholeness, harmony, and radiance (160). The foundational referent of all literature is life, its mystery and its meaning. To be consumed with desire and fear (or loathing) in the reading of a work of literature blinds us; it prevents us from seeing the whole, bright, harmonious picture. A truly creative artist will put us in touch with the human, neither offering us a solution nor an escape. It thus preserves the polar opposites essential to life and story. The gate to the paradise of the spirit is barred to didacticism and pornography, for example, for the former denies the tensions of narrative, and the latter is caught up in desire.

All too often in science fiction fantasy the desire presented overwhelms all other desire, creating a world which merely satisfies wishes. In fantasy, on the other hand, the desire presented ought to stand in critical relationship to the already existing desire, so as to purify that desire. When that happens, as Philmus argues, we can begin to talk about the content of science fiction fantasy, for then we can critically reappropriate the categories of the actual, the descriptive, the possible, and the normative. When that is done we can then begin to shift the discussion over into an apocalyptic mode of thinking, with its categories of promise and fulfillment.

In any discussion of the content of fantasy--that which is humanly desirable--the starting point (already underlying much of the above discussion) is J. R. R. Tolkien's seminal monograph, "On Fairy-Stories." Tolkien sees two functions to the fairy-story: 1) to explore the depths of space and time; and 2) to be united with all living things. However, Tolkien refuses to be drawn into a discussion of the truth or falsity of the world of fantasy, saying that fantasy is not re-presentational literature. Fantasy is rather a "Subcreation," a world which exists wholly and entirely within itself and for itself. "Fantasy, the making or glimpsing of other-worlds, was the heart of the desire of Faierie" (41). It is precisely this function of fantasy, the subcreation aspect, which critics

praise in Tolkien, particularly as it has been accomplished in
his monumental *Lord of the Rings*. But the tendency has been
(and is) more often to praise the geography and the sociology
(meaning here the peopling of that world), rather than the
history and temporal structure of the subcreation. Thus it is
refreshing to note the comment of Clyde S. Kilby that *Lord of
the Rings* "provides us with a dependable realization of time"
(70). And to note that Gunnar Urang devotes a whole essay to
"Tolkien's Fantasy: The Phenomenology of Hope."

Urang begins by describing the levels of meaning in the
work: the dimension of wonder, the dimension of import, and
finally the "dimension of incipient *belief*, which is a function
of the 'rhetoric' of this fiction" (97). Urang equates this
last dimension with the desirability of the subcreation, as
over against merely its possibility. Furthermore, the desirability of the subcreation is due more to (happy) endings than
it is to (happy) locales or (happy) people. For the world of
story does not exist outside the story, and so must concern
itself with the possibility and desirability of a happy ending.
The real question story raises in its very structure is whether
there are any grounds for hope. In an attempt to answer this
question, Urang describes the "hopeful patterns" found in *Lord
of the Rings*. He argues they constitute "something like a
theology--not a philosophy, but a theology--of history" (103).
These patterns include: 1) a "providential" design in which
all events are inter-related; 2) an eschatology, a movement
toward a definite end and a "decisive" struggle of cosmic
scope; 3) a composite hero; and 4) a series of lesser rescues
and happy endings which prefigure the final end. From these
patterns Urang works out a phenomenology of hope, in which the
explicit theological and metaphysical questions are bracketed,
and the question is simply put: What is it like to come face
to face with the impending destruction of the existing order,
and yet to have the experience of hope? Urang concludes:

> I have said that this experience (1.) presupposes an
> ordering of the historical process to some end and
> (2.) that it comes to be based on "signs" and para-
> digm-events within that history (107).

Such an understanding precludes reading *Lord of the Rings*, or

any fantasy for that matter, as allegory in which there is a
one-to-one correlation between image/symbol and referent.
Rather, Urang argues, what we have here is "mythical allegory,"
in which there exists much unassigned imagery. For as Myth it
is concerned with the totality of things, their space and their
time. Urang cites a statement of Tolkien to strengthen his
point: "For myth is alive at once and in all its parts, and
dies before it can be dissected."

B. Fantasy: The Normativity of Desire

        This brief look at the understanding of fantasy in
Tolkien's theory and practice leads us to the conclusion that
what is desirable in fantasy is a world in its totality; that
is, that we be told the whole story. Fantasy, in this light,
is a restructuring of the temporal world according to promise,
providence, paradigm-event, and end. In this it stands as
counter to the "time" of a simple linear extrapolation issuing
in utopia which ignores or denies history. Fantasy restructures
the temporal world by the very fact that it tells a story; it
is not, as utopia is, a plan or an explanation. What is further
desirable in fantasy is a sense of time which includes the sense
of an ending. We have suggested above that the transcendental
drive of future expectations in the future history model sees
the ending as final (or, at the outside, merely as the beginning of another cycle); while the "we are not alone" model
posits the introduction of extra-terrestrial intelligent beings
as the "ending" which gives meaning to human life. Involved
here are two different forms of expectation. In the future-
history model expectation is immanent; the end or goal is always
present within the understanding; and time becomes the medium
through which the passage occurs. In the "we are not alone"
model, expectation is imminent; duration becomes the barrier to
an ending never seen in its entirety. Time is not the enemy to
be overcome in that latter model, duration is. Therefore the
measurement of time will not be done according to the steady,
even rhythms of duration; time will be measured by signs, inter-
ventions, paradigm-events and miracles.
        These differentiating conceptions of time show up in the
very structure of narrative. In linear extrapolation which

issues in utopia the unexpected does not occur. And in the perfect society utopia is the unexpected is not allowed to occur. For this reason many critics deny that utopia is story in any sense and prefer to call it plan rather than story. In fantasy, on the other hand, imminent expectation demands the introduction of the unexpected. As with the term disbelief, the "unexpected" may benefit from more critical dissection. Eric Rabkin, in his study, *The Fantastic in Literature*, provides this. He distinguishes the "unexpected" which may simply be the introduction of a new character) from the "disexpected" (what the text has led us not to expect, but which later is seen as fitting) and the "anti-expected" (the introduction of a person or event which "reconfigures" the narrative world). (8-10) For Rabkin the fantastic is the reversal of the ground rules, established in the narrative, through the introduction of the anti-expected.

The tendency in criticism is often to disregard the reversal of the temporal ground rules which the narrative has established. The tendency is to view narrative as a model of how things happen, not when things happen; to see the recon- figuration in social or spatial terms, not in temporal terms. If fantasy is characterized by a willingness to believe, then what it signifies is a desire to transcend the slow, evolution- ary passage of time in favor of time measured by breakthroughs to new understandings. Now is important, not because the present is all there is, but because the present is when the breakthrough will occur: the radically new (understanding) will come soon. There is no other meaningful way to measure time. The hidden desire in fantasy is for miracles; for mira- cles have never signified primarily the overcoming of natural laws. Such an apologetic derives from a theology which has lost the sense of hope as imminent expectation. Miracles have always been more aptly understood as the overcoming of temporal laws: the kingdom of God is among you; the prophecy has been fulfilled. Once the anti-expected, the startling new perspec- tive, the miracle occurs, the story is never the same; and the reader's sense of time is altered radically. Progress is no longer conceived as a simple linear process, the logical and methodical unfolding of what has always been expected to reach finally some already perfectly imagined end. Progress, in the fantastic state of affairs, does not depend on the logic of extrapolation; it depends on the "logic of the miraculous," to use the phrase of Julius Kagarlitski. He continues: "The story of a miracle is completely contemporary. Technology grows old; magic does not" (39). In prior times the supernatural filled that role; in our times science does. For science to succeed, it must be miraculous, not just logical and progressive. It must exceed, in the stories it tells, the expectations it logically creates. Such is the function of the science fiction fantasy.

Fantasy, then, among other things witnesses to the desire for the radically new that will give meaning to the story of human history. The future-history model which issues in utopia is seen in the end as unsatisfactory. Although its possibilities may exceed the possibilities which are currently our limits, its desires never exceed the desires which have always existed. Not so with fantasy. The desires of fantasy, particularly regarding time and its passage and measurement, always exceed the desires of evolutionary humankind and are the mirrors revealing the true nature of those desires. This is true almost without qualification in the fantasies of J. R. R. Tolkien and C. S. Lewis, for example; significantly less so in the works of Isaac Asimov and Arthur C. Clarke; and almost non-existent in the stories of Robert Heinlein and A. E. van Vogt. The works of the latter two create present desires, rather than mirror their inadequacies.

C. S. Lewis writes: "To construct plausible and moving 'other worlds' you must draw on the only real 'other world' we know, that of the spirit" (12). The statement may also be taken as a comment about the promise that we are not alone, and the sense of imminent expectation which is its narrative ally. The promise that we are not alone, in the science fiction fantasy, is made to rest on the scientific rationale; that is, it is science which creates the means through which contact will be made. Contact, in that kind of story, however, is never of the kind which stands in critical relationship to the contact with the "other" always imminently expected in our own lives, whether it be with the dark side of our own being, with the other person,

or with a transcendent principle or being we call God. Contact
with the alien in science fiction fantasy is too often reduced
to a drama of technical expertise (or in the films, of technical
virtuosity). Murray Leinster's *First Contact* suffers from some
of this; although the mirror of the aliens does reveal some
human depth-dimensions. The clearest example of the techniques
of contact overwhelming a structurally flawed story is found in
The Mote in God's Eye, by Jerry Pournelle and Larry Niven. At
the other end of the spectrum is Stanlislaw Lem's *Solaris*, in
which the whole story is about the utter inability of man to
fathom the other, and the resulting painful and terrifying self-
examination which takes place.

Consequent upon the empty promise in science fiction
fantasy is, logically, the empty fulfillment, the fulfillment
that does not critically relate to present understanding and,
in the end, only reinforces the fear that we are alone--after
all! The resulting transformation of the promise into the much
more abstract and formless promise of cosmic friendliness, wherein the desire for the other is no longer even personal, ushers
in a post-historic era; for history is constituted by a personal
presence. In addition, promise loses its normativity when it
is totally emptied of a personal presence. It can no longer
function as the mirror which reveals the inadequacies of human
desire. What this amounts to when transposed into the categories
of life and death is the heretical position that life comes after
death (in a simple sequential process), instead of out of, or
through death. The introduction of the alien, or the extra-
terrestrial intelligence, functions in this understanding as a
denial of all human desire and personal presence in the same
manner that the pie-in-the sky belief denies the value of human
life and the struggle to overcome. Both symbolize, in terms of
future expectation, a radical discontinuity between this age
and the age to come.

When utopia and fantasy, finally, are seen in light of
the promise-fulfillment dialectic, the following results obtain.
In the science fiction utopia fulfillment is the negation of
the promise; and in the science fiction fantasy promise is the
negation of fulfillment. To reach the perfect state envisioned
in utopia is to achieve a static condition of being, the

post-historic era. The promise, in being fulfilled, is negated.
This is why so many utopias read as dystopias; for the future
is ripped out of their world and meaning is destroyed. In fantasy, on the other hand, promise is the negation of fulfillment.
So vague are the promises of an "end to cosmic loneliness," so
caught up are they in technical virtuosity, that "fulfillment"
only succeeds in further emptying them of any content. A fuller,
more satisfying dialectic of promise/fulfillment is obtained
when we trace the contribution of apocalyptic. Promise retains
its normativity, not by being emptied of specific applicability
when fulfillment might surpass or render promise obsolete;
rather promise retains its normativity by remaining promise.
Fulfillment is only the negation of negation; the promise becomes more clear by becoming less specific. Apocalyptic is an
understanding which can mediate the dialectic between promise
and fulfillment that utopia and fantasy, pushed to their limits
cannot. The form of this mediation we will take up in Chapter
Four; and the ramifications of it in Chapter Five.

Postscript: A Return to Story

For now we must retrace our steps one more time to
isolate a feature of science fiction obvious in its simplicity,
but profound in its consequences. Science fiction is story.
When all other considerations have been made and exhausted--
science fiction as didactic literature, protest literature,
admonitory utopia, escape literature, product of hack writers,
structuralist fable, cognitive estrangement, and so forth--
science fiction is still story. And it is precisely under this
aspect that the critical study of science fiction must be undertaken with more vigor if its radical ties with apocalyptic are
to be explicated in full, and if this explication is to benefit
the critical appropriation of apocalyptic by systematic theology.

The tendency in most narrative explications of science
fiction is to treat of the story as being *about* something else.
Thus, *Dune* is about the necessity of living in harmony with
one's environment; *Stranger in a Strange Land* is about the
powerful forces inherent in human nature (telekinesis, levitation, metabolic slow-down) and which can be harnessed through

the rigorous practice of meditation and "grokking;" *Imperial Earth* is about the urgency of systematically searching for extra-terrestrial intelligence; *Stand on Zanzibar* is about the finite nature of the present human condition and the desirability of a genetic mutation issuing in a new humankind. And so forth.

There is, of course, a legitimacy to the critical work which explores what a science fiction story is about. For all literature has a pragmatic function--whether that function is thought of as catharsis, a release through which the harmful emotions are purged and an equilibrium is restored; or whether its function is more an intellectual sharpening of the reader through an interchange of ideas which challenge pre-conceived patterns of thought. To remain on that level of critical explication, however, is to treat of literature only as allegory. In this there is only a one to one correspondence between symbol and idea, or character and idea; that is, the referent is always and only outside the world of story. Such critical interpretations, while not without use for certain purposes, short-circuit the fuller analysis of the structure of story. Story, if it is about anything, is first of all about itself, about story. The elements of story (the events, characters, situations) have a role, a function, a meaning entirely within the world of story. Story is not about a world, rather story presents a world.

The confirmation of this is found in the common practice of summarizing in an almost automatic response to the question of what the story is about. There is a critical distinction implied here between what the structuralists call the plot and the narrative, or the narration of that plot. The meaning carried by the plot is always polyvalent; while the meaning of the narration (how the story is told, to whom, in what context) is usually very limited and specific, and is contained in the structures of communication. Oftentimes the meanings of plot and narration work at cross purposes. Thus, for example, while Heinlein's stories pretend to be about the wonders of science, the dignity of personal initiative and responsibility, the glories of human freedom, and the radical debunking of dearly held social beliefs, the plots also carry the meanings of rugged individualism, preoccupation with self-aggrandizment, exploitation of other peoples and resources, and an obsession with immortality. For Heinlein's plots are structured inevitably around a strong, central, worldly-wise, male-dominating individual who triumphs over all the obstacles placed before him. Science has little, if anything, to do with structuring of the plot, and thus with the world of his story.

We discussed above how the function of fantasy is to present a world standing in critical relationship to the present world, the existing order of things. What this means, among other things, is that the present world also can be seen as story. And this, we have argued in the preceding chapters, is precisely the appeal of science fiction--in spite of what the self-understanding of early science fiction claimed.

Let us retrace some of the points made thus far, to see why this is so, and why science fiction has resisted this reading. Science fiction from the beginning has had a particular problem with its designation as romance; while it has always felt at home with its roots in fantasy. The reason for this is that fantasy, characterized as being dependent on a willing suspension of disbelief, has always raised the question of a credibility to be argued and defended on the grounds of a scientific rationale which undergirded that suspension of disbelief. Thus, the sudden, coincidental introduction of a secret ray gun, of time travel, of teletransportation, of the Vulcan death grip, of parallel worlds, for example--all these can be defended scientifically as not beyond the realm of possibility, someday. The working thesis is not that they be shown to be scientifically possible and/or explained in terms of presently known scientific laws or theory, but only that they be presented as not impossible and/or contradictory to them. The same sudden, coincidental, unexplained introduction of these devices or events, when viewed according to the structure of story, however, present a totally different meaning, or possibility of meaning. And when the credibility rests not on some scientific rationale (or pseudo-scientific rationale), but on a critical relationship to the present world, that is, on the relationship between the world of the story and the story of the world, entirely different possibilities of interpretation result. The story becomes incredible, not because the devices and events themselves cannot be explained "scientifically," but because the whole structure, the unfolding of the story, is impossible. At least it is impossible according to the temporal structure which underlies most of our story-telling.

Because science fiction has consistently dealt with the "willing suspension of disbelief" theme by arguing for a credibility which rests on a scientific rationale, science fiction has felt relatively at home with fantasy, and relatively uncomfortable with romance. The fact is, however, that science fiction is romance (a popular literature) because it is story above all. The critical study of science fiction has to proceed along these lines, as well as thematic and allegorical lines. We are led, thus, back to a consideration of Northrup Frye's study of the structure of romance, *The Secular Scripture*. At the beginning we noted Frye's functional definition of romance as a popular literature which people read "without guidance from their betters." We also noted his contention that there is "no structural principle to prevent the fables of secular literature from also forming a mythology, or even a mythological universe...a single integrated vision of the world, parallel to the Christian and biblical vision." Frye argues this is so because structurally there is no difference between fable and myth; they differ only in authority and social function (8). Myths are those stories which "stick together," achieve a central place in a society, and are needed to explain and give meaning to that society. Fables, on the other hand, are peripheral, loosely connected, and primarily intended to amuse and entertain.

Because there is no structural difference between fables and myth, there is no structural principle which prevents fables from becoming myths or even a mythology, and forming a mythological universe. People know what they need "without guidance from their betters" And what they need is story; they do not need plain facts and isolated pieces of information. In the terms used above: the displacement which occurs is the displacement of story, not what the story is about. Frye speaks in this context of the two poles of literature, romance and realism. Romance tends toward the displacement of story;

that is, the "adjusting of formulaic structures to a roughly
credible context," and thus ultimately toward metaphor and
myth (36). Romance searches to tell the story people want to
hear about their lives; and continues to tell it over and over
again until it achieves some kind of social authority. Realism,
on the other hand, tends toward the displacement of reality and
nothing more; and thus tends ultimately toward naturalism.
Realism ends by upholding the present order of things, insofar
as it cannot go beyond what is given. The "reality" which
romance works with, then, is never the same reality realism
works with; for the containing forms of romance transform the
matter which is its content. The "reality" romance works with
is the "conventions of literary structure." The referent of
romance is not the world outside, but the world of story; all
stories are made up of old ones; all plots are about other
plots. Frye writes:

> It is still not generally understood...that 'reality'
> in literature cannot be presented at all except with-
> in the conventions of literary structure and that
> those conventions must be understood first (43).

We have attempted in the above pages to illustrate some
of the literary conventions relating to science fiction precisely as it is a secularized transformation of biblical apocalyptic. For we have seen in both biblical apocalyptic and in
science fiction a vision of reality that is concerned with the
hopes, anxieties and fears of a people. Among the literary
conventions of science fiction we have isolated thus far are
the following: 1) the vision of the new age, and closely
associated with that, the understanding of the writers and the
readers and the literature itself as vehicles for the mediation
of its coming; 2) the theme of a period of crisis and transition;
3) the role of science and the scientist as the saviour of
humankind; 4) the dream of an achievable perfect human society,
symbolized in the utopian city; 5) the re-writing of the past
and/or appropriation of it through mythic history; 6) the
fashioning of a future history which creates living room in
space and time; 7) the techniques of extrapolation from existing knowledge; 8) extraordinary voyages to distant lands and
(increasingly) to distant times; 9) plausibility devices,

formerly dreams and ecstatic visions, now time travel and
parallel worlds; 10) the longing to make contact with the other;
and 11) the story's end which recapitulates and gives meaning
to all that has gone before. In his treatment of the structure
of romance Frye isolates further conventions. Of particular
note are the parallel themes of descent and ascent. The
resulting spatial world-view is a four-decker world, not the
usual three-decker one. Between heaven and earth there is
paradise, which is the symbol of human desire. To ignore the
legitimacy of human desire is to end up either in the effort,
often repeated in the bloody history of the millennialist movements and their secular counterparts, to inaugurate the reign
of heaven on earth; or in the equally futile attempt to deny
history and life in favor of eternity, whether it is understood
in post-terrestrial or in post-historic terms. Also of note is
the literary convention of the "happy ending," treated briefly
in our discussion of Tolkien. Frye's position is that the
happy ending is symbolic of the desire to continue to "struggle,
survive, and where possible to escape" (1976:132). He states
the point even more clearly:

> The feeling that death is inevitable comes to us from
> myth and fable. The latter is therefore both more
> true and more important (132).

When this understanding is joined with our concern for the
appropriation of story (myth, fable, romance or apocalyptic)
as a temporal art form, and when all the literary conventions
are viewed in light of this understanding (that the world of
story is a temporal world as well as a spatial one), then the
critical relationship to the present existing order (the story
according to which we live in time) takes on a new dimension.

A final cautionary note: Our concern here is not to
take sides in the current debate about whether or not "there is
only story." All we claim is that there is always story.
Further, since science fiction is story, and since apocalyptic
is story, it would be foolish not to undertake a critical
analysis of both under this aspect. A certain amount of reductionism occurs in such a process, to be sure; but it is our
hope that in reducing science fiction and apocalyptic to the
aspect of story, we will heighten the understanding of both

precisely as they shed light on each other. What we endeavor
to avoid through this is the kind of claim for science fiction
Scholes and Rabkin make in their study: "Notice that one defines science fiction by what it has in it, by its elements;
one defines fantasy by how it presents what it has in it, by
its structure" (170). Our contention, on the other hand, is
that structure transforms the elements; it is in the analysis
of the structure of apocalyptic and science fiction that we see
how very closely the two are tied together. Neither of the two
has any privileged status exempting them from comparative
analysis.

IV

APOCALYPTIC:
THE LANGUAGES OF FUTURE EXPECTATION

> As linear extrapolation admits the complexity and
> interdependence of society, the extrapolative
> enterprise becomes more difficult, less plausible
> in itself. If one is aiming at realistic projec-
> tion and lacks the religious or political faith
> that would provide a teleological end-point, lin-
> ear extrapolation is viable only in the short run
> ...Linear extrapolation which focuses on particular
> aspects of social reality cannot dwell on those
> aspects of present reality left unchanged without
> a loss in surface plausibility, but it avoids them
> only at the cost of a certain thinness of the
> social scene. It is therefore even more dependent
> on the intellectual appeal of its leading idea.

> --Robert H. Canary

Introduction

It would aid our study immeasurably if a treatment of
apocalyptic literature could follow along lines similar to
those used in the discussion of science fiction: the self-
understanding of apocalyptic, followed by the critical understanding. But the self-understanding of apocalyptic can, for
all practical purposes, be limited to the statement that apocalyptic saw itself as a successor to prophecy. Thus we begin
with a discussion of the critical understanding of apocalyptic.
Within this we seek to isolate an understanding of apocalyptic
as story. For it is precisely as story that we seek to arrive
at a structural analysis of the languages of future expectation;
and it is precisely as story that we will eventually discuss
the critical insights of narrative theology, insofar as these
insights bear on the temporal re-structuring of world. Different conceptions of future, of hope, of promise and fulfillment
result in a different story being told; and, conversely, listening to a different story (and living according to that story)
eventuates in a different appreciation of the function of
future, hope, promise and fulfillment.

There are additional understandings and presuppositions undergirding this chapter. Among these is the belief that history does not interpret itself. This is the great legacy prophecy has given us. But there is a further step to be taken: the interpretation of history (especially as it comes to us in the transcribed words of the prophets) does not interpret itself. The written word itself becomes a portion of history. Apocalyptic is a literary event, as much as a doctrinal and/or sociological event. Martin Buber comments on the apocalyptic writer that "he speaks into his notebook. He does not really speak, he only writes; he does not write down speech, he just writes his thoughts--he writes a book" (1957:200). This is said in a highly negative tone; yet the fact that apocalyptic is a written literature, as distinguished from prophecy which is transcribed speech, is a factor not lightly to be dismissed. J. J. Collins, in *The Apocalyptic Vision of Daniel*, argues that a whole new understanding of revelation (as interpretation) is signified by the literary nature of apocalyptic, especially insofar as revelation is given in cryptic forms: dreams, visions, mysterious writings. "The reception of revelation calls not for the obedience of the prophet, but for the wisdom of an interpreter" (1977:75).

This conscious literary dimension is of critical importance for apocalyptic, since its whole *raison d'etre* is to retell the story of God's promise. One reason why apocalyptic does not concern itself immediately with "plain history and real politics" is that it is a re-telling of a story; it is story about story. Apocalyptic takes another step back from immediate involvement and response, in the same way that all writing does. The problem of pseudonymity, long a *bete noir* for critics, highlights this factor. To establish the true author and his/her real intention does not settle all issues: the text has to be dealt with as a separate entity.

Finally, it is my contention that if it is possible (and desirable) to go from biblical apocalyptic to an analysis of the 16th century millennialist movements (a là Cohn), and even up to analyses of contemporary apocalyptic (a là Nathan Scott), then it is also possible to go back from present manifestations of apocalyptic to biblical. The warning of Paul Hanson, for example, that "we must temper our enthusiasm with an appeal for a rigorous application of the historical-critical method as a corrective to the type of errors which modern analogies can deliver" (4), is certainly valid; but it does not prevent even him from using the sociological categories of Weber and Mannheim to strengthen his own analysis. Hanson is correct, in this regard, to dismiss "subjective fantasies" as the referent of both biblical and contemporary apocalyptic. For the result is not only that biblical apocalyptic is misread; contemporary apocalyptic is also misread.

The aim, then, of the present chapter is to formulate a typology of the languages of future expectation enabling the reader to appreciate biblical apocalyptic and contemporary manifestations, insofar as both share similar structures of narrative, and insofar as in both the re-structuring of the temporal world is accomplished along similar lines. To arrive at this, we must begin with a brief analysis of biblical apocalyptic, in order to isolate those factors which are the components of apocalyptic narrative. Once this is done, it will become clear that the images, symbols, and devices of apocalyptic do not function in the same way as in ordinary discourse. The "revelation of things to come," for example, does not function in apocalyptic as prediction (as threat or promise), but as information. To misread apocalyptic on this point is to confuse it with prophetic eschatology, and, further down the line, to read the "revelation of things to come" as referring to plain history and real politics.

The Critical Understanding of Apocalyptic

David Ketterer says of the term, apocalyptic, that it is "carelessly and inconsistently employed in critical discourse" (xi). His book, as argued above, is an attempt to spell out a definition of apocalyptic and employ it as a critical counter in the subsequent analysis of apocalyptic science fiction dimensions in American literature. John R. May, in *Toward a New Earth*, a study of "apocalypse in the American novel," states as his purpose to "discern what elements of these language traditions have been and are still so universally true of the apocalyptic form that they can be said to be essential to its

purpose and meaning and thus serve as a canon for describing
contemporary American variations"(4). In order for each to
accomplish his task, ostensibly literary criticism, but mani-
festing also larger concerns, some kind of controlling
description/definition of apocalyptic must be formulated--it
could hardly be otherwise. Apocalyptic is everywhere recognized
as a literary genre, and must therefore justify its usefulness
by exhibiting some common characteristics attributable to the
many examples which constitute the genre. Nor has there been
any lack of attempts to do this, especially among scripture
scholars. These attempts will be our immediate concern in what
follows; and for our purposes I will classify them according to
the following categories: 1) internal considerations, the
literary characteristics, thematic and stylistic, which set
this genre apart; 2) external considerations, the historical
situation(s) which gave rise to apocalyptic; 3) considerations
of genre, what distinguishes apocalyptic from prophecy; and
4) moral/pragmatic considerations, of what use apocalyptic is.

Following this very brief review, which provides us with
the controlling elements of apocalyptic, we will attempt 5) to
make a structural analysis of those elements, particularly
promise and fulfillment, and of the languages of future expectation. What we are aiming for is a new way to read apocalyptic,
according to which the availability of apocalyptic for use in
systematic theology will be enhanced. One final note is in
order: The four categories are not exclusive, nor are they
exhaustive; nor finally is the fifth definitive. Each is
merely an emphasis, a perspective.

A.   Internal Considerations

The simplest, easiest, and often the most misleading
method of isolating the nature of apocalyptic is to describe
it, with a focus on the literary characteristics, its stylistic
and thematic features. Klaus Koch states:

> If we are to succeed at all in the future in arriving at
> a binding definition of apocalyptic, a starting point in
> form criticism and literary and linguistic history is,
> in the nature of things, the only one possible (23).

His survey of the apocalyptic writings, composed in Hebrew or
Aramaic, yields the following characteristics: 1) great

discourse cycles, carried on in dreams and visions between seer
and guide; 2) spiritual turmoil, caused by those dreams and
visions; 3) paranetic discourses to the readers; 4) pseudonymity; 5) use of mythical images rich in symbolism; and 6) the
composite nature of the work, usually a reduction of multiple
existing tests. Koch goes on to say that this body of literature seems to justify that we "pre-suppose something like a
movement of mind" behind it (28). Thus he goes on to list the
themes which comprise this movement of mind: 1) an urgent
expectation of the "end time" in the immediate future; 2) the
portrayal of this end as a cosmic catastrophe; or to say it
another way, 3) the passage from this age to the next, both of
which ages have been pre-determined from all time; 4) the use
of angels and demons to explain the course of events of the
end time; 5) a post-catastrophe existence in "paradise" which
is a conjunction of primal period and end time; 6) this transition (to the new age) will take place through an act of God;
but 7) is frequently mediated by an earthly messiah; and
8) this final age is a manifestation of God's glory (28-32).

     P. Vielhauer, in *New Testament Apocrypha*, submits a
similar list of literary characteristics, but with the addition
of "Surveys of History in Future-form." Since the work is
attributed to an author who lived in the past, that fictional
author had always to look ahead and prophesy. This description
of history in future form served to "arouse confidence in [the
actual author's] predictions of the future." Vielhauer's list
of themes likewise is similar, but again with one significant
addition: the issue of universalism and individualism. In
apocalyptic, history is universal in scope, with the result
that the concept of the chosen people is no longer operative.
Mankind is a unity. At the same time, apocalyptic insists that
the person stands as an individual before the throne of God.
The emphasis in this life is on law and righteousness (586-90).

     By far the most exhaustive list of apocalyptic features
is that compiled by D. S. Russell. Russell cites the list
formulated by Lindbloom: transcendentalism, mythology, cosmological survey, pessimistic historical surveys, dualism,
division of time into periods, teaching of two ages, numerology,
pseudo-ecstasy, artificial claims to inspiration, pseudonymity,

and esoterism. To this Russell adds: unity of history, source
of evil, conflict between powers, emergence of the "son of man,"
life after death, judgement, and resurrection. In addition to
the four pre-suppositions of apocalyptic, given by Staufer
(primordiality, conflict, eschatology and universalism), Russell
adds: determinism, and supernaturalism. Finally Russell
summarizes the nature of apocalyptic literature as: 1) esoteric
in character; 2) literary in form; 3) symbolic in language; and
4) pseudonymous in authorship (105-06).

Different combinations of the above listed characteristics account for nearly all such description/definitions of
apocalyptic. But what immediately strikes one upon having gone
through the above compilations, and other similar lists, is the
fact that they indiscriminately mix together stylistic and
thematic devices. Koch's plea for a "starting point" in form
criticism and in literary and linguistic history, seems to have
been disregarded even by himself. For alongside the literary
feature of "discourse cycle" Koch lists "spiritual turmoil."
Similarly, Russell, with his interminable list, includes everything anyone has ever claimed to be a characteristic of apocalyptic, without any regard for trying to order the features
according to their functions.

The problem of listing the characteristics is compounded
by the problem of defining the corpus of apocalyptic. But even
if critics were able to agree beforehand on the extent of the
corpus, the nature of apocalyptic cannot be derived from a mere
compilation of literary characteristics. Nature, even in literature, is not a sum of attributes. Somehow a definition of
the nature of, or, as we will suggest below, a description of
the structure of apocalyptic will have to be formulated to
account for the appearance and the use of all the above listed
characteristics. More importantly, such a definition/description
will also have to account for the fact that apocalyptic can be
still read meaningfully in our day and age; and indeed is still
being written. No simple listing of characteristics, no matter
how exhaustive, will account for those two phenomena.

The mere listing of the literary characteristics of
apocalyptic fails the most elementary test: it does not issue
in an adequate description of apocalyptic, one that will account

for its relevance both to its contemporaries and to those who
read it in the present. Typical of the attempts to derive a
definition from a compilation of characteristics is that of
Russell: "It [apocalyptic] claims to possess secret knowledge
of the future, and in particular of the manner and the time of
the End, which it is able to disclose under divine inspiration
and by supernatural means" (37). Such a genre of literature
would be no more than a curiosity for us today; and it could
hardly be expected to be other than that for its contemporaries
--unless we are committed to the facile distinction between the
modern and the primitive mind. In addition, it is no wonder
that, armed with such a description, some would compile a list
of characteristics stressing the most extreme and bizarre
elements of apocalyptic. And further, that in writing a history
of the rise of apocalyptic, they would seek out those situations
which account for the introduction of "foreign" elements into
the purity of Jewish thought. The problem with attempting to
isolate the nature of apocalyptic according to internal considerations is that it leaves us precisely nowhere. It issues
in a dead, static description/definition; one which is unable
to bridge the hermeneutic gap, unless that bridging be accomplished by a romantic regression to the historical era.

      Before moving on to other considerations to be taken
into account when isolating the nature of apocalyptic, we should
recall the critical work done by Ketterer and Kermode treated
above. Recognizing the existence and the value of apocalyptic
(a starting point not shared by all contemporary critics) their
literary critical analysis can help to bridge the gap created
by those who merely categorize and describe. Kermode is concerned with isolating the fictions by which humankind lives;
Ketterer, in a more personalistic direction, seeks to describe
the "creation of other worlds" which exist in the readers'
heads. John R. May's treatment of apocalyptic in *Toward a New
Earth* is a much more consciously biblically grounded study than
either Ketterer's or Kermode's. At the close of a brief survey
of apocalyptic from primitive times to the Book of Revelation,
May writes: "I suggest that the elements that are normative
for traditional or classical apocalypse are judgment, catastrophe, and renewal" (24). But May's study is more than a listing;

it is an attempt to work toward a typology of apocalyptic
which will not merely describe by listing, but will evaluate by
relating the types to the normative function of (Christian)
hope, a hope which looks to the future, not to the past. May,
then, is concerned with the elements of judgment, catastrophe,
and renewal not as static elements, but insofar as they function
in the literature of apocalyptic. May, as well as Ketterer and
Kermode, is concerned with how apocalyptic is read. As literary
critics all three realize that one does not read a list of
characteristics, one reads a story. Thus the nature of apocalyptic will have to somehow be related to story. Before turning to that issue, however, it is necessary to discuss the
attempts to isolate the nature of apocalyptic according to external considerations; that is, to relate it to the larger
story of humankind.

B.   External Considerations

     As a pre-figuration of the larger story of humankind we
encounter at once the seemingly interminable series of crises
which afflicted Israel, from the founding of the kingdom under
Saul and David to the final dissolution of that kingdom by the
Romans in 70 CE. In the story of Western civilization, at
least, it would be folly to try to find one's bearings without
the readings provided by the Judaeo-Christian experience--read-
ings in both senses of that word. Whereas surrounding nations
read nature, Israel read history; and whereas the former wrote
myth, Israel wrote story. Countless have been the studies of
the legacies we owe the Judaeo-Christian experience, from this
very sense of history to the idea of realism in literature. It
is no less true that to Israel we owe the legacy of apocalyptic,
the "radical instance" of our fictions, according to Kermode;
and in our terms, story about story.

     The topic under consideration here is the question of
how the historical situation (story) in Israel gave rise to
apocalyptic (as story about story). That is, what factors within Jewish history and/or what factors from without may have
caused, or at least occasioned, the formation of the type of
literature we call apocalyptic? The further question is:
Does a consideration of these factors account in any way for

the nature of apocalyptic? A corollary to this consideration
is the issue of how apocalyptic relates to other literary forms
and genres, particularly prophecy. While it is almost impossible to treat these two issues separately, I will attempt to
do just that for reasons which I hope will be evident.

Of almost universal acknowledgement is the statement that
apocalyptic is a literature of crisis. But caution is advised
precisely at this point; for we have seen that although Ketterer
alludes to the fact that John wrote his apocalypse as a reaction
to the persecutions inaugurated by Rome, his further suggestion
that John may have suffered from paranoia should warn us that
the designation of apocalyptic as a crisis literature may lead
to unwarranted conclusions. At best the conclusions do not
follow inevitably; for the designation of apocalyptic as a
crisis literature does not account for the fact that a crisis
situation could occasion apostasy and/or rebellion as well as
apocalyptic. Even more serious drawbacks occur when scholars
look to Old Testament times and the situations therein which
gave rise to apocalyptic.

But there is a certain amount of understanding to be
gained from a review of scholarship on this issue. Of critical
importance in all these studies is the question of continuities
and discontinuities, crisis being the occasion for the emergence
of the question: What does one look for in a crisis situation?
The old or the new? This pushes the consideration of apocalyptic
as a crisis literature one step further back; for old and new
cannot be related to each other as the continuous and the discontinuous. By and large, scholars have tended to stress the
discontinuous nature of apocalyptic as a response to a crisis
situation. That is, not only does apocalyptic talk about the
"wholly new," it itself is a wholly new form of literature,
created in response to a wholly new crisis experience in the
life of a nation. Otto Ploger, for example, speaks of apocalyptic eschatology as a "new type of mentality which can only
be explained as a result of a new understanding" (29). Ploger's
basic thesis is that so many discontinuities were created so
often and so rapidly in the life of Israel that apocalyptic
left itself open to the influence of foreign ideas (Persian
dualism being the most notable) which subsequently gave

apocalyptic its distinctive nature. Many other critics of apocalyptic follow Ploger in the intent, if not in the content, of his observations.

The interpretation of the crisis, however, differs from one commentator to the next. The most general, all-embracing formulation of it is typified by Russell's statement: "The world is no longer God's kingdom; it lay in the hands of evil, cosmic forces which were bent on the destruction of mankind and of the world itself" (267). Thus the crisis was not merely a crisis of this world, its history, and its historical forces; it was a spiritual crisis--that is, a crisis of the "principalities and powers" ruling this world. God and Satan were the real protagonists. Most commentators, however, try to be more specific in their description of the crisis and its protagonists. Ploger's thesis is that the "new understanding" which occasions the crisis is the understanding of Israel as a cultic community, "a religious community, a theocracy instead of a nation" (29). Eschatological expectations, he adds, are going to be significantly different, and expressed in a significantly different form, than are those for a political nation. Thus Ploger lines up the Pharisees and the Pietists (forerunners of the Maccabees) against the high priests and the scribes. Paul D. Hanson, in *The Dawn of Apocalyptic*, using the sociological categories of Weber, labels the protagonists as the visionaries and the hierocrats. This allows him to argue that the roots of apocalyptic are embedded deeply within prophecy, for the loss of prophetic vision was the real crisis confronting the post-exilic community. In terms similar to Ploger's Hanson speaks of the "loss of nationhood" and the "threat to the unity of the community," due to the factionalism between the visionaries and the hierocrats. His thesis, therefore, is that "Apocalyptic eschatology is the mode assumed by the prophetic tradition once it had been transferred to a new and radically altered setting in the post-exilic community" (10). But by locating the crisis much earlier in Israel's history, he is able to discredit the influence of foreign ideas as contributing to the essential nature of apocalyptic. More recently J. J. Collins has moved even further away from such searches for historical protagonists and sociological categories in delineating the crisis-situation

which occasions the rise of apocalyptic. Collins does not even
allude to the portrayals of concrete crises mentioned above;
his aim is simply to arrive at the essential thematic notion of
apocalyptic. He dismisses out of hand the idea of a definitive
end, and the distinction of the two ages. Both prophecy and
apocalyptic, he argues, have something to do with future expectation. But it is the content of that expectation Collins
believes separates the two: "It is this hope for the transcendence of death which is the distinctive character of apocalyptic" (1974:30). Although Collins does not speak specifically
of the crisis situation giving rise to this hope and the writing
of apocalyptic, it is not too difficult to imagine the real
life crises: persecution and disillusionment, resulting in the
necessary re-formulation of the hope of the believers.

What Collins seems to be arguing toward, and a point
which needs attention in any analyses of the crises giving rise
to apocalyptic, is that if the crisis situation is interpreted
too narrowly and detailed too specifically, it then becomes
difficult to understand the appeal and the meaningfulness of
apocalyptic outside of that particular crisis situation. This,
in general, is the difficulty with the attempt to isolate the
nature of apocalyptic from external considerations; it forces
us to read apocalyptic only as a response, and a very limited
response at that: a flight into another world, a spiritual
world. Collins' own rejoinder to such a reading of apocalyptic
is to complement "future expectation" with "depth dimension" of
the present. Hope for transcendence of death is not only a
future expectation; it is also a depth dimension of the present;
they interpenetrate each other (41).

Apocalyptic, therefore, is not only occasioned by crisis,
it also, in its own way, occasions crisis by acting as a
critical counter to a shallow reading of the present moment and
the present world and its structures. It is in this latter
reading of apocalyptic that we must search for the appeal and
meaning it has in the time of no apparent crisis. Whether or
not "hope for the transcendence of death" exhausts the content
of apocalyptic as the occasioner of crisis is another question,
especially if it is an individualized, interiorized hope. It
would seem that, contrary to Collins' systematic groundings

(he cites Bultmann and Rahner), the transcendence of death has political in addition to existential ramifications. This becomes especially apparent when we take up the following considerations: prophetic correlations and moral/pragmatic uses of apocalyptic.

C. Considerations of Genre

In the attempt to isolate the nature of apocalyptic through a consideration of its relationship to other literary genres, the genre which immediately invites comparison is prophecy. Nor is this immediacy misleading. Biblical apocallyptic is most often seen as a continuation of biblical prophecy, both by its writers and by its critics. The major critical battles have been fought over whether this continuation is to be interpreted as a transformation (in the positive sense) or a corruption of prophecy. Our argument will be that a dialectical comparison of prophecy and apocalyptic works to clarify the distinctive nature of each, while not allowing either to be cast in rigid forms and formulaic definitions.

Before reviewing some of the major treatments of the relationship between prophecy and apocalyptic, however, it might be helpful to treat briefly the question of why this is such a volatile issue and why it has been handled so cautiously in New Testament exegesis. And, indeed, why it is still handled so cautiously in biblical and literary circles.

In his admittedly polemic monograph, *The Rediscovery of Apocalyptic*, Klaus Koch discusses what he believes to be the reasons New Testament exegetes by and large attempt to "save Jesus from apocalyptic." Early on in the first flush of the new method of historical criticism, the controlling analogy employed to account for apocalyptic was the spatial/temporal. Apocalyptic flourished during the intertestamental period, approximately 200 BCE to 100 CE. Apocalyptic, therefore, was seen as a bridge; the spatial/temporal bridge was also a bridge of ideas. Koch cites the Old Testament scholar Hilgenfeld as writing in 1857 that apocalyptic "conveys the historical connection of Christianity with the prophetic predictions of the Old Testament" (36). Hilgenfeld's thesis, however, never survived as he intended it. While other scholars talked of the "prophetic connection," as it came to be called, for them it meant only that after a hiatus of 500 years (dating from the time of deutero-Isaiah) did Jesus, and possibly John the Baptist before him, revive the method and the message of the prophets. Thus apocalyptic served as a connection only in the sense of a wall, or a wasteland, and not in the sense of a bridge. Apocalyptic in German scholarship, Koch maintains, has henceforth been consistently relegated to secondary status. It is hardly worthy of comment, except as an aberration. Even the history of religions school was unable to revive interest in it. /1/

Although initially intended as a corrective to this approach, Anglo-American scholarship also tells a tale of the slighting of apocalyptic. R. Charles, the greatest English-speaking authority on apocalyptic, and on whose critical editions all subsequent scholarship depends, summed up the result of his studies on this point as follows: "Before AD 70 Judaism was a church [sic] with many parties; after AD 70 the legalistic party succeeded in suppressing its rivals, and so Judaism became in its essentials a sect" (vii). At that point, Charles maintains, apocalyptic passed over to Christianity. He holds this as a positive development; for it is the passing on of a prophetic charge. Scholars following Charles have been generally agreeable to his citing of CE 70 as a turning point; they have been far less favorable in their comments on who exactly inherited the legacy of apocalyptic, and indeed of what that legacy consisted. Koch cites the Unitarian minister R. Travers Herford: "Apocalyptic is full of promises, but has never kept one of them" (51). The implication here is that apocalyptic was taken over by the zealots.

Koch believes that these two trends in the interpretation of apocalyptic account for all the subsequent attempts by scholars to save Jesus from apocalyptic; for the Gospels are filled with apocalyptic sayings attributed to Jesus. If apocalyptic is truly a corruption of prophecy, a corruption which flourished in (and some would even say which caused) the long hiatus between deutero-Isaiah and Jesus, then Jesus must be saved from being convicted by his very own words. If, on the other hand, apocalyptic was a viable alternative to the sect of the Pharisees, but after 70 AD passed over to Christianity when

the Pharisees prevailed in Judaism, then Jesus must again be
saved from apocalyptic, lest he appear to be merely the founder
of a shadow religion at best, or, at worst, a critical-negative,
deluded community grasping at salvation through God's intervention. These attempts are summed up in the "theory of the
non-apocalyptic Jesus and his apocalyptic church," a theory,
which Koch insists, still enjoys great favor in New Testament
exegesis (39).

It may be, setting the above formulation of the issue
just slightly to the side, that biblical exegesis has been
primarily concerned with saving prophecy from apocalyptic.
That certainly is the interpretation gained from reading certain
Old Testament scholarship on apocalyptic. But if, as is our
contention, apocalyptic is a legitimate development of prophecy,
what saving prophecy from apocalyptic amounts to is saving
prophecy from itself. This negates the very essence of prophecy,
leaving it incapable of fulfilling its stated task: mediating
the present into the future.

What are the considerations that constitute a comparison
between prophecy and apocalyptic? The schema of Martin Buber
provides a generally agreed upon starting point for delineating
the differences:

	PROPHECY	APOCALYPTIC
Eschatology	Native, monistic	Foreign, dualistic
Object of Hope	Fulfillment of Creation	Dissolution of creation by a different world
Judgment	Announced, but revocable, conditional	Unalterable, final, fixed and determinate

It would be difficult, seeing it stated so bluntly, to interpret this other than as an attempt to save prophecy from apocalyptic, the latter being merely a corruption, a decadent later
development. Nor would it be difficult, taking a closer look
at the schema, to see that it lies behind all attempts to trace
the beginnings of apocalyptic in soil other than prophecy.
Thus van Rad in his Old Testament theology seeks to locate the
roots of apocalyptic in wisdom literature (303-08), while
Ploger, Russell, and a host of others spend great effort in

tracing the foreign influences in apocalyptic, notably Persian dualism. All have in one way or another accepted the thesis that apocalyptic is a corruption of prophecy, thereby forcing the biblical scholar to search elsewhere for the distinctive characteristics of apocalyptic. Even the fact that the writers of apocalyptic saw themselves as carrying on the tradition of prophecy is dismissed. Vielhauer will grant that the writers possessed and articulated this self-understanding: "The self-awareness of the writer might then be described as follows: the prophets have disappeared; the Apocalyptists have taken their place and continue their work in other but better ways." But he falls back on the Buber thesis to deny that such is actually the case: "The dualism, determinism, and pessimism of Apocalyptic form the gulf which separates it from prophecy" (596). Walter Schmithals, in *The Apocalyptic Movement*, argues along the same lines, maintaining that apocalyptic creates a "decisionless future" because of its determinism. He does grant, however, that the "radical de-historicizing of the future" (history for him amounts to the ability to make decisions) is balanced by a "radical historicizing of the present" (39).

These efforts to isolate the nature of apocalyptic by comparing it to prophecy—and concluding that apocalyptic is nothing other than the corruption of prophecy—presuppose that there is a commonly accepted and universally valid definition/description of prophecy. Such would hardly seem to be the case, judging at least from the intense scholarship generated by this precise issue alone. Moreover, the notion of a closed and definitive self-understanding and of a closed critical understanding of the prophetic is foreign to present day biblical hermeneutics.

In this light Paul D. Hanson's book, *The Dawn of Apocalyptic*, assumes such importance. Hanson's thesis is that "apocalyptic eschatology found at the heart of the late apocalyptic can be found already fully developed in all its essentials in the works of the mid-fifth century." He claims that most commentators do not go back far enough in locating the roots of apocalyptic, with the result that their methodology is deficient for handling all subsequent interpretations. More specifically:

> 1.) The sources of apocalyptic are misunderstood; 2.)
> the period of origin is centuries off the mark, mean-
> ing that the resulting typology of apocalyptic liter-
> ature is grossly inaccurate; 3.) the historical and
> sociological matrix of apocalyptic is left unexplained;
> 4.) the essential nature of apocalyptic is inadequately
> clarified (7-8).

Hanson's whole study is an attempt to locate the roots of apocalyptic in prophecy; or perhaps, to state it more in line with
our contentions, the roots of both prophecy and apocalyptic are
in the promise which shapes Israel's future hopes. Hanson does
maintain that both apocalyptic and prophecy share the same
essential vision: "Yahweh's people restored as a holy community
in a glorified Zion" (12). If this were Hanson's only contribution, it would set his study apart from all others; for it
provides the basis for a dialectical comparison of prophecy and
apocalyptic, instead of the static comparisons given to us by
Buber and other commentators.

How does Hanson proceed on this dialectical comparison?
First, he offers a description of prophecy and apocalyptic from
a religious perspective: (11)/2/

PROPHETIC ESCHATOLOGY	APOCALYPTIC ESCHATOLOGY

Prophetic announcement
  to the nation
  of the divine plan
    for Israel and the world
	Disclosure (usually esoteric)
	  to the elect
	  of the cosmic vision of
	    Yahweh's sovereignty
	    as he acts to deliver the
	      faithful

witnessed by the prophet
  unfolding in the divine
  council	

and translated into
    terms of
  plain history
  real politics
    and
  human instrumentality
	no longer disclosed
	    in terms of
	  plain history
	  real politics
	    and
	  human instrumentality

	because of a pessimistic view of reality, due to post-exilic conditions.

This comparison has some similarities to the schema proposed by
Buber; yet it does bring the feature of "crisis-literature"
into the description. Hanson, however, does not stop here with

his comparisons. Employing the terminology and categories of
Weber's *Sociology of Religion*, Hanson goes on to talk of the
tension which always exists in a society between the visionaries
and the realists. He is able to do this, of course, since he
insists that they do share the same essential vision. If they
did not, all comparisons would be meaningless. Prophecy, living
and functioning in a viable structure (the monarchy) as it did,
saw its task as that of integrating vision with reality. With
the failure of that political structure, the role of maintaining
the vision fell into other hands, hands which had no vested
interest in maintaining the status quo. Gradually, then, apocalyptic relinquished the need to translate vision into "plain
history, real politics and human instrumentality." Locating
apocalyptic on a continuum shown below, Hanson situates Israel's
religious thought in relation to its neighbors, cult in relation
to history, and apocalyptic in relation to prophecy:(29)

1.) Early Myth (Egypt and Sumer):   Negation of history

2.) Classical Mesopotamia: History is the mere reflec-
                                    tion of the cosmic realm

3.) Israelite League (Judges):   Myth and history in tension

4.) Royal Cult in Jerusalem   History is a reflection of
    (Royal Messianism):   cosmic events

5.) Prophetic Yahwism: History affirmed as the
                                    context of divine acts

6.) Apocalyptic: Indifference to the re-
                                    straints of history

7.) Gnosticism: Negation of history

Prophetic Yahwism is the supreme achievement of Israelite religion; but insistence on history as the context of divine acts
carries the seeds of its own destruction. For history fails.
And just as Job interpreted the failure of his own personal
history as the failure of God, so did apocalyptic interpret the
exile and the post-exilic turmoil as the failure of God. Thus
goes the analysis of a summary reading of apocalyptic.

But grant that prophecy and apocalyptic share the same
essential vision, the same promise, and one will see that
neither the success nor the failure of history is the main concern of apocalyptic. Thus Hanson says of apocalyptic that it
is indifferent to the restraints of history. Apocalyptic is
concerned above all with the promise; it maintains that through

such a close association of vision and reality (promise and
history) one has already compromised the vision. In Hanson's
phrase "indifference to the restraints of history" we are re-
minded of Kermode's "indifference to disconfirmation." In
neither case is this to be simply equated with a negation of
history. For apocalyptic, in this understanding, has passed
beyond the question of fulfillment and/or a material realization
of the promise/vision. Yet, just as apocalyptic haunts prophecy
with the question of fulfillment, so also prophecy haunts apocalyptic with the very same question. Prophecy and apocalyptic
exist in a dialectical tension; they need each other as a
critical counter. And fulfillment operates as the rubric to an
understanding of this tension.

     With this discussion we come back to the treatment of
apocalyptic in the work of Ketterer. In his study Ketterer
maintains that, in apocalyptic, satire comes up against prophetic mysticism to provide a form of judgment. He argues
further that the creation of meaning and purpose collides with
the possibility of non-meaning and chaos (13). In terms of the
discussion above, Ketterer can be read as saying that apocalyptic functions as a critical negation, not of history, but of
the exaggerated claims made in the name of history by prophecy.
More specifically, present fulfillment is not a sign of the
validity of the promise. Still, the question of fulfillment is
of central concern, for it is what allows the tension to be
present. When Ketterer argues that "apocalyptic allows for a
dialectic, conflict, or tension of opposites," he is saying no
more than that apocalyptic allows the question of fulfillment
to remain open to a future. Prophecy tends to close off that
future by identifying "plain history, real politics, and human
instrumentality" with the actions of God. It is true that
Ketterer does not describe his dialectic as that which exists
between promise and fulfillment; instead he offers the pairings
of pragmatic/speculative, material/transcendental, and is/ought
to be (8). Hanson's dialectic is that which exists between
visionaries and realists. We believe, on the other hand, that
the dialectic between promise and fulfillment is the most
satisfactory statement of the tension. It allows for a dynamic
reading of apocalyptic as story; and it is capable of absorbing

the dialectic existing between prophecy and apocalyptic.

A final note on the consideration of apocalyptic as a genre is the contention that we are dealing here with a "genre" only in an analogous sense. We are all accustomed in this sense to apply the designation "prophetic" to novels, plays, poetry, speeches, essays, and even to courses of action. Apocalyptic is not a genre standing alongside other literary genres such as romance, allegory, fantasy, or speculative fiction. All these genres, rather, are capable of being apocalyptic. As noted above, a consistent description of apocalyptic was that it is "composite in nature;" and capable of using many a different and varied literary form.

Moreover, in noting the attempts to isolate the nature of apocalyptic from external considerations, we saw that it is often described as a crisis literature. Any consideration of apocalyptic as a genre, thus, will have to take into account the crisis. In fact, apocalyptic can in this analogous sense of a genre be defined precisely insofar as it stands in relation to a crisis, real or imaginary; and insofar as it either causes or is a result of that crisis. This aids in the attempt to specify just how it is that any literary form may be appropriated by apocalyptic. At the risk of simplifying, we might say that in addition to telling a story to the reader, apocalyptic tells a story about the reader. Apocalypse does not happen in the reader (as Ketterer maintains); the reader happens into apocalypse. Surely any literary text will engage the reader on both these levels; but in apocalyptic the engagement on the latter level is clear and conscious. For the story about the reader is a story of crisis, and the crisis is precisely of the experienced tension between promise and fulfillment, which it will cause and/or resolve.

D. Moral/Pragmatic Considerations

In this final perspective on the nature of apocalyptic, through a consideration of its moral/pragmatic uses, we come at length to the heart of the matter. For any amount of reading in and noting its manifestations in contemporary literature and popular culture yields an almost limitless number of explicit references: from John Barth to Charles Manson, from Alvin

Toffler to Bob Dylan, from Robert Heilbroner to Kurt Vonnegut,
Jr., from Norman Mailer to the Jefferson Starship, and, as we
have been arguing throughout this study, from the earliest
science fiction to the latest. The fact that stylistic and
thematic correlations between biblical and contemporary apocalyptic can be traced and documented (Ketterer and May are but
two examples of this); the fact that, however much one may disagree that there is a crisis, apocalyptic is today as in biblical
times a literature of crisis; and the fact, finally, that so
much of contemporary apocalyptic is so closely related to and
so self-consciously prophetic in character--all this necessitates a serious consideration of the pragmatic and moral uses
of apocalyptic. The question before us, then, is not only what
is apocalyptic, but what does it mean?

    If scholars have been stymied in their efforts to reach
a consensus on what apocalyptic is and what it means; and if
hermeneutics has bogged down in its deliberations over how
apocalyptic, or any text for that matter, can mean, still the
plain fact emerging from any cursory reading of present times
is that apocalyptic does mean, and it does mean in the present.
The heart of the matter, thus, does not lie only in the past
(What is biblical apocalyptic? How did it emerge?); it lies
also in the present.

    As noted above, the story of apocalyptic in relation to
prophecy is for many a commentator the story of the decline and
fall of Old Testament prophecy. The story has its counterpart
in the present day: Apocalyptic is irresponsible, narcissistic
doom-saying, indulged in by some precocious and spoiled children
of an age which has provided all their spiritual and material
needs. To read the analysis by Nathan Scott, Jr., for example,
of how the contemporary tone of modern literature is so
thoroughly apocalyptic is immediately to see how such a
critical contention is the literary equivalent to much of
recent liberal theology's ongoing exegetical critique of apocalyptic as the corruption of prophecy. Prophecy is the liberal
theologians' responsible stance toward the secular world, toward
"plain history, real politics, and human instrumentality;" the
mode of religious concern which balances vision and practical
realities. Conversely, apocalyptic is the ranting of the

rebels and the revolutionaries who have given up on the practical realities.

Again, the heart of the matter lies in the present:
liberal theology's definition of prophecy is static and exclusive, rather than dynamic and inclusive. The intertestamental
period saw that a similar static and exclusive definition of
prophecy led to its own appropriation by the legalistic sect of
Judaism. In the process, prophecy was de-eschatologized and
became the hand-maid of the Law. Salvation came through the
observance of the law (Charles:viii). A similar fate awaits
prophecy in liberal theology's emphasis on the individual,
interiorized, existential response to the word of God. Prophecy
de-eschatologized becomes the hand-maid of existential response.
Hope becomes an act of faith, rather than the form of faith.
Salvation comes through faith, an individualized and personalized encounter which is a-political. In both cases, apocalyptic
becomes the aberration which becomes in turn the outcast, and
eventually the scapegoat.

All this merely sets the stage for the re-appropriation
of apocalyptic by certain systematic theologians during the
last thirty years. Dissatisfied with the impasse reached by
liberal theology's "dialectical" mode of thought (for it meant
primarily "paradoxical"); theologians of the historical school
began to search for new models of transcendence which would
allow them to re-capture the dialectic from the paradoxical.
It was maintained that the transcendence of Aristotelian meta-
physics had long since been shattered by the natural sciences
and by critical philosophy. The succeeding model of transcendence as a subjective transcendence of existence, proposed
by Descartes and Kant, had long since evolved into the alienated
transcendence contemporary man faces in the quasi-nature of his
own structures. In the latter, transcendence becomes a flight
from objectified reality, an escape into mysticism. This had
led historical theology to propose "the future as the new
paradigm of transcendence" (Moltmann:1969). Eschatology plays
a central and critical role in the self-understanding of this
theology. The way is opened, thus, for a critical re-appropriation of apocalyptic, for one has critically re-appropriated
the future, or to be more precise, the function of the future.

Koch points out that in many regards systematic theology has taken the lead in the re-appropriation of apocalyptic. Such a point may be argued, of course; but what needs to be noted in any case is that biblical exegetes and systematic theologians are paying closer attention to what the other is saying. Thus Collins, at the conclusion of his article, when speaking of the "logic of apocalyptic eschatology," cites both Bultmann and Rahner in support of his contention that eschatological formulations are, from one point of view, projections of hopes experienced in the present (1974:41). The point is not the final formulation at which Collins arrives, but the fact that he does not attempt to speak of the "logic of apocalyptic eschatology" outside the present-day discussion of its meaning. This is the heart of the matter. This is why the mere listing of literary stylistic and thematic characteristics gets us nowhere in the end; why an historical understanding of the rise of apocalyptic by itself does not account for the relevance of apocalyptic in our day; and why a static comparison of it with prophecy is of no avail in helping us to understand either prophecy or apocalyptic.

Hanson also, although he warns against drawing parallels too freely, cites contemporary analyses of future expectation. As noted above, his use of the categories realist and visionary are taken from the work of Max Weber. In a later sociological analysis of the origins of post-exilic hierocracy, Hanson uses the categories of the ideological and the utopian, taken from the work of Karl Mannheim. Hanson maintains that apocalyptic symbols and features are not the possession of one particular party or sect, in any one particular age--they belong to the nation as a whole. "They are forms of conceptualizing the future" (228). They become available to and are used by any group who happens to see themselves as outcasts. The function, purpose, and meaning of apocalyptic, thus, is the re-solution of the tension existing between promise and fulfillment, precisely as it bears on the present experience and as it is seen in light of future expectations. Prophecy stands as critical counter to apocalyptic by reminding it of reality; while apocalyptic stands as critical counter to prophecy by reminding it of vision (promise).

How can apocalyptic mean? Certainly not by being merely a literature of certain features and themes. Certainly not by being a literature which has for its self-understanding simply that it has responded to a crisis. And certainly not by denying its relation to prophecy. Apocalyptic can only mean by fulfilling its function, that is, by being a story about the reader, caught up in a crisis revolving around promise and fulfillment, of which there is no totally adequate solution at the present. The question immediately arises: What good is a promise if it can never be fulfilled? Or a future if it can never be reached? A partial answer is that promise and future cause us to look critically at the present, which fulfillment rarely ever causes us to do. It fact, it often prevents us.

In conclusion, however, it must be stated that while the present day understanding of apocalyptic may expand the boundaries of our reading of biblical apocalyptic, it cannot dictate the meaning. This undoubtedly is what Hanson cautions against. But what he has done, as Collins in biblical exegesis, and Ketterer, Kermode, and May in literary criticism, is to clarify the structures of apocalyptic literature and imagination so that new meanings can emerge from the texts. Critical study never issues in one definitive meaning of a text; it should, however, come up with a description of the structures of the text able to carry many new meanings through allowing for new readings.

The question which emerges at this point, then, is: How can apocalyptic mean anything, not in spite of, but because of its literary styles and themes, its historical roots, and its generic differences? This question leads us to the consideration of the languages of future expectation, and the formulation of theoretical models, not for the writing of, but for the reading of apocalyptic.

The Languages of Future Expectation

What follows can only in the loosest sense be called a structural analysis. The phrase is used in the subsequent pages simply to make clear that the work done here is pre-hermeneutical. For as a literary critical method structuralism is not a hermeneutic; that is, it does not seek to assign a meaning to the text, but merely to make clear the conditions in which meaning can occur. Speaking of its linguistic base, and the methodology derived from that base, Jonathan Culler, in *Structuralist Poetics*, states that a "generative grammar" is a tool for the investigation of discourse, not a tool in the formulation of that discourse. A grammar tries to "account for the facts about language by constructing a formal representation of what is involved in knowing a language" (26). The purpose behind formulating a generative grammar is to isolate and make evident the operating rules which cover the composite elements of a text. Structuralism is concerned with understanding how a component operates within a system, a structure; for only through operating within a structure can meaning occur. Finally, on a much larger scale--one which pushes structuralism close to the charge of being an ideology-- structuralism posits the existence of a "universal grammar," in the sense that there is an unconscious awareness that meaning is shaped according to systems. Structuralism seeks to explicate those systems through the creation of rational models so that new meanings of discourse can emerge.

It is in this final sense that we seek to formulate a typology of the languages of future expectation. There seems, on a common sense level, to be different ways of expecting the future, different stories to be told, and different understandings of time, of memory, and of hope. If we are truly serious about isolating the nature of apocalyptic, then we must go beyond these common sense understandings and attempt to formulate a system which underlies the structure of the narratives of apocalyptic. At the same time, so as not to divorce ourselves completely from other critical work and from the narratives themselves, we must take into account the critical understanding of apocalyptic treated above. We will thus briefly recapitulate that treatment, with the aim of isolating those components critical to the structure of the languages of future expectation.

From internal considerations we learn that a listing of the literary stylistic and thematic devices, while adequately isolating the nature of apocalyptic according to its distinctive

features, concludes by isolating apocalyptic from itself. In
its own negative manner, then, it argues for the need to go
beyond the lists to story, that is, to a structure which somehow accounts for the components of the compiled list.

From external considerations we learn that the question
is whether there is something other than crisis which accounts
for the continuity of apocalyptic (that some apocalyptic is
continuous can be argued from the fact that the books of Daniel
and the Revelation of John have been accepted into the canon),
for crisis alone cannot account for it. No matter how that
crisis is described--spiritual, political, religious, cultic,
personal--and no matter who the protagonists of that crisis--
God/Satan, life/death, light/darkness, realists/visionaries,
hierocrats/prophets, rabbis/pietists--a simple binary pairing
alone does not account for the continuity apocalyptic manifests,
and yet the disjunctive nature of its expectations. In our
analysis thus far of both science fiction and biblical apocalyptic we have been consistently called to consider *promise* as
the factor which specifies crisis as having both a dimension
of past-ness and a dimension of future-ness to it. From memory
of promise arises the future expectation which promise implies;
and from hope arises the remembrance of the promise once given.
Crisis is what situates these dimensions in a peculiar tension
and enables apocalyptic to arise. The function of apocalyptic
is to re-solve the tension which the older forms can no longer
adequately resolve. Thus we are here driven to go beyond a
description of crisis, to seek the function of crisis. Crisis
must somehow result in a new configuration of the polarities
existing within a nation or society.

From considerations of genre we have learned that the
attempt to save prophecy from apocalyptic has unwittingly saved
prophecy from itself, thereby destroying its viability. For
prophecy without apocalyptic inevitably catches up in the
promise/fulfillment trap; and in the end cannot account for its
own future expectations. Both apocalyptic and prophecy share a
common essential vision allowing for a dialectical comparison.
Apocalyptic functions as a critical negation, not of history,
but of the exaggerated claims made by prophecy in the name of
history. Prophecy, however, continues as a critical counter to

the exaggerated claims made by apocalyptic in the name of vision/promise.

From pragmatic/moral considerations we have seen that the heart of the matter, when it comes to reading apocalyptic, lies in the present as well as in the past. The present is not its own justification or its own meaning; but the present is after all that alone of which we have immediate experience. It is in the in-depth experience of the present that we will have to locate the meaning of history and the justification (or condemnation) of the present. Apocalyptic helps us to do precisely this by forcing us to focus on promise, fulfillment, and future expectation. Apocalyptic can be read on many different levels, one of which is as a language of the future considered as a depth-dimension of the present. In fact, this is the summary conclusion drawn from a consideration of the pragmatic/moral considerations of apocalyptic. Apocalyptic is a language of disjunctive expectation which, when transposed into categories of temporal structuring, is understood as imminent expectation. The themes of apocalyptic point to the nearness of God's promise; the crisis which occasions the rise of apocalyptic seeks to be resolved very soon. The pragmatic uses of apocalyptic are best understood as accomplishing the re-solution of the present crisis in terms of a promised future which is awaited urgently.

The final conclusion of this recapitulation is that to understand apocalyptic we will need to understand the language of imminent expectation. Yet this is precisely where the analysis of apocalyptic considered thus far leaves off. It has given us all the components of the language, but has failed to formulate the grammar. Again, what follows is not an attempt to explicate what apocalyptic means, or what the author intended it to mean, but only to argue that apocalyptic can be read on many different levels, or better, translated according to many different languages.

A. The Future as Expectation

Before the future is known it is expected. Even on the most unreflective level of our existence the future is grasped as a dimension of the present. The issue at hand is not the

question of knowing the future as we know some object; it is
rather a question of knowing the future as a dimension of the
present. We know of the future through expectation. What we
know is not the future in itself; in its simplest terms we know
the future as an extension of the present. "Tomorrow will
follow today," we often say completely unreflectively, expecting the future to happen more or less on its own. "As sure as
tomorrow will follow today, we will create a new society."
With such an expression the expectation of the future involves
us as active participants in its creation. "Tomorrow will
follow today, God willing." Now the expectation of the future
involves us as passive recipients. Expectation of the future,
therefore, has no simple, univocal meaning. For there are
three different manners in which the future can be expected.
The languages of future expectation will have to account for
these three different possible structures of future expectation;
they will also have to provide for the fact that these three
possible structures may exist simultaneously in one text. That
is, they are inclusive, and can mean inclusively. The Revelation of John, for example, can be read according to any of the
three different languages, but it will mean differently according to which language is used. Borrowing categories from
Ketterer (but modified according to all that has been discussed
above), I will speak of the language of 1) simple expectation,
2) modified expectation, and 3) disjunctive expectation./3/
Each one of us speaks and reads all three languages; we are all
multi-lingual when it comes to the languages of future expectation.

The languages of future expectation are not exclusive,
but inclusive. The language of simple expectation will include
and give its own meaning to statements of simple, modified, and
disjunctive expectation. But the latter statements will be
understood differently than those uttered in the language of
modified or disjunctive expectation. "We will land a man on
the moon by the end of this decade," for example, will be understood and meant differently in all three languages, according
to the meaning intended and the meaning heard. In the language
of simple expectation, landing a man on the moon is a statement
about a future expected to follow from a simple continuation of

what is known and what is being done at the present. In the
language of disjunctive expectation, however, it is a statement
about a future event in the story of humankind, having consequences which are not able to be contained in the physical fact.

B. The Language of Simple Expectation

        In the language of simple expectation the future is
expected simply as a continuation of the present. All that is
known of the future is that it will happen. "It's the way
things are," is a statement which sums up the world-view of
this language. That the future should receive any special
consideration is foreign to its thought. The future is "the
way things will be," just as the past is "the way things were."

        Change, in this language, is a fact of reality; it is
not a function of human consciousness and/or interpretation.
The present undergoes change, and results in a future different
than the present, either in degree or in kind. Yet neither
difference, degree or kind, exercises any critical function in
relation to the present. For change is a medium impermeable
to human consciousness.

        Let us graph this language in the following manner:

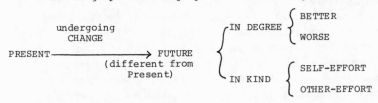

This is the simplest language of the future in relation to the
present. Operating as a straight-line projection of the present,
little or no feedback occurs. Change is the only link between
the present and the future; but change is not a living, conscious process. It is something to be undergone either blindly,
resulting in a future different in degree, or as the object of
manipulation, resulting in a future different in kind.

        What is obviously missing in this language is the dimen-
sion of past. The result is that the future also is not appreciated as a dimension of the present. The language of simple
expectation is the language of a people without a sense of
history, a people who have no awareness of any depth-dimension

in their lives. Both the present and the future are flat, one-dimensional. Continuity is sought on the level of material reality and sameness. Yet this is precisely where the difficulties arise. A future which is the same cannot be entirely the same, for this would completely eliminate it as an object of thought. Everyone is cognizant of change as a reality; the future, therefore, will have to be more like the present, or less like the present, than the present is like itself for us to even grasp it as an object of thought. The usual labels given to these projections are "better" or "worse." But in the depth-dimensionless language of simple expectation, the possibility of change for the better or the worse exercises no critical function. Change does that kind of thing, after all: it makes things better or worse. "That's the way things go." There does not exist in this language any control of meaning. What is, is; what will be, will be. This is perhaps seen more clearly from a consideration of the "future different in kind" where the language of simple expectation takes into account the statements of modified and disjunctive expectation. What counts in the future different in kind is the effort which goes into its formation; that is, it is a matter of will, control, and manipulation. Since there is no depth-dimension of the future in the present, will and control have no other meaning than that they are the means to bring about a future different in kind. "Things will be different," is all that matters. This is of more importance than whether the future will be better or worse. Indeed, it does away with that consideration entirely. In the end it not only makes no difference, there is even no way of determining or evaluating the future in terms of better or worse. These are judgments that the future will have to worry about.

The language of simple expectation speaks of the extrapolation and projection of existing trends or existing dreams. It expects only a future it can somehow see now, and over which it can exercise some kind of control. The future is in no way a transcendent reality; it simply has not yet arrived. Someday it will; and eventually all of it will. At that time life will be over, the book closed, and there will exist nothing.

Who speaks the language of simple expectation? Much of science fiction falls into this category; for it is the simple extrapolation of existing trends or existing dreams. The language says, in effect, "What you expect is what you get." Since the expectations can be either of a better world or of a worse world, the language speaks usually of utopia or dystopia, respectively. While it would be a mistake to categorize the bulk of utopian literature as a projection of a future different in degree, dystopian literature falls most often under that heading. "Things fall apart," is the way it is; that things get better usually requires some kind of effort. Thus utopian literature speaks the language of effort in science fiction, the language of will and control. Any cursory reading of utopian literature in science fiction bears out this claim. A utopian society is usually highly structured, centralized, dependent on a ruler or a ruling class; it generally exists temporally or spatially apart from the present society, that is, it is a-historical; it is established and remains in existence through an individual or collective act of the will. The structure of utopian society betrays the language of simple future expectation; it projects a material future accomplished through self-effort. Finally, the circle is completed in utopian science fiction with the underlying implication (often never explicitly stated) that a turn toward the worse is the result of other-effort, that is, outside interference.

Perhaps the clearest example of the language of simple expectation is *Walden Two*, discussed above. Like the majority of other utopias, Walden Two has no real history, because it has no collective memory of how it came into existence, nor any ritual institutions to preserve that memory. Likewise, it also has no discernable future, other than a perpetuation of already existing practices. There is a sameness to the community extending far beyond dress codes and behavior. In the recent film, *Rollerball*, to cite another example, we can gradually piece together that there were at the beginning football leagues, then three large nations, then the corporation wars, and finally "The Corporation." But we never come to any real understanding of the events leading logically to the coming into being of the society as depicted in the film. What is

really being said, thus, is that there is no understanding of
this process, no understanding of how we got from the past to
the present. Nor can there be any understanding of how we get
from the present to the future. There exists, therefore, no
depth-dimension of the present. Because there is no understanding of the "how," all that can be said is that we were in
the past, we are in the present, and we will be in the future.
We are prisoners of a chronology; there is an inevitability not
only to the future, but also to the present.

The language of simple expectation also characterizes
much of the work of Robert Heinlein. His stories, while often
engaging on the level of plot and characterization, fail to
challenge on the level of exploring the depth-dimension of the
present. In his preface to *The Man Who Sold the Moon*, Heinlein
himself says: "The stories in this and later volumes of the
series were not written as prophecy, nor as history...They are
of the 'What-would-happen-if--' sort." Heinlein continues:

> Technology races ahead while people remain stubbornly
> the same...It is a great and wonderful age, the most
> wonderful this giddy planet has ever seen. It is
> sometimes comic, too often tragic, and always wonder-
> ful. Our wildest dreams of the future will be sur-
> passed by what lies in front of us. *Come bad, come
> good,* I want to take part in the show as long as
> possible (1951:v).

The language of simple expectation is also the pre-
dominant language spoken by the "think tanks," particularly as
they move into "prospecting the future." There are many names
given to this policy research of the future: futures research,
prognostics, prospection, forecasting, futurism, futurology,
and futuristics. But central to the concern of all is the
necessity of control; either we will control the future, or it
will control us. John McHale's *The Future of the Future* is a
case in point. While McHale demonstrates a rather sophisticated
understanding of the dimensions of the future, speaking of the
varying relationships that exist between past and present and
future--in the end he comes down hard on the necessity of
control. Control is not only needed to survive, it is also
needed to understand. All the various views of the future have
today "crystallized around the idea that the future of the

individual and of society are within human control" (5). Although he does speak of humankind having moved beyond the belief
in the inevitability of progress, what he means is simply that
humankind can control progress.

It would be a mistake in all this to overlook the
positive features of the language of a simple expectation insofar as it makes use of extrapolative techniques. For this
is the language spoken by the empirical sciences: economics,
with its graphs of exponential growth; statistics, with its
laws of probability, and so forth. Much of the work being
done to curb the rate of pollution and the cancerous growth of
urban areas is the result of Environmental Impact Statements
written in the language of simple expectation. The language
also appears in ethical discourse, under the rubric of consequences. In his book, *The Moral Choice*, Daniel Maguire writes
that unless we know the consequences of our choice in the
matter at hand, we do not really know the object or situation
in its entirety. Consequences are a dimension of the moral
object (150-57). Finally, it would be difficult to imagine
the "discovery of the technique of discovery" as having taken
place without the language of simple expectation. McLuhan
cites this discovery, along with the "technique of suspended
judgment" as the two guiding principles of the modern era (68).

To read apocalyptic as the language of simple expectation, however, is to set up the possibility of attributing a
meaning to it which is fundamentally foreign to its intent.
This is not to say apocalyptic has not been (and is not at the
present) often read in this manner. To further complicate
matters, there are elements of simple expectation in apocalyptic.
That these writers were able to read the "signs of the times"
and from them extrapolate the impending collapse of the social
order should not surprise, unless we think that "futurology"
is solely a result of the enlightenment mentality. But it
would be a shallow reading of apocalyptic to read the entire
corpus as the language of simple expectation. What a reading
of apocalyptic on its own terms has to offer is the introduction
of an element which both presents a control of meaning, and
generates the future as a depth-dimension of the present. This
element, isolated above in our brief survey of the critical

understanding of apocalyptic, is *promise*. It is promise which
is the critical element of the language of modified expectation.

C. The Language of Modified Expectation

In this language the future exists as a depth-dimension
of the present. This depth-dimension we call future is known
because of promise; that is, it is promise which allows us to
know future as more than a simple mechanical extension of the
present. More importantly, it is promise which allows future
to exercise a critical function in relation to the present.
In the end this understanding is the heritage left to us by
prophecy. In our present day it is translated into such statements as: past and future, memory and hope, are subversive of
the present; that is, they exercise a critical function./4/

Let us graph this language in the following manner:

```
                 acted on by        ⎧ SIMPLE EXPECTATION
                   PROMISE          ⎪
PRESENT ─────────────↓──────→FUTURE  ⎨ MODIFIED EXPECTATION
a-temporal           a dimension of ⎪
consciousness of     the present    ⎩ DISJUNCTIVE EXPECTATION
time and space       understood as
```

It is promise which opens a dimension in consciousness we call
time, and creates a dimension in the present we call future.
It also creates a dimension we call past. These are available
to us through memory and hope, respectively. Promise is what
also breaks down the gulf between present and future; it allows
us to penetrate the reality we call change, and to perceive
continuity as other than material reality and sameness. Continuity is a function of human consciousness and interpretation.
Promise is the means by which the present is transcended; and
the future is transcendence.

To the language of simple expectation all of this sounds
merely like a fancy way of saying that the future is the promise;
this is exactly how that language understands talk about the
promise. Or, at the opposite extreme, talk about promise may
be taken to mean that the promise is the future, which would be
explained conveniently by the category: "Future, different in
kind through effort." Nothing could be further from the intent
of the language of modified expectation. The future is not the
promise; nor is the promise the future. The future is the

fulfillment (active or passive) of the act of creatively pre-
paring for the fulfillment of the promise. The future is the
future; it is transcendent and closely allied with hope. The
promise is the promise, it is immanent, and closely allied with
memory.

The language of modified expectation, therefore, is the
language of an historical people; and it creates an historicized
people. It functions to mediate the past into the present
(through memory), and the present into the future (through hope).
It is a conscious appropriation of change.

Having said this, we must go one step further and try
to understand why it is that this language can generate the
future, now understood either as simple, modified, or disjunctive expectation. The fact is that change can be appropriated
in different manners; and the controlling factor, deciding in
which manner change is appropriated, is the promise as understood. As noted above, the language of simple expectation
interprets talk about the promise as meaning that promise and
future are interchangeable elements of speech. To make a
promise is to create a future which will eventually be achieved
through the passage of time. Or, conversely, to talk of a
future is nothing other than to make a promise of how things
will be--if only we put our will to it. Thus, even when faced
with talk of promise, the language of simple expectation allows
neither promise nor future to exercise any critical function.

The language of disjunctive expectation, on the other
hand, tends to interpret talk about promise in terms of fate,
luck, or chance. It is true that sometimes this is precisely
the meaning intended. When a threat is made, for example, it
is to be understood as a promise without content; this creates
a feeling of a future disjunctive from the present. While the
threat may be very specific (saying death will occur under such
and such circumstances), it is nonetheless without content in
the language of future expectation, since it does not signify
the means by which this threatened change can be appropriated.

There is a sense, however, in which the language of
disjunctive expectation has served to allow future and promise
to exercise a critical function. Fate, luck, chance, if perceived as promise without content, and future without

specification, at least force us to admit that the present does not sum up all there is to reality. Disjunctive expectation's appropriation of change, therefore, has an unsettling effect, in that it gives lie to an over-rationalized and over-objectivized appropriation of change, capable of very efficient, technical manipulation. This language is not used to account for the phenomena as yet unexplained by scientific knowledge; it is used rather to keep alive the possibility of radically new knowledge through a radical questioning of every known postulate. It may be that fate, luck, chance are not the best words to use; but they have served that purpose, and they will continue to serve--as long as they are not decoded by the language of simple expectation to mean that fate is our future, or our future is due to pure chance.

In its appropriation of change, modified expectation allows both promise and future to function as critical counter to the present. Promise makes us responsible to the present by making us responsible to the future, through the realization that the future exists as a depth-dimension of the present.

Given the structure of the language of modified expectation, it is possible not only to work forward from a promise to an expected future; it is also possible to work backward from an expected future to the promise necessary to create it. In the Bible it is sometimes difficult to see this happening, since we are all quite knowledgeable of the promise to begin with. But in the literature of science fiction this critical tool is of immense value, particularly in utopian/dystopian science fiction. Given the society of Walden Two, for example, it is possible to work backward to the "promise" which is Skinner's real message to us: We can and will modify and control human behavior to ensure a perfect society. So also with the thousand and one other utopian societies: We can and will create a society free from tension and conflict, free from want and need; we can and will create the technology necessary to provide for all the material needs of all the people. So also with the ever-increasing literature of dystopia: Machines are a threat to the creative life of man; cities are a threat to humankind's social interaction; technology is a threat to the ecological balance of nature. And so on.

Carrying the analysis one step further: It is possible
to specify the type of consciousness which might be open to the
promise implied in an expected future. And, indeed, this is
where the real critical study of utopian literature needs to be
focused. For it is on this level that science fiction functions
as a feedback mechanism, insofar as it allows the future to
function as a critical counter to the present. It can only do
this, however, if it creates somehow a new consciousness of the
present. Future alone cannot do this (as we have seen in our
discussion of simple expectation). We need the mediating
presence of promise, implied in the expected future, to create
this new consciousness of the present.

An expected future utopia which is merely a dream-fantasy,
a satisfaction of primitive and primal urges, is a promise made
to a consciousness which views the present as an agglomeration
of circumstances frustrating those urges. Much of science
fiction's early fascination with robots, it would seem, could
be read in this light, especially those which project the creation of a robot to serve as a sexual partner./5/ On the other
end of the spectrum, an extrapolated future dystopia, which is
merely the nightmare-fantasy of uncritical fears, is a promise
made to a consciousness which views the present as the breakdown of all spiritual, moral, and aesthetic values, the negation
of all that is true, and beautiful, and good. It plays to all
the worst in humankind. The clearest examples in the literature
of science fiction are those which describe the future city.

It would be impossible to defend all biblical and inter-
testamental literature against the charge that it too plays to
the worst in humankind; or that none of it is an escape from or
a capitulation to the "terror of history," which is another
label for the process described above. Nor would all science
fiction be safe from this indictment. But to say that all
apocalyptic and all science fiction have only this meaning would
necessarily infer that there is only one consciousness of the
present: the present is an obstacle to the fulfillment either
of the promise or threat. It would also imply that the future
is not a critical category, but only a negative one.

These considerations force us to take a further step in
our analysis of the languages of future expectation, a step

which must be taken to preserve the present in its own integrity, and allow the present to play its own critical role. For the present must be allowed to offer a critique of memory and hope, or else humankind is at the mercy of those two facets of consciousness. It is the language of disjunctive expectation which allows precisely this to happen. It answers the questions asked about the present, insofar as the present is often seen as the fulfillment of the promise.

D. The Language of Disjunctive Expectation

The language of disjunctive expectation is the language of crisis. The immediate implication is that it is here where we will isolate the structure of apocalyptic. This structure will allow apocalyptic to be read on its own merits, not according to the formulae of simple or modified expectation.

To begin with, disjunctive expectation allows us to see that promise is just as normative (if not more so) for the present as it is for the future. It does this by refusing to allow fulfillment to become the ultimate test of the validity of promise. Given a promise, there is always a dimension of crisis in the present, for the present exists as the (partial) fulfillment of promise. It is this which generates crisis: the real or imaginary conjunction of promise and future in the present. To accept the present on its own terms and in its own integrity through memory and hope (that is, as witness to the dimension of crisis) is to accept the fact that there will always be an incongruity between promise and future when measured in terms of fulfillment. This conjunction of promise and future renders the present impermeable to the promise as originally stated.

Here we encounter the motivating factor of apocalyptic: it is to render the present open to the promise, not to seek delayed fulfillment in some fantasy future. The crisis which occasions apocalyptic is not disillusionment with the present as an obstacle to the future, but with the present as an obstacle to the promise; that is, with the present as the conjunction, real or imaginary, of the promise with the future measured in terms of fulfillment. Disjunctive expectation is needed to overcome that conjunction. There exists in disjunctive

expectation a different consciousness of the present, therefore, a consciousness which means that all apocalyptic need not
be read as an escape from, or a capitulation to, the terror of
history. The incongruity between promise and future takes
place only in the present; hence the fact that all apocalyptic
literature is intensely concerned with the present, and how to
live in the present. It is story about the present!

Let us graph the language of disjunctive expectation as
follows:

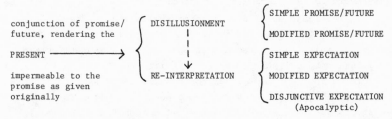

conjunction of promise/future, rendering the

PRESENT ⟶ impermeable to the promise as given originally

DISILLUSIONMENT
↓
RE-INTERPRETATION

SIMPLE PROMISE/FUTURE
MODIFIED PROMISE/FUTURE
SIMPLE EXPECTATION
MODIFIED EXPECTATION
DISJUNCTIVE EXPECTATION
(Apocalyptic)

In this language disjunctive expectation itself is able
to carry a new and different meaning because it rises out of a
new and different consciousness, which gives rise to disillusionment and ultimately to re-interpretation. Disjunctive
expectation, moreover, is one step further removed from the
appropriation of change through modified expectation. For
whereas modified expectation was a reading of the process of
change as history, disjunctive expectation is a re-reading of
history, and its critical assessment. It is, as we will argue
later, a temporal re-structuring of history.

What the language of disjunctive expectation immediately
makes clear is that it has its roots in, and cannot be divorced
from, the worlds of simple and modified expectation. It is able
to appropriate the movements of these two languages insofar as
1) it recognizes the process of change (it sees, that is, that
disillusionment follows upon a specific consciousness of the
present, and that re-interpretation follows upon disillusionment); and 2) it is aware that change is a series which can be
repeated indefinitely unless modified expectation is comple-
mented by disjunctive expectation.

Through its insistence on the "nevertheless" of life and
language, disjunctive expectation seizes upon the promise in

its pure state; fulfillment is no longer a condition of its
validity. Disjunctive expectation, therefore, is a hedge
against a future present in which the conjunction of promise
and future would again inevitably result in disillusionment,
thereby repeating the cycle. It is possible, therefore, to
read disjunctive expectation on one level as an attempt to
break out of a cycle, created not by history, but by exaggerated claims made in the name of history. In the simplest terms
this claim is that God's acts are to be equated with the events
of history, and vice versa; and, further, that the present is
the fulfillment of God's promise given to us in the past.

Because it has its roots in simple and modified expectation, disjunctive expectation recapitulates the stages of the
preceding two languages before it passes from speaking of fate,
luck, and chance as being determinative of human destiny (in a
disjunctive manner), and begins to speak of imminent expectation (as that which welcomes the interruption of the ordinary,
the plain, and the real). When it has done this, moreover, it
is then able to account for new meanings of simple and modified
expectation.

Consciousness of the present as the conjunction of
promise and future leads first of all to a formulation of
crisis as "the supposed failure of the promise." This is disillusionment proper as portrayed in the graph. The immediate
reaction, in this state of affairs, is to deny the failure,
maintain that the promise still holds as originally given, and
overcome the crisis by an act of the will. When it comes to
the crisis of disillusionment, the language of simple expectation is caught in the structure of its own meaning. Due to a
mechanical view of the future in relation to the present (a
simple linear extension), there is only one way to overcome
crisis: to insist upon the promise as given, i.e., as end and
goal. To achieve the end (fulfill the promise) is only a matter
of implementing the means and making the act of will to put the
means into practice. If any adjustment has to be made, it will
only be to change the content of the means. The end goal
remains the same, as does the form: a willingness to action.

As graphed in the structure of this language, the simple
and modified promise/future merge in the creation of utopia;

for, as noted above, in utopia will predominates. Strong ruler/narrator imposes his will on subject/reader. In utopia, as child of disillusionment, we see the perfect marriage of matter and form. In this language moreover, utopia is a realizable world; for failure is never a failure of vision, but always and only a failure of will. This is the peculiarly American guilt trip, the paradigmatic example of which is Vietnam. Formulation of the crisis as the "supposed failure of the promise," therefore, leads either to a future of simple expectation (in which the dystopian model prevails), or to a future of modified expectation (in which the utopian model prevails). Both have failed to allow the present to exercise its critical function in relation to the promise and to the future.

For that reason, formulation of the crisis as "the failure of the supposed promise" is a preferable description of the consciousness of the present. This formulation allows for reinterpretation. By accepting the present on its own terms, through memory of and hope in the promise, the language of disjunctive expectation accepts the fact that there will always be an incongruity between promise and future when measured in the terms of fulfillment. For this reason, it literally sees no future in repeating endlessly the cycle projected by simple or modified expectation. There has to be an end--in both senses of the word! Given the promise, and given the refusal to reinterpret the promise (which simple and modified expectation refuse to do), how could things turn out differently?

Re-interpretation of the promise, however, is not in itself to be equated with disjunctive expectation; for there has always existed the possibility of moving from re-interpretation of the promise into a future of simple or modified expectation. In the language of simple expectation, disillusionment is caused by the fact that the present is so totally new and different that there is no way in which it can be compared to the past, and no way in which it can be compared to the future. Every means of comparison fails. But though the language is ostensibly disjunctive, the meaning is none other than that of simple expectation. The most readily available example of this is Alvin Toffler's *Future Shock*. Toffler's

book is a case of heightened consciousness of trends; it never
penetrates to the deeper levels of promise. This is why in the
end it does not, and cannot, offer any consistent analysis of
what is really "out of joint," and what is needed to cope with
a future we cannot completely control. And all the while the
futurologists debate the topic of how to control a future
which is so shocking, the present wreaks havoc on our sensi-
bilities./6/

Re-interpretation of the promise can also lead to a
future of modified expectation. But in the end this too does
not satisfy, for it follows down the same path. In the future
of a re-interpreted modified expectation, the promise is constantly being made over in light of current disillusionment.
But no matter how strong the desire for it to be otherwise, as
soon as the content of the promise is specified (which is what
happens in the process of re-interpretation), there follows
inevitably the fulfillment which fails. Although modified
expectation allows the present to function as critical counter
to the promise, it does not do so on a profound enough level
to preserve the integrity of either promise, present, or future.
In the process the promise tends to be completely changed and
eviscerated; the present tends to become simply the battleground of promise and future; and the future tends to become
the projection of present hopes, instead of its creator.

It is our contention, therefore, that only when the re-
interpretation of promise issues in the language of disjunctive
expectation are we able to apply the name apocalyptic to it.
Let us briefly review some of the considerations of the languages
of future expectation, to see how they bear on the question of
isolating the structure of apocalyptic. The roots of both
prophecy and apocalyptic are in the promise which shapes future
hopes. But apocalyptic goes beyond prophecy in that it is
"indifferent to the restraints of history," or to put it another
way, it is characterized by an "indifference to disconfirmation."
This, as we have insisted throughout, does not mean that apocalyptic is a critical negation of history, but only of the
exaggerated claims made in the name of history. Apocalyptic is
indifferent to fulfillment of a promise whose content has been
explicitly stated in overly positive terms. Yet there does,

and must, exist a dialectical tension between prophecy and apocalyptic--else both tend to solidify into polarized opposites, mutually exclusive, instead of inclusive. Prophecy de-eschatologized becomes subservient to the law. But apocalyptic without a prophetic dimension becomes escape from, or capitulation to, the terror of history. Static and polarized, both forsake the present. Now the present is not its own justification, nor its own meaning; nor, finally, does history explain itself. It is in the in-depth experience of the present where the meaning (or absurdity) and the justification (or condemnation) of the present will have to be located. Apocalyptic helps to do precisely that by focusing on the relationship between promise and present, and between present and future, without reducing the whole matter to a question of fulfillment.

The final question is, therefore: "How does apocalyptic provide a new focus on the relationship between promise and present, and between present and future?" To answer this we must go back to the language of simple expectation and its interpretation of disjunctive expectation. There we noted that for simple expectation a disjunctively expected future followed from a giving of a promise without content. Such a future is often characterized as fate, luck, or chance. The genius of apocalyptic is that it transfers the promise without content from the past into the future--through a critical process called the negation of negation. This is what it means to say that apocalyptic seizes upon promise in its pure state. Disillusionment and re-interpretation relentlessly strip away all the specific content of the promise, until only the promise (and the one who gives it) itself remains.

Fulfillment, in this language, takes on an entirely different meaning, if indeed the word can be used at all. Fulfillment is no longer understood as in the languages of simple or modified expectation, where it is reduced to a more or less mechanical process through which promise is validated sometime in the future. Such an understanding, if applied here, would uphold the charge that the adherents of apocalyptic eschatology are merely waiting for a future in which there will be a full revelation of the truth, since truth will never be fully known in this life. If fulfillment means anything in the language of

apocalyptic, it means the act of discovering and naming the
content of the promise as it is lived out in the praxis of the
people. Fulfillment, therefore, is always real, but it is
never complete. It validates neither the promise nor the future,
but the present; for the present is all that is immediately
known in apocalyptic. The promise is known only as it exists
in the present, and the future is known as the depth-dimension
of the present. The result is that in the future it is not the
future that will be better known, it is the promise that will
be better known; as will also the present be known better.
The validation of the promise, then, is not in its material
realization, but in the knowing of it. The future is no longer
a mere projection of present hopes; it creates hope by giving
the present more room to grow in knowledge and wisdom.

Knowing the promise, moreover, is mostly a process of
unlearning through disillusionment. Such is the story in Old
Testament times; there is no reason to imagine that the story
can be told any differently today. All the promises projecting
a future glorious in details and accomplishments must needs be
painfully unlearned as we encounter again and again *in the
present* the tragedies of repression, racism, alienation, sexism,
manipulation, despair, and sin. Through this process of unlearning we learn that this present is not the promise; and we
come to understand what the promise does mean: a challenge and
a chance for redemption, through hope and trust and loving
action which strip away the false veneers of fulfillment. The
promise without content, as understood in the language of simple
expectation, longs to be filled in the language of disjunctive
expectation.

In the language of apocalyptic, then, we encounter a new
configuration of promise, present, and future: one which allows
us to avoid the pitfalls of fulfillment becoming the ultimate
test of validity. The control of meaning for this language
does not lie in the content of the promise as explicitly stated
in the beginning; nor does it lie in some remote or near fulfillment in time. It lies in the present understanding of the
promise precisely as it is open to a new and deeper understanding through reflection upon praxis. The promise is simply and
profoundly the promise of *more*. The promise of more cannot be

bounded spatially or temporally, it cannot be limited to deduc-
tive logic, extrapolation, possibility, or the techniques of
manipulation. *More* can be understood and affirmed, for example,
in the simple action of Rosa Parks sitting down in the front
of the bus; for in that action we understand anew what promise
means, what present means, and what future means.

The final consideration concerns the promise "without
content." We must explore whether such a promise is an empty
promise, or whether, due to the one who gives the promise, it
is without content but not empty. At stake is an understanding
of history as personal. In biblical and intertestamental times
the one who gives the promise is God. The question, therefore,
arises: With the "death of God" does not the whole structure
of the language of apocalyptic collapse? It is our contention
that the God-language collapses, but the language of apocalyptic
does not. It can further be argued that it is precisely because
of the "death of God" that apocalyptic arose in the first place.
One way to read the fall of the Israel nation, captivity, exile,
and the final destruction of the temple in 70 CE, is to read it
as the story of the death of God. God in this sense is to be
understood as the world-view which explained, justified, and
gave meaning to the political, social, and religious structures
of the Israel people. The collapse of those structures signified the death of God. This is not to be understood as an argument for the existence of God; but merely a statement that the
question of God cannot be treated apart from the social,
political, and religious life of a people. What remains after
the death of God is the promise alone. The one who gives the
promise moreover is not understood as one who stands apart and
aloof from the struggles of the people, but is only known and
understood in and through those very struggles. What crisis
and disillusionment do is drive a people back to a re-reading
of the history of their own struggle and a re-telling of it in
order to discover what the promise really meant. It is in this
process that apocalyptic arises. The one who gives the promise
is not known apart from those who have received the promise.
This is why apocalyptic continually goes over the history and
pre-history of the people.

That today it is no longer customary to speak of God as the giver of the promise in no way denies the fact that the promise as something received somewhere along the line (if only through the exercise of critical reason) is of vital concern for those who work for the emancipation of humankind. The death of the gods of rationalism, enlightenment, positivism, pragmatism, capitalism, of science and technology--all these deaths are the occasion for the flowering of apocalyptic, for each death in its own negative way clarifies the understanding of the promise. Apocalyptic, thus, is engaged in a constant and un-ending re-reading of history in order that someday the whole story may be told.

Imminent Expectation:
The Temporal Structures of Apocalyptic

The analysis thus far has focused on the "logical" and gramatical structures of the languages of future expectation. It remains to explore briefly, as a prelude to Chapter Five, the temporal structures implied in these models.

To begin with disjunctive expectation. In the logical, semantic structures of that language meaning is carried by such words as: but, nevertheless, however, on the contrary. We are forced to await something new, a reversal, a turning around, an opposing viewpoint. There occurs a break, an interruption, a shattering of the expected end (and meaning). But there also occurs a transition--a moment belonging neither to the meaning which has gone before, nor to the meaning which follows. It is an in-between state. So also with the temporal structuring of disjunctive expectation, hereafter referred to by the more commonly accepted designation: imminent expectation. Imminent expectation signifies a breakdown of the usual configurations of time as conjunction or cause/effect, the former being the outlook of simple expectation, the latter that of modified. Imminent expectation disavows a simple before/after, cause/effect perception of time and duration. It throws together by radically disjoining.

The usual reading of apocalyptic is done according to simple or modified expectation. The result is that in the logical structuring the dualism contained is read as God *and*

Satan, life *and* death, good *and* evil. In temporal structuring
this reads as follows: After Satan, evil and death have had
their day, then God, life and good will overcome. Or, according to the temporal structures implied in modified expectation,
it reads as follows: Due to the inevitable superiority of God,
good and life, through their efforts Satan, evil and death will
be overcome. Both temporal structurings are linear projections,
and can be measured by discrete points on a continuum of time.
It is possible to tell where we are "historically" according
to those models.

Imminent expectation, being disjunctive, forsakes those
models. There are still the elements: God/Satan, good/evil,
life/death. But they are joined disjunctively: Satan, nevertheless God; evil, nevertheless good; death, nevertheless life--
or the opposite, if we are sensitive to the negative charge of
apocalyptic. Just as there is no "logical" process that leads
one to expect that one will follow (rise out of, break into,
transcend) the other; so also the temporal (re-)structuring
denies any simple conjunctive or causal explanation. *It is
imminent expectation alone which throws the two together*. As
though by expecting the sunrise we "cause" it to happen. Everyone "knows" that waiting does not cause the sun to rise; neither
is one "surprised" when it does. Yet the meaning of the whole
structured event comes from the very waiting, the expecting.
It is imminent expectation which makes the waiting a meaningful
act by disjunctively throwing together darkness and light.

Disjunctive expectation, thus, is a relinquishing of
control over the logical structure of events. It is a refusal
to be bound by the past-ness of history, or the future-ness of
history; that is, by what is given as having happened or as
going to happen on a continuum of "same" time. It is remarkable,
in this sense, how critics of apocalyptic give credence to the
"Two world, two age" theme of apocalyptic and still come down
on a continuum of one time. Imminent expectation is, more
significantly, a relinquishing of control over the future-ness
of history. In this sense it is a "radical dehistoricizing" of
the future, in that it refuses to control (or manipulate) the
future through the imposition of a theoretical model. More
properly it might be called a radical de-evolutionizing of

history and the future; where evolution is the theoretical model which radically de-historicizes the present. Evolution is unable to interpret the present except in terms of before/after and/or cause/effect. In evolutionary theory everything can be accounted for in the present, except the radically new--either as given or expected.

Apocalyptic, far from telling the reader simply what to expect (soothsayers, diviners, astrologers and the like could do just as well--and indeed the label "doomsayer" has been applied to apocalyptic precisely because of that misreading), tells the reader how to expect. It temporally re-structures the world by introducing the mode of imminent expectation. For only imminent expectation allows the closed fabric of time to open for the radically new. And the time most closed, ironically, is the present; especially when the present is seen as the sum of all which has gone before, or the beginning for all which follows. Imminent expectation, therefore, is a "radical historicizing" of the present, this in-between time.

To prevent this transition from becoming merely another duration (which Kermode argues has, in fact, happened), apocalyptic continues by telling the end of the story in the same literary forms of myth as it told the beginning. It does not end with a "nevertheless." How to expect is never emptied of what to expect; but the emphasis is clearly on the former. This reading opens up new levels of meaning in the interpretation of the kerygma, the proto-gospel, as found in the Acts of the Apostles. Peter's story of the passion and death of Jesus is interrupted by the "nevertheless" of God's raising him up. The radically new has broken into the closed time of the world. The narrative structures and literary devices of visions, dreams, and ecstasies (the literary equivalents of science fiction's time travel and parallel worlds) likewise collapse onto the present. One can go anywhere (anywhen) from here now. But the point is that one must begin in the present if the radically new is to be expected. Determinism also, long another foil for critics of apocalyptic, is the narrative assurance that imminent expectation is not entirely devoid of content, that how to expect is never emptied of what to expect. But in the narrative structure of apocalyptic it is significant that what is expected is never human in origin, in choice, or in resolution. It devolves from the mighty works of God. What is determined, therefore, is never humankind's response; the present always remains open to the radically new. And, further, imminent expectation is the medium through which the radically new breaks into the present. (This is also one of the many points made by *Close Encounters*.)

Imminent expectation, through the "re-adjustments made in the name of reality," actually so limits the what to expect that it arrives ultimately at a point similar to that of critical theory: what we can expect is the negation of negation. Collins, as we have seen, labels this the "transcendence of death." But there exist in apocalyptic much more concrete images.

We read in the *Secrets of Enoch* (Charles):

> There will be amongst them neither labour, nor sickness, nor humiliation, nor anxiety, nor need, nor violence, nor night, nor darkness, but great light. And they shall have a great indestructible wall, and a paradise bright and incorruptible, for all the corruptible things shall pass away, and there will be eternal life. (65:9-10)

And in *4 Ezra* (Charles):

> The present Age is not the End...But the Day of Judgment shall be the end of this age and the beginning of the eternal age that is to come:
> wherein corruption is passed away,
> weakness is abolished,
> infidelity cut off,
> while righteousness is grown
> and faithfulness is sprung up. (7:112-114)

And in *Revelation*:

> This is God's dwelling among men. He shall dwell with them and they shall be his people and he shall be their God who is always with them. He shall wipe every tear from their eyes, and there shall be no more death or mourning, crying out or pain, for the former world has passed away. (21:3-4)

These images are to be taken *literally*; that is, they function in a critical way in the narrative structure of apocalyptic literature to prevent the "content" of expectations from sliding into personal revenge, individual triumph, and self-seeking gratification. All these charges have been made against apocalyptic and science fiction.

Finally, imminent expectation sheds new light on the problematic of possibility versus desirability, discussed above in Chapter Three in connection with utopia and fantasy. To focus solely and exclusively on what to expect, and to read apocalyptic and science fiction simply as a catalogue of the possibilities of things to come depends on perception of the temporal structure as a simple linear projection closed to the introduction of the radically new. This is the ultimate trap of reading science fiction as extrapolation and prophecy as prediction. Imminent expectation, on the other hand, is a temporal re-structuring which opens narrative to the desirability of the radically new--for the sake of story. How to read story becomes a matter of how to expect. And following upon that, how to live also becomes a matter of how to expect.

Briefly noted, such are the temporal structurings capable of being accounted for by an analysis of imminent (disjunctive) expectation: Time becomes focal and disjointed; history a matter of relinquishing control; the present an openness to the radically new; and the end a negation of negation. The challenge apocalyptic (read as the language of imminent expectation) hurls at the usual configurations of time, change, history, and development is obvious. Likewise, the challenge apocalyptic hurls at the usual reading of science fiction. Both of these will be addressed in Chapter Five.

APOCALYPTIC: THE HORIZON OF THEOLOGY

> Like history and the novel, much biblical narrative
> in explicative interpretation is not "system" or
> pure factual description, but the cumulative render-
> ing of a temporal framework through realistic depic-
> tion and chronological continuity.
>
> --Hans W. Frei

Introduction

Science fiction (at least in its pulp origins) is best
understood as an apocalyptic literature. It involves an intense longing for a new age and a new world. It views the
present time as a time of crisis and a time of great (imminent)
expectation. In this context we note the following parallels
between science fiction (as a secular apocalyptic) and biblical
apocalyptic: Both 1) purport to be a revelation of things to
come; 2) are built upon a body of (secret) knowledge and tend
toward gnosticism; 3) re-appropriate the myths of origins and
ends; 4) create a future history (which historicizes the cosmos) and re-write past history according to its faith; 5) arise
in similar social and political settings; 6) become the gathering point for the strange, the occult, the para-normal understandings of life and history; and 7) look for salvation and
deliverance from something or someone beyond present reality
(of which both despair). The failure to ground the criticism
of science fiction in its early self-understanding leads to a
confusion of forms. Romance tending toward myth is an inade-
quate theoretical model for encompassing the whole science
fiction phenomenon. The self-understanding of science fiction
(as a new literature for a new age) is a clue to the understanding of its enduring appeal. Subsequently we explored
some ramifications of this claim, focusing particularly on the
temporal structuring in narrative and on the languages of
future expectation. Of particular interest were the literary

critical categories of fantasy and utopia. In utopia we en-
countered the limits of rational extrapolation (in the form of
future history); and in fantasy the dialectic between possibility and desirability (in the form of the "we are not alone"
theme). Neither was able to re-solve the tension between promise and fulfillment which stands at the core of apocalyptic.
Our analysis of the languages of future expectation was offered
as a means to do just that--to learn to read science fiction
and biblical apocalyptic as story which re-solves the tension
by a temporal re-structuring of time, change, development and
history (i.e., of the temporal world) in terms of imminent
expectation, rather than extrapolation.

It is this latter issue, however, which brings us face
to face with the critical concern of our study: How is it
exactly that an understanding of science fiction as secular
apocalyptic furthers a deeper appreciation of biblical apocalyptic? How, in turn, does a deeper appreciation of biblical
apocalyptic ground the work of systematic theology? And
finally: How does imminent expectation figure into these considerations as a critical category?

Popular Culture and People's Religion

In a thoroughly enjoyable and iconoclastic book, *The
American Monomyth*, Robert Jewett and John Shelton Lawrence
systematically debunk the selfless super-hero of popular literature and culture, from Buffalo Bill to Captain Kirk of *Star
Trek* and the saviors in *Jaws*. Central to their argument is
the claim that whereas classical monomyth (a là Joseph Campbell)
was based on rites of initiation and passage, the American
monomyth is a secularized version of the Judaeo-Christian
redemption dramas, "combining elements from the selfless servant who impassively gives his life for others and the zealous
crusader who destroys evil" (xx). When this particular monomyth
is joined with an analysis of the "Werther effect"--"the form
of voluntary behavior alteration produced by interaction with a
powerful artifact of popular culture"--the result is a redefi-
nition of the boundary between fact and fantasy (36). In other
words, the reader's perception of the real world is a hopelessly

tangled mixture of the two; motivation is as dependent on fantasy as it is on fact. The "Werther effect" is Jewett and
Lawrence's answer to the "bubble gum fallacy" which says that
popular culture, while often merely a form of entertainment,
can offer a necessary means of escape, or a means to work out
hostile, aggressive feelings. This fallacy also claims that
popular culture has not the power to corrupt or destroy.
Jewett and Lawrence argue to the contrary: if it can work for
good, it can also work for bad.

There is much to commend in *The American Monomyth*; the
brief statement above merely gives the opening argument. It is
in the practical criticism that Jewett and Lawrence strike at
the heart of the monomyth, and the need for tools to critically
assess it. But there is also something missing in the book.
While Jewett and Lawrence are certainly correct in questioning
the "value-free" sociological analysis of popular culture; still
there is something to be said about keeping a critical distance.
In particular they are critical of the work of Herbert Gans in
Popular Culture and High Culture. Gans himself is partly at
fault; his admittedly "arbitrary" and "stylistically poor"
division of "taste publics" into five classes (high, upper-
middle, lower-middle, low and quasi-folk low) does little on
the surface to overcome the positive/negative connotations of
the terms themselves; nor does it provide an adequate methodology
for isolating the dialectic that exists between popular and
high culture (41). The common sense division between the two
(popular and high) is in no way made more clear, nor is the
evaluation (Gans' stated aim) made any more easy by means of an
arbitrary continuum running from low to high.

A closer reading of Gans, on the other hand, does provide
a critical differentiation between popular and high culture; it
deepens the common sense understanding (by allowing us to go
beyond it), while at the same time providing a handle on that
dialectic. In writing about the "critique of mass culture,"
Gans distinguishes between "creator-oriented" and "user-oriented"
culture. Gans states:

> The critics of mass culture are creator-oriented; they
> argue that differences of perspective between creators
> and users should not exist because users must bend to

the will of creators, taking what is given to them,
and treating culture from the creator's perspective (25).

At stake is the question of the homogeneity of the audience;
and, indeed, of society. To be creator-oriented in culture is
to insist on the didactic nature of culture and its socio-
political role in legitimating existing institutions and
structures. User-orientation, on the other hand, signals a
breakdown in the homogeneity and a denial (through non-accep-
tance) of the values promulgated by the high culture. Gans
locates the transition from creator-oriented to user-oriented
in the lower-middle culture. Homogeneity in social structure,
if our treatment of utopian literature tells us anything,
results from a creative principle which has the place of primary value in society. The very existence of popular culture
then, signals a minority viewpoint and a challenge to the
legitimating values as "taught" in high culture.

There is a danger, of course, in trying to make Gans'
distinction do too much work. It is sufficient here if we
allow it merely to keep before us the facts that 1) the primary
distinction in culture is that between public and high, and
2) this distinction does have socio-political ramifications.
The danger of ignoring this distinction is the trap Jewett and
Lawrence have difficulty avoiding: a near total dismissal of
popular culture, predicated on a creator-oriented analysis of
a user-oriented culture. To avoid this danger in our subsequent treatment of apocalyptic and science fiction as manifestations of popular culture we will introduce into the discussion
some different perspectives on this very same distinction, trying to illustrate how it cuts across varying fields of study:
biblical studies, systematic theology, and spirituality.

Northrop Frye describes popular literature as that literature which people read "without guidance from their betters."
In Gans' terms it represents users refusing to "bend to the will
of creators." But the dichotomy between high and low should
not be allowed to obscure other significant processes at work.
Frye's study of the secular scripture is the study of the
tendency of romance toward myth. Myth, we have learned from
the structuralists and particularly from Levi-Strauss, is
authorless. Understood in Gans' terms, myth is user-oriented.

This does not mean, however, that here we have a user-oriented culture which seeks to legitimate existing institutions. It simply means, using another of Frye's distinctions between myths of concern and myths of freedom, we identify popular myths with the latter. Myths of freedom are authorless, in the sense that they arise from what the people have always considered desirable (1971:54-56).

This myth-making process in our times is obscured by the fact that we know the identity of the author--here referring specifically to science fiction--and tend to interpret the process from the viewpoint of the author. Thus Heinlein is categorized and critiqued as one who perpetuates the myth of the rugged individual; Asimov as one who re-fashions the myth of (galactic) empires; Clarke as one who gives voice to the myth of total breakthrough and/or god-like transformation. And so on. All this is a legitimate field of study--to take in the whole body of a writer's work, sort through the themes, isolate the stylistic devices, penetrate the author's psychological make-up, and carefully delineate the world-view grounding his or her literary enterprise. But the mythopoeic process is hardly appropriated through such literary critical devices. The process is best understood when we turn the whole thing on its head; when we start from a basic acceptance of a user-oriented culture and the authorlessness of myth. The most an author can suggest are some possibilities; what is desirable can only be ascertained through a careful reading of the user-oriented culture, i.e., through what is popular. This, as we will see, is what it means to have a "view from the bottom."

This device of standing the mythopoeic process on its head also sheds light on the tension between extrapolation and expectation. Whereas the majority of critics single out extrapolation as one of the key features of science fiction, in reality it is expectation which more fruitfully grounds a critical study of the genre. The critique of expectations from the standpoint of author's intentions results in the psychological literary studies which in the end tell us little about the mythic power of their work. It is only another example of user-oriented culture being critiqued according to the norms and values of creator-oriented culture. This is not dismissing

out of hand such examples of critical enterprises; it is merely
to argue that a vast reservoir of meaning is missed and ignored
if only such kind of criticism is engaged in.

Extrapolation, as argued above, is concerned primarily
with possibilities and probabilities. Expectation, on the
other hand, while it may be grounded in extrapolation, transcends it. Thus, for example, contact with extra-terrestrial
beings rests on a very high probability according to those
astronomers and astro-physicists working in the area. But all
the scientific possibility and probability in the universe cannot move such extrapolation over into expectation. Nor can
possibility and probability account for the meaning which the
expectation of contact with extra-terrestrial beings (not the
actual contact, but the expectation of it) has for the people
who share the expectation. It is almost as though a "leap of
faith" is involved; as though extrapolation based on scientific
possibility and probability were a necessary but not sufficient
condition for the expectation involved. Much of science fiction
can be read according to the dynamics of such apologetics.

But there is another facet to this phenomenon. There
exists a body of critical work which focuses on the "type" of
person who reads science fiction or who encounters UFOs. Much
of it is based on the psycho-sociological categories of discontinuity, marginality, and alienation. "In short," Ted
Peters sums up such arguments, "psychic tension causes deviant
behavior and a UFO experience is an expression of such deviancy"
(262). Much the same kind of argument has often been made to
dismiss the readers of science fiction. The value of Peters'
study, however, is that it does not concern what people are
moving away from as much as it attempts to explore what they
are moving toward. Peters argues that the eidetic structure
of the UFO experience symbolizes a desire for transcendence,
omniscience, perfection, and redemption. He concludes:

> Covert UFO theology is the attempt to relieve the tension
> [between science and religion] and make peace with sci-
> ence. It is the attempt to construct a wholesome unitary
> horizon for self-understanding--a myth which incorporates
> both our religious feelings and our naturalistic assump-
> tions (278).

Two things ought to be pointed out before moving on.
First, Peters here is talking about myth (covert UFO theology);
and the UFO myth(ology) is a prime example of myth as authorless. Second, the unitary horizon needed is one which must
take science into account. This does not refer primarily to
the attempt to explain UFO technology according to scientific
possibility and probability. It refers to the fact that
scientific study and investigation can neither verify nor fal-
sify a significant number of UFO experiences. The recent
television series, *Project UFO*, thus serves primarily an apologetic purpose. It is necessary to establish the fact that when
talking about UFOs we are engaged in an entirely different
language game--that of religion/theology.

To return: Peters' argument seems to lack a final explicit step, although it is there behind what he says. The UFO
experience does not merely symbolize the desire for transcendence, omniscience, perfection, and redemption; it symbolizes a
desire for, and a movement toward, a community of people who
share those very same beliefs. To refuse to make that step in
the "hermeneutic of secular experience" explicit leaves Peters'
study open to the possibility of further analysis moving only
in the direction of the privatized and individualized reductionism of psychological and existential investigations.

Expectations are a shared belief, or they are simply the
individual projections of an alienated person. Extrapolations,
on the other hand, are an individual work. Peters writes:
"The goal of UFO belief is to overcome the stress due to the
sense of alienation we feel in a world that is not truly a
home" (278). Now, the reason this world is not truly a home is
not only because it lacks the dimensions of transcendence, omniscience, perfection, and redemption; it is also (and primarily)
because it lacks community, people who share those beliefs and
those expectations--and who hold that they are desirable, no
matter how much the literature of absurdity, rugged individualism and solipsism hold sway. The UFO cultists, and the science
fiction readers, have found a home--now. The home is built out
of the expectations and beliefs they share; and it is constructed
according to the means which alone can withstand the assaults
of skeptics and scoffers--story. We will discuss below the

critical importance Metz attaches to the narrative dimension in
theology. For now we want to explore another perspective of
the basic distinction between popular culture and high culture,
this time according to the distinction Harvey Cox makes between
story and signal.

Cox's work, *The Seduction of the Spirit: The Use and
Misuse of People's Religion*, is not a systematic treatment of
the topics suggested in the title. Instead, it is his story.
What "theory" it contains has been stated often and elsewhere;
but Cox does crystallize in lucid terms and with a challenging
resonance what others are wont to hide in stiff analysis. He
begins his preface: "All human beings have an innate need to
tell and hear stories and to have a story to live by. Religion,
whatever else it has done, has provided one of the main ways
of meeting this abiding need" (9). In the category of story
Cox distinguishes between autobiography and people's religion.
The former is "my" story; the latter "our" story. People's
religion includes, for Cox, both folk and popular religion.

Set apart from and over against people's religion (as
story) is religion as "signal," religion which is "coded,
systematized, controlled, and distributed by specialists" (10).
Again, the danger lies in making a too facile correlation with
Gans' distinction between user-oriented and creator-oriented
cultures, and drifting from there into the popular pastime of
assigning values: Story is good, signal is bad. Cox does not
succumb to such easy judgments. He argues for the necessity
of religion as signal, but against its exclusivity. More
importantly, however, Cox's whole book is an argument for the
present existence of people's religion, over against a view
that religion has already been reduced exclusively to signal
and is no longer able to function as story, i.e., that it is
capable of study only as an historical phenomenon. Among the
tools for the study of people's religion (or as Cox would argue,
"learning from" rather than merely "investigating") are "participant hermeneutics" and "experimental liturgies." In a later
chapter Cox also calls for an "iconography of popular culture."
It should also be noted that in order to distinguish himself
from much of the work done previously in the field of theology
and culture, Cox places particular stress on popular culture

as a most fertile source of study. Finally, in a chapter
treating of people's religion and radical theology, Cox argues
that radical theology is correlated more fruitfully with
people's religion than it is with the "Death of God" theologies.
The preoccupation with secularization has merely obscured the
fact of a wholesale displacement of religion and religious
themes from institutionalized forms to people's religion. "To
be radical in any sense today," Cox writes, "means to be in
touch with those people who are ordinarily seen as 'losers'"
(169-70). Cox critiques much current theology as being culture
bound, elitist and provincial. Because of this it is closed
to the emergent cultural awakening of the third world. But
one need not go to the third world (as Cox had done) to be in
touch with "those people who are ordinarily seen as 'losers'."
This is often merely another form of elitism, available only
to those who have the time, the opportunity, and the money
available to them. The real challenge lies much closer to home.
In fact, it lies at the very heart of the culture we all share.
We have endeavored in this study to explore popular literature,
culture, and religion as manifested in science fiction--pre-
cisely insofar as science fiction is story about the 'losers
and marginals,' those who exist at the edge of (high) culture.
We are not claiming in any way that science fiction exhausts
the content and/or meaning of popular culture; nor that it is
even the most obvious way of getting at the story of the losers.
We are simply saying it is one way among many. But, since the
parallels to biblical apocalyptic are so striking, our analysis
has endeavored to show that by "learning from" science fiction
we can more fruitfully appropriate biblical apocalyptic, precisely as it too is a popular literature, culture, and religion
of the losers. And as is being more and more argued today,
apocalyptic lies at the heart of the "high" culture of biblical
studies (Käsemann; Betz).

There are no simple means available for us to ground
unequivocally our contention that biblical apocalyptic was a
"popular literature" in its day. On the one hand, we could
cite the number of apocalyptic writings still extant, and deduce
accordingly that there must have been a far greater number in
circulation at the time. Or we could cite the testimony of

some biblical scholars that apocalyptic was indeed a very popular form of literature during the inter-testamental period.
On the other hand, popular literature is not such merely because of numbers; nor does the opinion of scholars alone serve
to ground such a designation. We must approach it from our own
experience of popular literature and religion.

Apocalyptic becomes more available to us the more it is
seen as a people's religion. Surely this has been the lesson
of history--as is graphically documented in Norman Cohn's *The
Pursuit of the Millennium*. But it is also seen in a more careful reading of the biblical and inter-testamental apocalyptic
literature. Using some of the considerations discussed above
we can say that apocalyptic is user-oriented, rather than
creator-oriented literature. Pseudonymity is one form of
anonymity, and in turn a way of underlining the authorlessness
of apocalyptic myth. What characterizes apocalyptic is not the
predictions made by the pseudonymous author (i.e., his or her
extrapolations), but rather the expectations voiced in the
literature. The "escape" often seen as the appeal of apocalyptic is not an escape from the harsh realities of this life;
it is an escape into a believing community. This community
shares a belief in transcendence, omniscience, perfection, and
redemption--and perceives that all four of these beliefs are
inextricably joined. Finally, apocalyptic is much more story
than it is signal, to use the terminology of Cox. More importantly, it is the story of those at the bottom, the losers.
To use the sociological term: it is the story of a marginal
people. All the critics, those who are disposed favorably
toward apocalyptic and those who see in it the worst features
of human history, agree on this point: in apocalyptic (whether
biblical, inter-testamental, chiliastic, revolutionary or even
literary) we are confronted with the "(hi)story of the losers."
If the statement of Marx ("Religious suffering is at the same
time an expression of real suffering and a protest against real
suffering. Religion is the sigh of the oppressed creature, the
heart of a heartless world, and the soul of soulless conditions.")
has ever been applicable in any other sense than his subsequent
statement ("Religion is the opium of the people"), it is
applicable to the literature of apocalyptic.

We have argued in the above chapters that this is true because apocalyptic has preserved the dialectic between promise and fulfillment, refusing to buy into the complete identification of the two--now, or in the future. We see in this "(hi)story of the losers" the much needed corrective to the "(hi)story of the winners," that account which dominates the consciousness of existing institutions and structures of power. A consciousness which settles for immediate goals evaluated only in terms of preserving the entrenched power of those who have been victorious, and concludes by blaming crime on the criminals, poverty on the poor, racism on the blacks, the browns, the yellows, the reds, welfare on the recipients, and disease on the sick. It ends finally by seeking to implement programs to eliminate the latter.

Yet it has been the latter who have kept the promise alive by consistently denying that the present be seen as a simple fulfillment of some past promise. It is the latter who have kept alive the function of the future. The future as a dimension of the present (not as a controlled extension of existing conditions) allows the dialectic of promise and fulfillment to continue in a meaningful way. Eliminate the future as openness to the radically new and the dialectic dies. Hope then becomes as act of faith, rather than its form. Hope becomes something to do when everything else has failed.

In the above chapters we concentrated on one particular facet of the apocalyptic imagination, the temporal structuring of the world. We argued that the languages of future expectation needed a careful analysis in order to avoid reading apocalyptic as simple or modified expectation. For both of these rely on a more or less simple linear view of time progressing along a common path toward a future rising out of the present according to simple conjunctive or causational patterns. There is only one *time* in these languages. We suggested, however, that in disjunctive (imminent) expectation there is not only a new world, there is also a new time. Time, in disjunctive expectation, cannot simply be appropriated according to the configurations of before/after, cause/effect. It is caught up also in the configurations of the already/not yet, the now/ nevertheless. The language of fate, chance, and luck (what

simple expectation resorts to when faced with the radically
new) and the language of responsibility, decision, and control
(the catchwords of modified expectation when contemplating the
new) are transcended and transformed in the language of disjunctive (imminent) expectation. We suggested that imminent
expectation accounts for many of the temporal structures and
structurings of apocalyptic literature, offering an alternative
to the temporal structures implicit in the narratives of simple
and modified expectation. These latter narratives, of course,
are the narratives of the "winners," those who have been lucky
and fated to win, those who have made the right decisions,
controlled their lives, and accepted responsibility for *the*
future. In imminent expectation, however, time becomes focal
and disjointed, history becomes a matter of relinquishing control, the present becomes an openness to the radically new,
and the end becomes a negation of negation. These themes we
now want to explore, particularly in light of Metz's recent
call for a movement "from a church of an evolutionistically
softened eschatology to a church of the imminent expectation"
(1978:143).

Apocalyptic and Political Theology

In a short exploratory work, *Christ and Counter-Christ:
Apocalyptic Themes in Theology and Culture*, Carl Braaten seeks
to spell out some implications which a renewed interest in
biblical apocalyptic has, insofar as it holds the key to a
number of problems that face the theological enterprise today.
1) It deals with the problem of Christian origins, insofar as
apocalyptic is a marginal literature. 2) It throws light on
the transition between the Old and the New Testament, since the
"New Testament is a literary occurrence largely within the
medium of apocalyptic." 3) It serves to provide a more complete picture of the historical Jesus, insofar as it fills in
the background of his times. 4) It suggests that the history
of Christianity be written as a story of the search for the
Kingdom. 5) It counters the excessive personalism (individualized and privatized interiority) of Christianity with a universalism. 6) It looks at society from the bottom up. 7) It
challenges Christianity to trandscend itself. And 8) it has

an apologetic purpose, insofar as it argues for a belief in
the future *in* Jesus (v-viii).

In the course of his work Braaten (following Moltmann)
employs the distinction between *futurus* and *adventus*. The
former signifies the future actualization of potentialities
within things; the latter, the appearance of something new not
yet within things, not even potentially. The former, Braaten
concludes, allows for extrapolation, the latter for interpola-
tion. We have made a similar distinction (following Rowley)
between the future rising out of the present, and the future
breaking into the present. Braaten concludes his argument:
"Christian eschatology is not metaphysical finalism but apocalyptic adventism" (11).

Braaten, however, does not follow up his conclusion with
a systematic analysis of "apocalyptic adventism" (what we call
imminent expectation); but this is precisely what is called
for if we are to see its real implications for systematic
theology. Metz's call for a rejection of "evolutionistically
softened eschatology" (which is comparable to "metaphysical
finalism," but which is more profoundly aware of the scientistic
bent of our times) and the appropriation of imminent expectation
highlights this precise issue: The re-structuring of the world
must proceed along temporal as well as spatial lines. Without
a careful explication of the significance imminent expectation
has for systematic (political) theology, the result is a program
of worthy aims, but one not grounded radically in the praxis of
the "losers" it purports to verbalize. The conclusions of
Braaten's study illustrate how he fails to follow up on the
implications of naming Christian eschatology "apocalyptic
adventism." The following list is not really a program for
action "in the world;" but it does outline his program for
systematic theology. His bottom line is the formulation of
(apocalyptic) categories which made Jesus' revolution more than
political. 1) Jesus' revolution included the concept of the
totum, total change. "For the new that is coming means a complete break with the present order. Politics presupposes too
much continuity." 2) It includes the concept of the demonic;
what we are fighting against is not flesh and blood, but
principalities and powers, i.e., against the 'isms of modern

culture. 3) It is based upon the belief that the present is
not exhaustive of reality; any awareness of the "signs of the
times" tells us that. 4) It demands a radical (not merely a
psychical or intellectual) conversion if the kingdom is to
come. 5) It also calls for an unconditional surrender to
absolute love of God and fellow humans. 6) It is based on the
"proletarian principle" of the gospel; it looks for the lowly
to be raised. 7) It calls for a reversal of roles: the last
shall be first; the mighty shall be thrown down. and 8) It
proclaims that the hopelessness of 'now' is the birthpangs of
the future (111-12).

From this list arise the critical questions: How and
where in all these programmatic conclusions does one draw the
line between God's intervention and humankind's responsibility?
Who is to take the initiative? Does 'conversion' precede or
follow the coming of the kingdom? Is it humankind's task to
cast down the mighty and raise the lowly? Are we to hasten a
state of hopelessness so that the new can come? Is humankind
to destroy the old so that the new can be born? Whence comes
redemption?

These are the critical questions thus far not addressed
in our discussions. They have also been lacking in the current
spate of articles and studies of apocalyptic and theology. The
choice has too often been merely one among the chiliastic
excesses of the 16th century revolutionaries (and their counterparts in modern terrorism), the subjective, hallucinogenic cop-
out of the solipsistic world of drugs and the literature of
silence, and the passive surrender made by the outcasts in the
face of overwhelming complexity. We have tried throughout this
study (at the cost of being vague sometimes, and deliberately
arbitrary at others) to resist such options. Braaten's programmatic conclusions have forced us to finally confront the issue
head on. And the only way out, the only means through which to
preserve some notion of God's intervention and humankind's
responsibility is through a further explication of imminent
expectation.

In a remarkably cryptic paper (Metz's writings bear out
the adage that less is more) delivered at a colloquium (Notre
Dame, 1977), and subsequently published in the proceedings:

Toward Vatican III: The Work That Needs to be Done, J. B. Metz ties together more than ten years work developing a political theology, and in one swift and short thesis moves ahead to explore the relationships between apocalyptic and political theology. I will not attempt to summarize what already must be considered as tight a summary as could be made of the work of Metz. But I will try to highlight those elements of it that bear on our study of apocalyptic in terms of imminent expectation.

The title of Metz's paper is "For a Renewed Church Before a New Council: A Concept in Four Theses." Each thesis proposes a direction in which the Church must move if a new council is to take place, and to be transformative. Thesis One: "From a church of the West to a church of the North-South axis; or, the church in changing from a citizen's church to a church of class conflict" (1978:137). Metz is here reviewing the literature of the sociology of knowledge, insofar as it bears on the unity of the church. And he is suggesting that the more credible self-understanding is one which sees the church engaged in a dialogue with itself (North-South, rich-poor), rather than in dialogue with other world-views (East-West, Christian-Marxist, capitalist-socialist). The latter divisions only invite a view of class conflict that is projected onto the world, and/or a tendency to identify the church with one or the other of the pairs.

Metz's second thesis clarifies the issue significantly. In it he calls for movement "From an over-adapted church to a church of discipleship; or, the church in transition from a popular 'church for the people' to a radical 'church of the people'" (139). Before any other comments on this thesis, it needs to be pointed out that a "people's Church" is the necessary correlate to a "people's religion."/1/ Cox's program of experimental liturgy to complement participant hermeneutics simply does not go far enough in this direction. Cox is correct, however, when he draws the connection between radical theology and people's religion, thereby transcending the debate over the death of God and the secularization of modern culture.

In explicating this thesis Metz contends that only "practical [i.e., based on praxis] identification," not interpretation and hermeneutics, can be the ground for the church's

identity and its social legitimation. But there are all kinds
of praxis. Metz therefore makes it clear where he draws the
bottom line: "That praxis whose intelligible and indentity-
securing power cannot be replaced by an interpretation is
called discipleship" (139). Metz is careful to point out, however, the double structure of this discipleship: the mystical-
political and the practical-political. To be radical in one
means to be radical in the other; to buy into one as the sole
realm of praxis is to sell out the other totally and completely.
Examples do not abound in recent history, but they are to be
found: Gandhi, Martin Luther King, Daniel Berrigan--and Jesus
Christ. These people do not simply present one option among
many, nor are their principles to be reduced to ethical liberal-
ism: what all good people everywhere stand for. Such reductionism leads to a "truncated" discipleship, with the consequence
that "What results is either a reduction of discipleship to a
purely social-political dimension of action or a reduction to
a private-religious spirituality" (139). We are brought back
here to Metz's previous statement that the praxis which can
never be replaced by interpretation is discipleship, for the
reduction of discipleship to the social-political order or the
private-religious sphere is precisely the interpretation which
seeks to replace discipleship. At stake is not only a church
of the people (as opposed to a church for the people); also at
stake is a God of the people (as opposed to a God for the
people).

In this latter transformation, moreover, we begin to see
how the theses of Metz bear on the questions raised by Braaten's
programmatic conclusions. For this is precisely the issue
between emancipation and redemption: How and where do we draw
the line between God's intervention and humankind's responsibility? Whence comes redemption? Metz argues that the resolution to these questions can never be replaced by theoretical
models; but can only be re-solved by practical knowledge; that
is, through commitment and through the stories of discipleship
that are handed down. But praxis always has a social and
political dimension; and so any discipleship (truly such) must
inquire into the social and political context of that discipleship.

These considerations (surely the heart of Metz's paper) lead to two further movements which must occur within a renewed church. Thus Thesis Three: "From an ecclesial authority based on juridical-administrative competency to an ecclesial authority based on religious competency; or, the leadership of the church in transition from a leadership that 'has' authority to a leadership that 'is' authority" (142). Specifically Metz is here arguing for a legitimation of the church's leadership through discipleship, rather than through juridical-administrative competency. "Religious competency results from radical discipleship" (142). Metz does not explicitly relate this issue to the questions raised above, but some lines can be drawn. Any description of a leadership/authority which 'has' authority is a theoretical model, insofar as the "consent" of the people has been by-passed in favor of legitimating that authority through intellectual and/or legal arguments. The questions concerning emancipation and redemption thus are completely lost in the praxis of domination; the church is experienced as no different from any other institution dominating and controlling the lives of people. Only a leadership grounded in radical discipleship has the religious competency to speak of redemption; juridical-administrative competency leads often merely to talk of emancipation (if not by advocating it, at least be serving as that from which people are to be emancipated). Thus, when Metz argues that "such an understanding of authority [as grounded in radical discipleship] could finally effect that transformation of 'domination' that is necessitated by our world-society if we are to survive humanly" (143), he is talking of more than reversing the roles of master and servant (the "proletarian principle of the gospel"), he is talking of the possibility of the church talking of redemption--not as something to be handed out by authority, but as something to be experienced in the praxis of the whole church. Transformation of domination, in this understanding, is not merely a reversal of roles, it is a transformation of closed-ness into openness--an openness to the message of Jesus: the radically new kingdom of God.

There is no way to speak of a transformation of domination without speaking of an openness to the radically new.

We will see further in his fourth thesis how Metz follows through
on this by urging that the church appropriate imminent expectation. Here we want briefly to explicate the closed-ness of
domination, in terms of how control of the future functions as
an essential ingredient of the process of closure.

Ever since the dialectic of Enlightenment, in which the
fundamentally new possibilities of freedom, on the one hand,
are contrasted with the enormous threats to that same freedom,
on the other, the tension between domination and freedom has
been resolved by appeal to the future. Future emancipation
justifies present decision. Freedom is the freedom to control
the future, rather than be controlled by it. Freedom is seen
to be limited if the future is allowed to offer any critique of
present decisions. Thus, the only future allowed to the "truncated" modern technical Enlightenment is a "decisionless future."
That is, control is exercised from the present over the future;
movement is allowed in only one direction. The leadership model
flowing from the enlightenment bears this out: bureaucracy
allows movement in only one direction, from the top down. The
decisionless present gives rise to the decisionless future.
The same analysis in terms of what leadership model follows
can be made of the "truncated" classical theoretic Enlighten-
ment--monarchy allows movement in only one direction; its
decisionless present gives rise to a decisionless future./2/

Does our reading of science fiction throw any light on
this? Aside from the content of so many of the stories of
science fiction--a content that speaks consistently of a perfect, just, logical, scientific structuring of human society
which eliminates disease, poverty, war, and suffering--a critical explication of the structure of the science fiction story
based only on the techniques of extrapolation underlines the
preoccupation the present Western mind has with control and
domination. In light of this we discussed above the relation
of science fiction to utopia and fantasy. More specifically,
in light of the temporal structuring implicit in science fiction
utopia and science fiction fantasy, we concluded that there
existed two distinct forms of the science fiction narrative:
the "future history" model (which extrapolates possibilities
based on present knowledge) and the "we are not alone" model

(as symbolic of an openness to the radically new). We also
discussed the relationship between utopia and fantasy in terms
of possibility and desirability. It becomes all the more clear
as we progress in our study that openness and desirability,
much more than possibility, are constitutive of the very structure of human history. Possibility alone cannot serve as the
condition of possibility grounding the hope of humankind. The
temporal structuring of the "future history" model is limited
by seeking to ground new possibility in already known possibility (just as it seeks to ground freedom in freedom). It speaks
and hears only the language of simple and/or modified expectation. The future is *only* that which humankind can control, or
which controls it. On the other hand, the temporal structuring
of the "we are not alone" model is open to the desirability of
the radically new. It speaks the language of imminent expectation. Domination is transformed. The closed-ness of control
(whether experienced as master or servant) is no longer the
logic of history; openness is. More specifically, openness to
the present gives rise to openness to the future as a radically
new dimension of the present. A transformation of domination
cannot occur without an openness to the radically new. This
leads us to a consideration of the fourth thesis of Metz's
paper, a thesis which can now be seen as an integral part of
his argument.

The movement in Thesis Four is "From a church of an
evolutionistically softened eschatology to a church of the
imminent expectation: or, the church in a field of tension
between apocalyptic and politics" (1978:143). The comments on
this thesis by Metz are so compact it is hard to add anything
without saying what he has already said, but more poorly. The
church, Metz argues, is by and large perceived as a negligible
factor in society, because nothing is expected of it any longer.
Further, it gives the impression of being the "secret accomplice"
of the resignation and hopelessness permeating modern consciousness due to the dialectic of Enlightenment. Why has this
happened? Because discipleship has degenerated. Why has
discipleship degenerated? Because it no longer is grounded in
imminent expectation; it has been cut off from its roots.
Time in Western consciousness has become a "homogeneous

continuum that contains no surprises." Even eternity is emptied
of promise, because an evolutionistically softened eschatology
denies the possibility of the radically new. "The apocalyptic
symbol of the breakdown and end of time has been exchanged for
the pseudo-religious symbol of evolution which in its impene-
trableness so much permeates us all that we scarcely perceive
any longer its irrational quasi-religious domination over us"
(144). This is seen particularly in the reduction in evolutionary thought of imminent expectation to constant expectation.
For in that reduction we have already acceded to an evolutionary consciousness of time, change, development, and history.
In terms of our discussion above, how we expect becomes determined by what we expect and vice versa. Both theology and the
church, Metz continues, become anti-apocalyptic institutions,
insofar as they absorb the expectations of people and provide
a stabilizing effect. On the other hand, once imminent expectation has been freed from its reduction to constant expectation, it is seen as that which "does not paralyze political
responsibility but establishes its foundation [for it] provides
the hope that has been appeased and seduced by evolution." It
is evolutionary consciousness which cripples discipleship.
Metz concludes: "Apocalyptic imminent expectation is and must
remain the mystical correlative to an experienced political
reality" (144-45).

Now, it would be misleading to take the fourth thesis of
Metz and consider it on the same level as the other three; or
to see it as a conclusion to (in the sense of a logical deduc-
tion from) them. Metz's fourth thesis is on the order of a
step transcending the other three, by providing a ground on
which the whole analysis rests. We will attempt in the following pages to explore exactly how it grounds the work of Metz by
referring to the work of Jurgen Moltmann and Langdon Gilkey.
Both have been noted for their efforts to formulate a theology
of history (and of time, change, and development). We wish to
establish through this brief comparative analysis that any
discussion of emancipation and redemption (in terms of temporal
structuring) must move beyond a critique of the "structures" of
history, to a discussion of the "horizon" of history. This
last distinction comes from the recent work of Gilkey; to him

we turn first.

Gilkey's theological enterprise has centered primarily on the hermeneutic of secular experience as a prolegomenon to theology proper (God-talk). Gilkey is mistrustful of the claims of the revisionist theologians that the truth of God-talk can be verified by metaphysical language. Such argumentation rests on the presupposition that language reduplicates thought, and thought reduplicates reality. But it is precisely these rationalist presuppositions which have been called into question in the modern era. At best, a hermeneutic of secular experience can serve as a prolegomenon to theology proper in that it fulfills two important functions: 1) it underlines the priority of faith in human existence in general; and 2) it is a necessary supplement to the insight of faith. These conclusions are argued at length in his early work, *Naming the Whirlwind*.

In a more recent book, *Reaping the Whirlwind*, Gilkey moves closer to an ontological and metaphysical discussion of human existence and meaning. But he still distinguishes two steps in the process of "faith seeking understanding." There is, he says, "a break between prolegomenon and constructive or systematic theology" (117). He does acknowledge that one can, through reason, come to an ontological understanding of the structure of human existence: "The fundamental ontological structure of our existence as temporal and historical...[is] expressed by the polarity of destiny and freedom, the given actualities from the past and the response to that given demanded of us in terms of new possibility." Even so, even though one can isolate this fundamental ontological structure, still the question of ultimacy is not resolved. "The ontological structure of destiny and freedom which structures history is set within a horizon that is religious; and it is in that ontological structure within that horizon that the passions of political action, the mythological character of political speech, and the ultimate ambiguity of all political enterprises find their ground" (119-20). The remainder of Gilkey's book is an attempt to explicate that horizon in terms of the symbolic-theological language of providence, history, hope, and eschatology.

One may disagree with the ultimate expression of Gilkey's systematic theology, with his attempts at retrieving the notion of providence particularly, and with his attempt to provide an overview capable of integrating providence and eschatology. Our brief review of his theological enterprise is offered merely to point out what we believe is a valid methodological procedure--that Gilkey speaks of a distinction between ontological structure and horizon, and that he insists the two be kept separate. The religious horizon of history grounds the being and the understanding of the ontological understanding of human existence; but it is not, in turn, grounded by anything other than itself, least of all by human understanding.

This distinction between structure and horizon helps assess the meaning and importance of Metz's paper on a renewed church, particularly insofar as it clarifies the type of theologizing separating the fourth thesis from the first three. In the fourth thesis Metz is clearly talking of the horizon of political theology, while in the first three he is discussing the structure. His proposal then (and one not clearly spelled out in the paper) is that apocalyptic serves as the horizon of political theology. To read apocalyptic as entering into the structure of political theology invites the repetition of the chiliastic/revolutionary excesses which have characterized the manifestations of apocalyptic down through the centuries. We will take up this theme later.

We turn now to the work of Jurgen Moltmann for another perspective on the topic of apocalyptic as the horizon of (political) theology. There is no doubt that Moltmann (and Metz also) sees 'eschatology' as the horizon of theology. Moltmann's seminal book, *Theology of Hope*, is subtitled, "On the Ground and Implications of Christian Eschatology." It is too much here even to begin to attempt a summary of this major work. Much of our analysis of the languages of future expectation, particularly the designation of the centrality of promise, is dependent on Moltmann's argument. We are concerned here with his comments on apocalyptic.

Moltmann deals only slightly and in passing with the specific topic of apocalyptic. Most comments are of a general nature, using the term apocalyptic to signify the content of a

particular type of eschatology: that which treats of the last
days, the end time, the final victory. Only in one short
passage does he tackle head on the problem of apocalyptic insofar as it signifies a form as well as a content. In short,
Moltmann is concerned to clarify how apocalyptic stands in
relation to prophecy, a topic discussed above. Moltmann runs
through the usual arguments for viewing apocalyptic as a corruption of prophecy: it is deterministic, dualistic, fatalistic
concerning this world, and (in Hanson's terms) removed from
"plain history, real politics, and human instrumentality."
Is it then, Moltmann asks, radically non-historic thinking?
And is it thus radically flawed? For Moltmann the answer lies
in whether or not one conceives of "universal history" (the
form of apocalyptic) as being non-historic thinking. The
further question is whether in doing "historic" thinking, one
must be situated in a particular concrete time and place.
That is, can history be anonymous, or pseudonymous? Moltmann
suggests that apocalyptic is not non-historic thinking; it is
firmly rooted in the mode of historic thinking common to all
the Israel people. But the perspective of the apocalyptic
thinking of history has changed: "In place of a historic eschatology comes an eschatological contemplation of history" (1975:
135). The attempts of biblical theologians to critique apocalyptic according to prophetic categories misses this point; it
ends up claiming that apocalyptic is prophetic eschatology
poured into the mold of cosmological myth.

     There is another possible interpretation, Moltmann
argues; it could be that what is involved here is not at all
"a cosmological interpretation of the cosmos" (136). The result
is that history, not the cosmos, is the horizon of the promise.
History then does not become cosmological, but the opposite
happens: the cosmos becomes historical. The whole world, not
just the world of the Israel nation, becomes involved in the
sufferings and the glory of the last days. The point is that
the *totum* of apocalyptic supersedes even that of cosmological
mythology--in present day terms, there is a perspective here
which goes beyond even the astrophysical theories about the
origin and preservation of the universe, the "big bang," the
"bang-bang" cycle, or the "steady-state" theories. Moltmann

concludes:

> This historifying of the world in the category of the
> universal eschatological future is of tremendous im-
> portance for theology, for indeed it makes eschatology
> the universal horizon of all theology as such. With-
> out apocalyptic a theological eschatology remains
> bogged down in the ethnic history of men or the exis-
> tential history of the individual (137-38).

Moltmann's argument is on a much wider scale than Metz's;
and it does not have the particular focus of Gilkey's. But the
essential movement in all three is the same: there is a structure to history and to historical (political) activity which
somehow must be grounded in a horizon of history and historical
(political) activity.

This has ramifications reaching through all the many
levels of this study. In regard to the theses of Metz it means
that apocalyptic is the horizon of political theology. To
explicate apocalyptic in terms of the structure of political
activity leaves one the task of picking up the pieces after the
"millennialists" have destroyed the old in order to inaugurate
the new age. Or, as is the more usual case, explaining that
imminent does not mean constant expectation, nor does imminent
mean immanent. Imminent expectation grounds provisional
eschatology (insofar as it related to present praxis) and so
grounds and is the foundation for responsible political activity
(freedom grounded in freedom leads to the abolition of freedom),
but always in a horizon which is the condition of its possibility. Hope becomes the form of faith, in this analysis, not the
act of faith. In terms of a distinction used above, apocalyptic
is much more concerned with how we expect than with what we expect. How we expect is related to our existence within a horizon of history; what we expect is perceived within our understanding of the structure of history. To confuse the two, as
Metz makes clear, results in one or other of the two determining
both; in our own day an evolutionistically softened eschatology
has become both how *and* what we expect--more of the same.

The ramifications of understanding apocalyptic as the
horizon of political theology extend also to a critical analysis
of the programmatic conclusions of Braaten. One cannot fault
his isolation of the critical apocalyptic themes in the teaching

of Jesus, themes which made his revolution more than political:
the *totum*, the demonic, signs of the times, radical conversion,
unconditional surrender to love, the proletarian principle,
present hopelessness as birthpangs of the new. But what bothered
us then, and what still bothers us, is Braaten's uncritical
appropriation of these themes—which seems to accept them in
terms of a cause/effect perception of change, as though "doing"
these things will hasten the coming of the new. Thus we
suggest that Braaten at this critical point in his analysis
fails to transcend the consciousness against which the counter-
Christ stands: conjunctive eschatology which proceeds along a
linear path to an end goal in a process determined according to
the categories of before/after, cause/effect. Such categories
as these do not help in any way to resolve the critical questions of how and where one draws the line between God's intervention and humankind's responsibility. That is, one correlates
emancipation and redemption. The resolution (re-solution) of
these questions must somehow take into account the fundamental
distinction between the structure and the horizon of history,
between what we expect and how we expect. To resolve the
questions in terms of cause/effect leads to the inevitable
positing of a double-structure of causality: one acts as
though everything depended on oneself, one prays as though
everything depended on God. To resolve the questions in terms
of before/after leads to the positing of the double-structure
of time (and of history): eternity comes after time, history
ends and the kingdom takes over. Both these configurations
have been applied to the dualism of apocalyptic and result in
a resolution of the critical questions in terms of a determinism;
a determinism, moreover, which ultimately eviscerates the praxis
of the people.

　　　The question, then, comes down to this: Do people live,
act, and expect within a horizon of conjunctive expectation or
within a horizon of disjunctive (imminent) expectation? Does
not positing a praxis of conjunctive expectation lead to the
inevitable transformation of that praxis into a technique, and
issue finally in an appropriation of time, change, development,
and history in terms only of that which can be extrapolated,
manipulated, and controlled; only of that which is seen as

possible?

We have argued above that science fiction provides one
of the means available through which to engage in a hermeneutic
of secular experience on this precise point of the horizon
within which praxis is grounded. We have seen, further, that
whereas the typical reading of science fiction interprets its
horizon within which people live, act, and expect to be one of
conjunctive expectation, on the other hand, there is ample
evidence that science fiction also and more fundamentally is
grounded in the horizon of imminent expectation.

From the very beginning, before any discussion of content,
plotting and style, the self-understanding of early science
fiction suggested that a correlation with apocalyptic literature
presented opportunities for analysis broadening the base of
critical study and allowing for an appropriation of science
fiction as a popular literature, instead of the usual glossing
over of that fact and/or a dismissal of the bulk of science
fiction in favor of treating a relatively few "classics."
(Such tactics are similar to theologians refusing to be responsible for heretical and/or ideological uses of religion; and
scientists refusing to be held accountable for the (ab)uses of
their "pure" scientific discoveries. And so forth.) At the
heart of the self-understanding of early science fiction was
the enthusiasm which characterized it as "something entirely
new." However crass and commercial were the interests of
Gernsback and other science fiction publishers, science fiction
was a popular literature which caught the fancy of those who
looked forward to a new age and who felt indeed that they were
standing on its threshhold. And however scientific were the
presuppositions of this new literature, however much it tried
to hold to what was scientifically possible and/or probable,
science fiction from the beginning was a literature of wonder.
The titles of the early pulps bear this out, using and re-using
the vocabulary of the wonderful, strange, marvelous, amazing,
fantastic, and astounding. The ordinary matter of scientific
fact and discovery was transformed, not only by being made the
content of the scientific romance, but more simply by being put
between the glossy covers. Even the stories themselves were no
longer read as romances (although structurally they were those);

instead the story and narrative were seen as testimonies of
those who had seen the future, who had seen tomorrow. Time was
no longer perceived as being composed of a past, present, and
future, stretching along a logical and chronological line which
progressed according to fixed laws. Time consisted of today
(this present time) and tomorrow. It was measured not according to the ordinary events of the real world, but according to
the extraordinary events: according to invention, discovery,
journey, in terms of contact with extra-terrestrials, friendly
or hostile, as a result of catastrophe or breakthrough. Each
event ushered in a totally new age; it was not continuity which
characterized time, it was discontinuity: tomorrow was a new
age. All the political institutions of this age would pass
away when the new age came. But even within the world of this
story (the story of early science fiction) there was still the
possibility of the new. Science fiction from the very beginning never capitulated to the temptation to settle for one
particular formulation of the new. The new worlds of Doc Smith
became the old worlds of Isaac Asimov; just as today the new
worlds of Robert Heinlein (*Starship Troopers*) become the old
world of Joe Haldeman (*The Forever War*). The political is at
the mercy of the cosmological; and both, in turn, are at the
mercy of the historical--that future of choices, of decisions,
and more fundamentally, of expectations which swallows up all
the small worlds we call home.

Such is the world of early science fiction, a world of
imminent expectation. It is to this world the critic of science
fiction must return if there is to be any ultimate resolution
of the confusion of forms which has characterized (and still
does) the critical study of science fiction. One is tempted to
draw easy parallels between the domestication of imminent
expectation (in the literary critical study of science fiction)
and the domestication of eschatology (in the doctrinal development of Christianity). There are none. But there are some
things which can be said by way of comparison. Of particular
interest is the tendency toward privatization characterizing
both literary criticism and theological reflection. Meaning
and salvation become affairs of the radically privatized heart.
Even conscience, that most political of ethical categories,

becomes a moment to "be alone with our God, who speaks in our heart." And, of course, all literature is read similarly: it is Shakespeare who speaks directly to me through the medium of the drama.

In the literary critical study of science fiction this emphasis has resulted in dismissing the social world of tomorrow people expect in favor of considering the private future world the writer extrapolates according to scientific and/or literary laws and structures. How to expect has been almost completely overshadowed by what to expect. The classifying of science fiction according to the usual genres of fantasy, utopia, romance, philosophical tale, cognitive estrangement, or structural fabulation does nothing to resolve the confusion of forms. For each category is exclusive, rather than being inclusive. In our review of the critical understanding of science fiction we saw J. O. Bailey unable to assimilate science fiction as romance into his larger critical framework. We saw Kingsley Amis, having noted and then dismissing the fanaticism of early science fiction, consequently unable to account for the fantasy roots and dimensions of science fiction. But even as critics moved out to incorporate larger frameworks for their critical study (we noted especially David Ketterer and Robert Scholes), the temptation to domesticate the radical nature of science fiction's imminent expectation proved to be irresistable. Thus, Ketterer reduces science fiction to a head-trip by reducing apocalyptic to the same. And Scholes, through the mechanics of structuralism, subordinates literature to the scientific control of the future--and reduces the imminent expectation of apocalyptic science fiction to a structural principle of action. Although neither Ketterer nor Scholes clearly intend their work to serve as such, Ketterer's reduction of apocalyptic to a head-trip and Scholes' reduction of it to a structural principle of action, can function as supporting arguments for dismissing science fiction as private fantasy and/or as public fantasy. The former is fantasy proper, the latter utopia; both are viewed as a means of escape from the harsh realities of the present. Fantasy is seen as escape through privatized daydreaming, a purely subjective state of existence, living in one's own world. Utopia is seen as escape through public

day dreaming, wanting everyone else to live in one's own
world; dreaming the unattainable and settling for the possible
both at the same time, while completely ignoring the category
of the desirable as revelatory of the human.

What the domestication of imminent expectation in science
fiction criticism results in, therefore, are two options:
either apocalyptic is reduced to a subjective fantasy, or it is
reduced to a structural principle of action. It should come as
no great surprise that a similar reductionism is evident in the
theological, critical treatment of apocalyptic in the development of religious thought. Apocalyptic is the strange, bizarre,
subjective, esoteric, symbolic literature of a certain type of
people who have given up on the usual political and historical
processes, and who escape into their own fantasies about imminent deliverance by the intervention of God. Or, apocalyptic
is simply the literature of chiliastic zealots and millennialist tyrants who seek to destroy the old order completely so as
to inflict their wild visions onto a hapless world.

In science fiction as a popular literature we do not see
this happen, at least not to any large extent. Dianetics
(Scientology) and Technocracy, Inc., are not large factors in
the private lives of the majority of readers. People who read
science fiction have, by and large, resisted the reduction of
imminent expectation to either subjective fantasy or objective
manipulation through structural principle for action. In
other words science fiction over the years has operated on an
entirely different level; and imminent expectation, so radically
a part of science fiction, has operated on an entirely different
level. Despite the best efforts of literary critics, and even
theological critics, *Star Trek*, *Star Wars*, *Close Encounters*,
2001, and the works of Asimov, Heinlein, Clarke, van Vogt,
Sturgeon, Bester, Blish, Herbert, Anderson, Lewis, LeGuin, Lem,
and the hundreds of other science fiction writers, function as
the horizon within which the reader lives his or her social
and political life. It is on this level that science fiction
must be subjected to critical scrutiny; not on the privatized
level which seeks to criticize the escape of each particular
reader, nor on the privatized level which seeks to critique
the extrapolative techniques of the writer.

Current biblical scholarship on the origin, nature, and purpose of apocalyptic, and current systematic theology, treating of the eschatological foundations of all theological enterprise, have reinforced this understanding of apocalyptic as the horizon which grounds political and social life. Also, and more significantly, it has allowed for the retrieval of apocalyptic literature as a popular literature, a literature of marginal people, the outsiders, the losers-- a literature which functions more as story than as signal. In literary critical work this means that as much attention must be paid to the reader as to the writer. And we have attempted to do just that throughout, especially in our analysis of the languages of future expectation. Science fiction criticism focusing on the craft of the writer has tended to concentrate on the techniques of the fictional craft, especially on the techniques of extrapolation--to the point where even the "introduction of a startling new *donne*" is seen as just another technique. There is no attempt here to dismiss or deny the value of such literary critical work; merely to stand it on its head, as it were, and suggest that similar categories may be used to analyze expectation as are used to analyze extrapolation. The result is that the control of meaning is much harder to isolate and immensely more difficult to manipulate. It is not merely in the "radically new" where meaning resides; it is in the "radically new which is imminently expected" where meaning is found. The former allows for control by the narrator/ruler/technician; the latter shifts control over to the new, the unknown, the longed for, the desired which is expected imminently. Waiting is what creates. For to relinquish control is the pre-condition (the necessary, but not sufficient condition) for the coming of the new.

In the models of extrapolation (and the mirror models of expectation) in which time is viewed as evolutionary progression along a linear path, time becomes a barrier, an obstacle, a gulf separating one point from another. Or, it becomes a medium through which control is exercised. All popular literature (and popular culture) is a search for immediacy. This can best be seen, perhaps, in a closer look at the religious manifestation of popular culture: people's religion, wherein the search is

empts leave the resulting theological reflection un-
ly aware of the totalizing (and incipient totalitarian)
f emancipatory history.

It is precisely this latter concern which leads Metz to
the correlation of emancipation and redemption "within
mework of what I term...'the history of human suffering'"

For it is precisely insofar as emancipatory history has
to come to grips with human suffering (and indeed has
ibuted to it as the result of that failure) that a discus-
of suffering provides a context in which to speak of
mption. Suffering and the (hi)stories of suffering raise
t of all the question of guilt. Emancipation, conceived in
ms of a universal historical totality--i.e., humankind as
subject of history--soon retreats into the "exonerating
hanism" of abstractions when faced with the question of
ilt for suffering. The subject soon becomes again an object;
is time not of God's actions, but of the processes of tech-
ological and economic progress. The result is a "painfully
amouflaged heteronomy" (327). Anthropodicy has replaced
theodicy. A Christian soteriology, on the contrary, does not
flee into abstractions, but demands participation in guilt, in
the concrete praxis of life. Such a participation opens one to
the possibility of redemption not as a process confirming
innocence, but rather one which redeems us from complicity.

Suffering and the (hi)stories of suffering also raise
the question of "deadly finitude"--i.e., what to do not only
with the dead but with death itself. Emancipation justifies
the dead who have died to make us free; but it does not help
the living who still face the same finitude. Thus the cynicism
with regard to the dead whose death has been meaningful, when
compared to the living whose death is still perceived as a
negation and nothing more. Emancipatory progress becomes an
ideology to which humankind is sacrificed generation after
generation. A Christian soteriology, on the contrary, offers
no simple justification of the dead, and so faces head on the
finitude of (our) death and the meaning of (our) freedom. Metz
sees in Jesus' "descent into hell" an example of this--insofar
as it prevents a history of redemption from being reduced to
emancipatory progress looking only to the future. The history

for the immediacy of the spiritual, transcendent dimension of
life./3/ People's religion and apocalyptic are statements
against the heavy burden of evolutionary time used by those in
power to enslave the people. But whereas the protest has most
often been read as one against an institutional presence and
for a *spatial* immediacy (the nearness of God, Christ, love, the
inner self, nirvana, i.e., immediacy in the spiritual, transcendent dimension of life has been reduced to the immanent),
the protest ought also to be read as one against evolutionary
presence and for *temporal* immediacy (the nearness of the radically new, i.e., the imminent). What is called for in apocalyptic is indeed a de-historicizing of the future, when that
future is merely the *futurum*, the rational extrapolation of
existing trends. For that kind of future only de-historicizes
the present by robbing it of the possibility for the sudden
coming of the new. All that remains in the present is the
suffering, impotence, and futurelessness of humankind. A
simple reliance on rational extrapolation does not create the
future, it destroys it as a dimension of the present. And by
destroying it, it not only de-historicizes the future, it
de-historicizes the present. It leaves us, as many others have
commented, at the brink of (if not in) the post-historical era.

All this is why the "we are not alone" model in science
fiction is of such critical importance. For it suggests not
merely another model of the science fiction story (thus, criticism of the writer's craft); it suggests a whole new way of
reading science fiction. It suggests that science fiction be
read not only as a medium for the expression of new ideas and/or
scientific data in a palatable form (although it can be that),
nor only as a tool for criticizing the present and/or visions
of the future (it can be that, too); but it also suggests that
science fiction be read as the horizon within which people live
and act socially and politically. The former two ways of
criticizing science fiction, we repeat, focus on the writer's
craft; the latter on the readers' attitudes. Or to put it
another way: the former two try to isolate what stands behind
the text (as the author stands, literally, behind it); while
the latter is more concerned with what stands in front of the
text (as the reader does).

This last description also has the advantage of suggesting that the only way to get at the meaning out front is through
a critical analysis of the readers. Thus again we are in debt
to popular literature, for it is a literature eminently concerned with the reader. It is a user-oriented literature, in
the terminology of Herbert Gans. This orientation, moreover,
concurs with the analysis of the theory/praxis relationship
which has been the focus of much recent systematic (political)
theology. Of particular interest is the opposition between
those theologians who explicate human experience according to
the disclosure models of limit-experience and/or transcendental
experience, and those who are concerned with the very structure
and meaning of lived human experience insofar as it has a transforming value (Lamb:1978b). The praxis of reading is not
valuable merely because it discloses the meaning (theory) intended by the author. Reading itself has a transforming value.
There is in this a parallel to the search for the meaning behind
the text (i.e., the meaning already present, explicitly or
implicitly) as opposed to the meaning out front, which cannot
be appropriated except by a participation in the experience of
reading.

Finally, we might note that the phrase, "we are not
alone," has a double meaning. The "other" is also the other
believer. The statement is a testimonial about "we" not "I."
There is in this belief ("we are not alone") a proclamation not
only that the future as extrapolation is not enough, but also
that the present as a private experience is not enough. We see
on further reflection that the two are indeed linked: that the
most efficient means for political and social oppression is to
reduce all experience to private experience, to cut people off
not only from the future, but also from each other. This has
led us to suggest above that in addition to the desires Ted
Peters claims the UFO experiences symbolize (a desire for transcendence, perfection, omniscience, and redemption) we ought
also to add the desire for community, for shared faith.

This desire for community and for shared faith leads us
in our concluding analysis to the centrality of story and the
primacy of narrative theology, both of which are necessary in
the discussion of the relation between emancipation and

redemption. Indeed, the correlat
experiences recapitulates the main
the dialectic of religious and secu
established the communal, shared nat
lays it open to the coming of the rad
now is whether this faith can in any w
seemingly unbridgeable gulf lying betwe
redemption. And if so, it remains to se
story are critical to the enterprise.

Emancipation and Redempt.

If there is any formulation of the pl
across all facets of the concern of the conte
enterprise to correlate critically human exper
tian faith, it is Metz's formulation of it in
relationship between emancipation and redemptio
ience's current controlling metaphor is emancipa
theology's is (and always has been) redemption.
here a new perspective on the problem of critical
But, Metz insists, the critical correlation is not
which correlates question and answer, systematic the
historical theology, history and dogma; but rather on
correlates theory and practice, the understanding of 1
social practice. Emancipation is not the question to w
redemption is the answer; nor, on the other hand, is red
the earlier understanding of emancipation. There can be
baptizing of emancipation; nor can there be a "theologica
foothold in the crevices of this dialectic of emancipation
(1977:323). There can be no argumentative soteriology which
tacks God onto the human process of emancipation, which says,
in effect, in the future we will see the two processes as one.
To do so is to take away from both the understanding of emancipation and the understanding of redemption: for both must be
accepted as mediating a totality, as telling the whole story.
Nor, Metz continues, can there be any compromising theologies
which attempt to assimilate this emancipatory totality, such as
the two-kingdom paradigm or the paradoxical soteriology of the
transcendentalist or existentialist theologies, respectively.

of redemption calls for "backward solidarity" as much as it
calls for "forward solidarity." Our death must justify (redeem)
those who have died in the past, as much as their death justifies (emancipates) us. Further, "backward solidarity" prevents
us from reading history as an account of the triumphant; but
instead forces us to view it from the standpoint "of the conquered and the victim in our history." For, having failed to
redeem those who have died in the past, we will have failed to
confront our own finitude. Thus the existence of "subversive
histories...which again and again disperse and disavow as abstract the spell of a total emancipatory reflexion on history"
(329-30). The "conquered and the victim" remind us that humankind's emancipation is not adequate justification for what they
have suffered; only redemption will suffice. We must also
descend into hell.

Now, the questions raised by suffering, and the (hi)sto-
ries of suffering, also throw the "pure argumentative" soteriologies of classical Christian theology into disarray. For they
tend to revert to an a-historical position by placing themselves
outside and above history, and therefore cannot adequately
address the dialectic of emancipation and redemption. Redemption
becomes either "futuristic," or suffering becomes "suffering
between God and God." In neither case is there an identification
with the (hi)stories of suffering; for either the story of
suffering becomes a story about someone else, or the story becomes a story of the eternal (a-temporal) struggle between good
and evil, or the story is reduced to its conceptual referents.

For these reasons Metz advances a soteriology which he
calls "explicitly narrative, a fundamentally memorative-narrative
soteriology." Its advantages are twofold: 1) it is able to tell
one story which is at the same time a story of redemption and a
history of suffering; and 2) it is able to actualize (through
our telling and re-telling of that story) not only the history
but also the process of redemption, because it is the "communication of the experience of faith...[of an] original experience
of something new, something never before present" (332-33).

In another short essay on narrative Metz discusses the
practical and performative aspects of narrative. In the first
(practical) there is the "narrative self-enlightenment about the

very interest which underlies the narrative process" (i.e., in
the telling of the story it becomes our story); in the second
(performative) we have the sacraments (particularly Eucharist
and Penance) which are "incorporated within the framework of a
narrative action" (1973:87). Although Metz defends a time and
a place for argumentative soteriology, he insists that a treatment of redemption in conceptual terms alone and a continued
reliance on a mediation of it in those terms alone prevents its
continual and necessary renewal, which a memorative-narrative
soteriology can provide. (Thus also in the area of science
fiction, we see that the stories told of the "scientific understanding" of the universe are in the end just as important if
not more so, than the understanding itself.) Metz ultimately
grounds his critique of an argumentative soteriology and his
proposal for a memorative-narrative soteriology on the "narrative structure of critical reason." Memory, in light of this,
is not just another form of "knowing," such as the computer
"remembers" historical facts. A computer, since it cannot forget, cannot really remember either. It knows a-historically.
There is no interest in its knowledge; there is nothing at
stake. Not so with memory for humankind; its remembering is
subversive and dangerous, for it is an identification with the
(hi)story of suffering which it narrates. Metz concludes:

> These dangerous stories break through the spell of a
> historical reconstruction based on abstract reason and
> repudiate any attempt to reconstruct man's conscious-
> ness from the abstract unity of "I think" (1977:330).

Returning finally to science fiction, we are confronted
with the many stories which are not based on the abstract unity
of "I think." Although some of the "future history" science
fiction stories break out of the mold of conjunctive temporal
structuring and sweep far into space and time by means of disjunctive "warps," still it is the "we are not alone" stories
which shatter most often the spell of historical reconstruction
and historical projection. Emancipation in science fiction is
most clearly linked with conjunctive modes of temporal structuring, i.e., with future history and its progeny, utopia; while
redemption is most often linked with disjunctive (imminent)
modes, i.e., with stories reminding us "we are not alone." How

we expect, that is, what kind of temporal structuring we live
within, does have a bearing on the dialectic of emancipation
and redemption, and indeed on the dialectic of religious and
secular soteriologies. It does not exhaust the dialectic, to
be sure; but it does provide a thoroughly contemporary means
of exploring it. It may be that all emancipatory thought more
closely adheres to conjunctive logical and temporal structuring,
while redemption reminds us of the disjunctive aspect of salvation. Most particularly it reminds us that passivity (*Passion*,
in the Gospel narratives) is the human mode of its appropriation.

It would give me no greater satisfaction nor pleasure
than to say Metz has once and for all (re-)solved the dialectic
of emancipation and redemption, thereby leaving us a simple
mopping up exercise vis-a-vis our analysis of science fiction
and apocalyptic. But even his proposals are tentatively offered;
and his essays more often than not conclude with suggestions and
questions: How precisely do we define narrative? How does
fictive (hi)story relate to story? How can we say that story
is authentic? True? What is the relationship between narrative
and "real" time? Does the presence of the story-teller mean
that narrative cannot be reduced simply to a textual problem?
Is there a narrative aspect to science? To logic? In addition
to theology? Finally, what about the obvious narrative structure
of the Scriptures?

These questions suggest many different avenues for further
work. Some of the questions have been explored tangentially in
our study of science fiction and apocalypse. But it must be
admitted that indeed we have only arrived at the beginning, the
point at which serious study can begin. The task now, in brief
summary form, is to take Metz's analysis and concluding questions, and propose in turn our own set of questions, our own
guiding concerns. We offer these as an aid in the future
critical study of science fiction from a theological point of
view. In light of the scope and the aim of this present study,
in light of political theology and a memorative-narrative
soteriology, and in light of apocalyptic as the horizon of
(political) theology, the following areas of concern seem to me
to be critical in the on-going dialogue between theology and
science fiction.

Three Critical Concerns

A. Redemption in Science Fiction

Although it is tempting (and a temptation too often
yielded to) to state simply that the reference of science fiction is emancipation, and the referent of theology is redemption, a central concern of our study has been to suggest that
the relationship between emancipation and redemption is one
found within the body of science fiction itself. That relationship may not mean the same thing as it does in the analysis of
Metz (to determine that much more critical work remains to be
done); but it does mean in the same way. The abstract, totalizing stories of science fiction utopias and future history
have served too often as mechanisms for exonerating the guilt
of social planners, technological tyrants, and scientific
saviors, who have declared war on the poor (instead of diseased
institutions), on ethnic identity and pride (instead of racial
prejudice). The stories of this kind of science fiction are
stories about the wholesale sacrifice of humankind for the sake
of some "idea" of freedom, equality, justice, economic success,
or intellectual awakening.

On the other hand, the hope for redemption (as the form
of a basic human faith, not the act of that faith) has been
kept alive in the stories which "remember" we are not alone.
Desirability and waiting inform historical consciousness more
so than does possibility, choice, and control. For the former,
more so than the latter, ground the unfolding of history in the
successive affirmations of the dignity of all human persons--
especially those who suffer and who wait. The "we are not alone"
theme, we suggest, refers not only to the longing for a redeeming
intervention, but also has for its referent the solidarity of
all humankind, past, present, and future. Thus science fiction's
often ignored, but highly significant, preoccupation with the
past, the myths of origins, most of which do "remember" that we
are not alone. Science fiction criticism must grapple with this
as an integral part of the genre, not an aberration or a red
herring.

B. Science Fiction as Popular Literature

      The form of science fiction criticism shaped according
to a creator-oriented view of culture, and moving from that to
a concern primarily with science fiction as extrapolation (i.e.,
which isolates the extrapolative techniques of the writer) reinforces the reading of all science fiction as emancipatory
(hi)story. Our contention that science fiction should be read
as a popular literature forces the critic to view it from the
perspective of a user-oriented culture. The result is that
expectation emerges as the central illuminating characteristic,
and thus, science fiction should also be read as redemptive
(hi)story. A preoccupation with extrapolative techniques
(whether in terms of Ketterer's apocalyptic imagination, Scholes'
structural fabulation, or the think-tank variety of future
prognostics) cannot adequately account for the narrative consciousness of either the writer or the reader, nor for the fact
that both perceive the science fiction story as story about
selves rather than others. The turn away from the critical
treatment of science fiction as popular literature to science
fiction as social commentary, literary creation, cognitive
estrangement, sociological analysis, philosophical speculation--
a turn seen from the beginning in Amis's refusal to take
seriously the science fiction fan(atic)--has only led in literary critical circles to a confusion of forms. The parallel in
theological circles is theology's rejection of narrative consciousness which has led to a state wherein "all linguistic
expressions of faith may therefore be seen as categorical
objectivizations or as changing symbols of what cannot be said"
(Metz, 1973:85).

      It is necessary for the critic of science fiction to pay
attention to and critically ground his/her work in an appreciation of science fiction as popular literature, and the whole
science fiction phenomenon as popular culture. For narrative
consciousness (the practical and performative aspects of narrative) has always been the heritage of a user-oriented literature
and culture. This is particularly the case insofar as narrative
consciousness manifests readers' expectations. A similar case
may be made for the work of the theologian, especially the

biblical theologian: his or her work should be grounded in an appreciation of the faith (the Scriptures) as an expression of popular literature and culture.

C. The Horizon of Imminent Expectation

Expectation cannot be reduced simply to its content (what to expect); for this is to fall back on extrapolation and, in the end, on an appreciation of apocalyptic as a structural imperative in (for, of) history, rather than its horizon. The inability of some scriptural theologians to see apocalyptic as anything other than a corruption of prophecy, and the similar inability for some literary critics to see apocalyptic as nothing other than revolutionary rhetoric and/or program, can be traced to this failure to distinguish between the structure of history and its horizon. That failure, in turn, confuses the relationship between emancipation and redemption; for it necessitates a reduction of the problematic to the question of where humankind's responsibility leaves off and God's intervention begins.

In science fiction the problematic resolves to the dialectical relationship between "future history" and the promise that "we are not alone." Does not the latter operate as the horizon of historical consciousness? And at the same time, does it not critique the absolutizing and totalizing tendencies of the former? Yes; but only, we conclude, in the framework of imminent expectation, wherein time becomes focal, absolute control is relinquished, and waiting is seen as creative. For only then is the radically new not able to be specified beforehand through the techniques of rational extrapolation. Only then is the "subversive-liberating memory of redeemed freedom among the systems of our so-called emancipated world" kept alive (Metz, 1977:224).

The meaningfulness of eschatological language in science fiction becomes at this point of critical concern. If it does thematize, shape, and direct a dimension of human experience (imminent expectation) which operates as the horizon of historical consciousness, then the "miracles" of the past are as close to us as the "miracles" of the future--that is, they are both of them dangerous and subversive of a present closed off

to the radically new. Miracles and the literary genre of fantasy have social and political implications; they are not all
of them reducible to the privatized world of "infinite subjectivity." The question of the meaningfulness of eschatological
language is of critical concern for the theologian as well as
for the literary critic. The argument for the "transformative"
nature of praxis "discloses" ultimacy or transcendence, bears
on this point. For if the eschatological language of imminent
expectation discloses a transcendence in terms of an end to (of)
history limiting all human desire and hope (an end which is
already present), then the subject of history becomes inevitably
the object of historical processes. Again, this is to view
apocalyptic as a structural program/imperative for action,
rather than as horizon of history. This is the trap of the
millenialist and the naive Marxist; neither of whom is liber-
ating or subversive. But if the expectation (the experience of
the eschatological language of imminent expectation insofar as
it is narrative) is transformative, then the future is always
open to the radically new because the present itself is.

If all this seems too favorable a reading of science
fiction, so be it. It pretends to be no more "favorable" than
Metz's reading of the Christian faith. I conclude with what
remains, after this whole study, the task of further critical
concern in the correlation of science fiction and Christian
faith: Science fiction has preached emancipation but longs
(at its core) for redemption; theology preaches redemption but
settles (often) for emancipation.

CHAPTER ONE

/1/   Gernsback's editorial in the first issue of *Amazing
Stories* is reprinted in full in Gunn (1975:120-21).

/2/   Philmus employs the device of "mythic displacement" in
his analysis of science fiction. His study is cited at vari-
our places in this work. Darko Suvin is the proponent of
science fiction as "cognitive estrangement." His article is
one of the more lucid and valuable interpretations of what is
going on in science fiction.

/3/   Bentley Glass cites a statement of H. G. Wells: "I am
only interested in people, in the mass; I'm indifferent to
the individual....The scientist himself is the dedicated tool,
the impersonal means to a magnificent end" (288).

CHAPTER TWO

/1/   Thus, Clareson (1971), Scholes and Rabkin, and Aldiss
(1975) all cite Amis' study as being of critical importance.

/2/   The following passage from Moltmann makes the point
very succinctly: "In this post-Christian legalistic apocalyptic, the present time becomes the moment of great decision:
the world is lapsing into the spiritual death of atheism,
atomic catastrophe, the death of the young from drugs or
ecological self-destruction. At the same time, it is the hour
in which the true church has to rise up as the visible place
of refuge in the disaster: 'Rise up for the final struggle.'
It cannot be denied that such visions of the future exist in
the New Testament, and that the crisis of history may come to
such a critical end. But nowhere in the New Testament does
the 'end of the world' bring about the second coming of Christ.
The New Testament looks forward to the very reverse, that the
second coming of Christ will bring the end of destruction and
persecution in the world. Anyone who reads the 'signs of the
times' with the eyes of his own existential anxiety reads them
falsely. If they can be read at all, they can be read by
Christians only with the eyes of hope in the future of Christ.
Otherwise the apocalyptic interpretations of the age will be
like the nihilistic attempts of the 'devils' of Dostoevsky,
who want to destroy the world in order to force God to inter-
vene, and who for romantic reasons regard chaos itself as
creative" (1974:21).

/3/   H. Bruce Franklin discusses the tension between mythos
(story) and logos (scientific knowledge) in the following
passage: "Science, a cumulative process which exists to be
superseded, and fiction, a series of individual attempts to
create matter which cannot be superseded, have vastly differing

relations to time. Insofar as any work of science fiction is
a form of science, it partakes of the temporality and imper-
manence of science and surrenders the timelessness of fiction.
...So that any story in this collection which has withstood
time or even triumphed over it has somehow managed to span the
chasm, or apparent chasm, between fiction and science" (ix-x).
The story (mythos) becomes the vehicle for the promise.

/4/ See Lamb (1978a:56-92) for a discussion of the foundational unity of lived inner experience. Lamb bases his work
on Lonergan.

CHAPTER THREE

/1/ This is basically Cohn's argument (1-32). He carries
it over into a sociological-historical analysis of the apocalyptic world-view, tracing it eventually to Naziism and Communism. But see also Nathan Scott. Scott's article treats
almost exclusively of the literary manifestations of the
negative charge of apocalyptic, although there are here, too,
social and political ramifications. For a more sympathetic
treatment of apocalyptic and millennarianism see Thrupp.

/2/ Tzvetan Todorov's structural analysis of the "fantastic"
is particularly relevant here.

/3/ Campbell's work is prodigious. His *Masks of God* series
covers the known world of myths and mythology. I will be
referring here only to one published talk, "Mythological Themes
in Creative Literature and Art." It is here that Campbell's
thought bears directly on the subject at hand: literature as
the vehicle which mediates our passage through the gates of
desire, on the one hand, and fear on the other. That is, even
prior to the critics' keeping distance, the reader also must
be kept at a critical distance. Thus Campbell, too, can be
helpful in formulating a theory of reading--although he is
primarily concerned with a theory of writing.

CHAPTER FOUR

/1/ Käsemann and Betz detail in more depth the plight of
apocalyptic in German (and indeed in most Western) theological
and scriptural scholarship.

/2/ I have schematized this and the following description
from Hanson for easier comparison.

/3/ Ketterer speaks of "extrapolation," not expectation. I
have turned the whole matter on its head, so to speak, prefer-
ring to discuss the readers' point of view, not the writers'.
The term "disjunctive" is used to contrast with "conjunctive."
I have been helped in this regard by an article by Graydon F.
Snyder. Snyder uses the phrase "radically disjunctive" to
describe the eschatology of Jesus and Paul.

/4/   Below it is argued that apocalyptic allows the present to exercise a critical function in relation to promise and future, thus creating a dialectic. Here I am indebted to Lamb for a discussion of the attempt by political theology to articulate the "foundations of theology in a future-oriented present praxis capable of integrating a critical mediation of both from the past into the present and from the present into the future" (1978a:57). Lamb later writes, "The critical presence of the future in the present is the openness of the present to the radically new" (64). See also Metz (1972) and Moltmann (1975:102-06).

/5/   Asimov's famous "Three Laws of Robotics" also appear to be a wish-fulfillment, a promise made to a consciousness which sees the present only as a hopeless morass of moral quibblings, to be set straight by a modified decalogue trimmed by science to just three laws. The Laws read:

1. A robot may not injure a human being, or, through inaction, allow a human being to come to harm.
2. A robot must obey the orders given it by human beings except where such orders would conflict with the First Law.
3. A robot must protect its own existence as long as such protection does not conflict with the First or Second Law.

/6/   While reading Toffler's *Future Shock*, for example, it struck me that here was a contemporary "Pilgrim's Progress." But after wandering through the slough of "future shock," the present pilgrim is left only to his/her own devices: there is no salvation except through an act of the will, forcing the person to "see" reality differently. Toffler's current *The Third Wave* suffers from the same fault.

CHAPTER FIVE

/1/   Cox makes this point in his book (226-27). But see also Baum (74-76).

/2/   See Lamb (1977) for a discussion of "truncated" enlightenments. See also Horkheimer and Adorno, and Gilkey (1977) for discussion of the inner limits of modern, rational enlightenments.

/3/   Huston Smith, Theodore Roszak, and Jacques Ellul, for example, all explore the compelling immediacy of popular religion. This immediacy, to be sure, is not always a positive feature; there are often negative dimensions to it. Thus the inclusion of Ellul's *The New Demons*.

WORKS CONSULTED

Aldiss, Brian W.
1974   *Billion Year Spree: The True History of Science Fiction.* New York: Schocken.

1975   "Magic and Bare Boards," *Hell's Cartographers*. Brian W. Aldiss and Harry Harrison, eds. New York: Harper & Row.

Alves, Ruben
1974   *A Theology of Human Hope.* St. Meinrad: Abbey Press.

Amis, Kingsley
1960   *New Maps of Hell.* New York: Harcourt and Brace.

Ash, Brian
1975   *Faces of the Future.* New York: Taplinger.

Asimov, Isaac
1969   *Nightfall and Other Stories.* Greenwich: Fawcett Crest.

1972   *The Early Asimov.* Garden City: Doubleday.

1974   *Before the Golden Age.* Garden City: Doubleday.

Bailey, J. O.
1972   *Pilgrims through Space and Time.* Westport: Greenwood Press.

Baring-Gould, W. S.
1946   "Little Supermen, What Now?" *Harpers* (September):283-88.

Barrett, C. K.
1961   *The New Testament Background.* New York: Harper.

Baum, Gregory
1975   *Religion and Alienation.* New York: Paulist Press.

Becker, Carl
1963   *The Heavenly City of the 18th Century Philosophers.* New Haven: Yale University Press.

Berdyaev, Nicolas
1952   *The Beginning and the End.* London: Geoffrey Bles.

Bestor, Alfred
1964   "Science Fiction and the Renaissance Man," *The Science Fiction Novel: Imagination and Social Criticism.* Basil Davenport, ed. Chicago: Advent.

Betz, Hans Dieter
1969   "On the Problem of the Religio-Historical Understanding of Apocalypticism," *Apocalypticism: Journal for Theology and Church* 6. Robert Funk, ed. New York.

Blish, James (writing as William Atheling, Jr.)
1964   *The Issue at Hand.* Chicago: Advent.

Bloch, Ernst
1970   *Man on His Own.* New York: Herder and Herder.

Bova, Ben
1974   "The Role of Science Fiction," *Science Fiction: Today and Tomorrow.* Reginald Bretnor, ed. Baltimore: Penguin.

Braaten, Carl
1972   *Christ and Counter-Christ: Apocalyptic Themes in Theology and Culture.* Philadelphia: Fortress.

Buber, Martin
1957   *Pointing the Way.* New York: Harper & Row.
1960   *The Prophetic Faith.* New York: Harper.

de Camp, L. Sprague
1975   *Science Fiction Handbook.* Philadelphia: Owlswick.

Campbell, John W., Jr.
1953   "The Place of Science Fiction in the Modern World," *Modern Science Fiction.* Reginald Bretnor, ed. New York: Coward-McCann.
1966   *Collected Editorials from Analog.* Harry Harrison, ed. Garden City: Doubleday.

Campbell, Joseph
1970   "Mythological Themes in Creative Literature and Art," *Myths, Dreams, and Religion.* Joseph Campbell, ed. New York: Dutton.

Canary, Robert H.
1975   "New Worlds for Old?" *Science Fiction Studies* 2:130-33.

Charles, R.
1913   *The Apocrypha and Pseudepigrapha of the Old Testament*, II. Oxford: Oxford University Press.

Cioranescu, A.
1972   *L'avenir du passé*. Paris: Gallimard.

Clareson, Thomas P.
1971   "The Other Side of Realism," *SF: The Other Side of Realism*. Thomas D. Clareson, ed. Bowling Green: Bowling Green University Press.
1977   *Many Futures, Many Worlds*. ed. Kent: Kent State University Press.

Clarke, Arthur C.
1964   *Profiles of the Future*. New York: Bantam.

Cohn, Norman
1961   *The Pursuit of the Millennium*. New York: Harper.

Collins, J. J.
1974   "Apocalyptic Eschatology as the Transcendence of Death." *Catholic Biblical Quarterly* 36:21-43.
1977   *The Apocalyptic Vision of the Book of Daniel*. Missoula: Scholars Press.

Cox, Harvey
1973   *The Seduction of the Spirit: The Use and Misuse of People's Religion*. New York: Simon and Schuster.

Crossan, John Dominic
1975   *The Dark Interval*. Niles: Argus Communications.

Culler, Jonathan
1975   *Structuralist Poetics*. Ithaca: Cornell University Press.

Dane, Clemence
1936   "American Fairy Tale." *North American Review* 242:143-52.

Dickson, Paul
1972   *Think Tanks*. New York: Ballantine.

Ellul, Jacques
1964   *The Technological Society*. New York: Vintage.
1975   *The New Demons*. New York: Seabury.

Farmer, Philip Jose
    1975   *Doc Savage: His Apocalyptic Life.* New
                         York: Ballantine.

Festinger, Leon, et al.
    1964   *When Prophecy Fails.* New York: Harper.

Feuer, Lewis S., ed.
    1959   *Marx and Engels: Basic Writings on
                         Politics and Philosophy.* Garden City:
                         Anchor.

Fiedler, Leslie, ed.
    1975   *In Dreams Awake.* New York: Laurel.

Finer, S. A.
    1954   "A Profile of Science Fiction." *Socio-
                         logical Review* NS 2:239-56.

Fiorenza, Francis
    1977   "Political Theology as Foundational
                         Theology." *CTSA Proceedings* 32:142-77.

Franklin, H. Bruce
    1966   *Future Perfect.* New York: Oxford
                         University Press.

Frei, Hans W.
    1974   *The Eclipse of Biblical Narrative.*
                         New Haven: Yale University Press.

Fromm, Erich
    1966   *You Shall be as Gods.* New York: Fawcett
                         Books.

Frost, S. B.
    1952   *Old Testament Apocalyptic.* London:
                         Epworth.

Frye, Northrop
    1970   *The Stubborn Structure.* Ithaca: Cornell
                         University Press.
    1971a   *Anatomy of Criticism.* Princeton:
                         Princeton University Press.
    1971b   *The Critical Path.* Bloomington:
                         Indiana University Press.
    1976   *The Secular Scripture.* Cambridge:
                         Harvard University Press.

Gans, Herbert
    1974   *Popular Culture and High Culture.* New
                         York: Basic Books.

Gibbs, Angelica
    1943   "Onward and Upward with the Arts:
                         Inertrum, Netronium, Chromaloy, P-P-Prut."
                         New Yorker (February 13):42ff.

Gilkey, Langdon
1969   *Naming the Whirlwind: The Renewal of
                    God-Language.* Indianapolis: Bobbs
                    and Merrill.
1977   *Reaping the Whirlwind.* New York: Sea-
                    bury.

Glass, Bentley
1957   "The Scientist in Contemporary Fiction."
                    Scientific Monthly 85:188-93.

Gougard, Henri
1974   *Démons et Merveilles de la Science
                    Fiction.* Paris: Julliard.

Greeley, Andrew
1977   "When Religion Cast off Wonder, Holly-
                    wood Seized It." *The New York Times*:
                    November 27.

Guiterrez, Gustavo
1973   *A Theology of Liberation.* Maryknoll:
                    Orbis.

Gunn, Giles B.
1975   "Threading the Eye of the Needle."
                    JAAR 43:164-84.

Gunn, James
1974   "Science Fiction and the Mainstream,"
                    Science Fiction: Today and Tomorrow.
                    Reginald Bretnor, ed. Baltimore:
                    Penguin.
1975   *Alternate Worlds.* Englewood Cliffs:
                    Prentice-Hall.

Hanson, Paul D.
1975   *The Dawn of Apocalyptic.* Philadelphia:
                    Fortress.

Hartley, Margaret L.
1953   "Is Science Fiction Subversive?" *South-
                    west Review* 38:244-50.

Heilbroner, Robert
1961   *The Future as History.* New York: Grove
                    Press.
1975   *An Inquiry into the Human Prospect.*
                    New York: Norton.

Heinlein, Robert
1951   *The Man Who Sold the Moon.* New York:
                    Signet.

Hillegas, Mark R.
    1967a   *The Future as Nightmare*. New York:
                     Oxford University Press.
    1967b   "The Course in Science Fiction: A Hope
                     Deferred." *Extrapolation* IX:18-26.
    1974   "Second Thoughts on the Course in
                     Science Fiction," *Science Fiction: The
                     Academic Awakening*. Willis E. McNelly,
                     ed. CEA Chapbook.

Hirsch, Walter
    1958   "The Image of the Scientist in Science
                     Fiction: A Content Analysis." *American
                     Journal of Sociology* 63:506-12.

Horkheimer, Max and Theodor W. Adorno
    1972   *Dialectic of Enlightenment*. New York:
                     Seabury.

Horowitz, Irving L.
    1977   *Ideology and Utopia in the United
                     States: 1956-1976*. New York: Oxford
                     University Press.

Illich, Ivan
    1978   *Toward a History of Needs*. New York:
                     Pantheon Books.

Jewett, Robert and John Shelton Lawrence
    1977   *The American Monomyth*. Garden City:
                     Doubleday.

Johnson, Roger A.
    1974   *The Origins of Demythologizing*.
                     Leiden: E. J. Brill.

Kagarlitski, Julius
    1971   "Realism and Fantasy," *SF: The Other
                     Side of Realism*. Thomas D. Clareson,
                     ed. Bowling Green: Bowling Green
                     University Press.

Käsemann, Ernst
    1969   "The Beginnings of Christian Theology,"
                     *Apocalypticism: Journal for Theology
                     and Church* 6. Robert Funk, ed. New
                     York.

Kermode, Frank
    1967   *The Sense of an Ending*. New York:
                     Oxford University Press.

Ketterer, David
    1974   *New Worlds for Old: The Apocalyptic
                     Imagination, Science Fiction, and
                     American Literature*. Garden City:
                     Anchor.

Kilby, Clyde S.
1969
"Meaning in *The Lord of the Rings*," *Shadows of the Imagination*. Mark R. Hillegas, ed. Carbondale: University of Southern Illinois Press.

King, J. Norman
1977
"Theology, Science Fiction, and Man's Future Orientation," *Many Futures, Many Worlds*. Thomas D. Clareson, ed. Kent: Kent State University Press.

Knight, Damon
1967
In Search of Wonder. Chicago: Advent.

Koch, Klaus
1970
The Rediscovery of Apocalyptic. Naperville: Allenson.

Kornbluth, Cyril
1964
"The Failure of the Science Fiction Novel as Social Criticism," *The Science Fiction Novel*. Basil Davenport, ed. Chicago: Advent.

Kuhns, William
1971
The Post-Industrial Prophets: Interpretations of Technology. New York: Harper.

Lamb, Matthew L.
1977
"A Response (II) to Bernard Lonergan." *CTSA Proceedings* 32:22-30.
1978a
History, Method, and Theology. Missoula: Scholars Press.
1978b
"Dogme, Expérience et Théologie Politique," *Révélation et Expérience*. E. Schillebeeckx and Bas van Iersel, eds. Paris: *Concilium* 133:99-111.

Lanternari, Vittorio
1963
The Religions of the Oppressed. New York: Alfred Knopf.

Lasky, Melvin
1976
Utopia and Revolution. Chicago: University of Chicago Press.

van Leewen, Arend T.
1968
Prophecy in a Technocratic Era. New York: Charles Scribners.

Levi-Strauss, Claude
1963
Structural Anthropology. New York: Basic Books.
1966
The Savage Mind. Chicago: University of Chicago Press.

C. S. Lewis
    1966   *Of Other Worlds*. New York: Harcourt,
                    Brace, and World.

Lonergan, Bernard
    1972   *Method in Theology*. New York: Herder
                    and Herder.

Maguire, Daniel C.
    1978   *The Moral Choice*. New York: Doubleday.

Mandel, Siegfried, and Peter Fingesten
    1955   "The Myth of Science Fiction." *Saturday
                    Review* August 27:7-8.

Mannheim, Karl
    n.d.   *Ideology and Utopia*. New York: Harvest
                    Books.

May, John R.
    1972   *Toward a New Earth: Apocalypse in the
                    American Novel*. Notre Dame: Notre Dame
                    University Press.

McHale, John
    1971   *The Future of the Future*. New York:
                    Ballantine.

McLuhan, Marshall
    1966   *Understanding Media: The Extensions of
                    Man*. New York: Signet.

McNelly, Willis E.
    1974   *Science Fiction: The Academic Awakening*.
                    CEA Chapbook.

Metz, J. B.
    1969   *Theology of the World*. New York: Herder
                    and Herder.
    1972   "The Future in the Memory of Suffering."
                    Concilium 76. New York: Paulist.
    1973   "A Short Apology for Narrative." *Con-
                    cilium* 83. New York: Paulist.
    1977   "Redemption and Emancipation." Matthew
                    L. Lamb, trans. *Cross Currents* Fall:
                    321-36.
    1978   "For a Renewed Church before a New
                    Council: A Concept in Four Theses,"
                    *Toward Vatican III: The Work That Needs
                    to be Done*. David Tracy, ed. New York:
                    Seabury.

Moltmann, Jürgen
    1969   *Religion, Revolution and the Future*.
                    New York: Charles Scribners.
    1970   "Theology as Eschatology," *The Future of
                    Hope*. Frederick Herzog, ed. New York:
                    Herder and Herder.

1975   *Theology of Hope*. New York: Harper.

Moskowitz, Sam
     1963   *Explorers of the Infinite*. Cleveland:
                              World.
     1966   *Seekers of Tomorrow*. Cleveland: World.
     1968   *Science Fiction by Gaslight*. Cleveland:
                              World.
     1970   *"Under the Moons of Mars"*. New York:
                              Holt, Rinehart, and Winston.
     1976   *Strange Horizons*. New York: Charles
                              Scribners.

Mumford, Lewis
     1972   *The Transformations of Man*. New York:
                              Harper.

Nozick, Robert
     1974   *Anarchy, State, and Utopia*. New York:
                              Basic Books.

Ommen, Thomas
     1978   "Verification in Theology: A Tension in
                              Revisionist Method." Marquette Univer-
                              sity: unpublished.

Parrington, Vernon Louis, Jr.
     1964   *American Dreams*. New York: Russell
                              and Russell.

Peters, Ted
     1977   "UFO's: The Religious Dimension."
                              Cross Currents Fall:261-78.

Philmus, Robert
     1970   *Into the Unknown*. Berkeley: University
                              of California Press.

Plattel, Martin
     1972   *Utopian and Critical Thinking*. Pitts-
                              burgh: Duquesne University Press.

Ploger, Otto
     1968   *Theocracy and Eschatology*. Richmond:
                              John Knox.

Pohl, Frederik
     1978   *The Way the Future Was: A Memoir*. New
                              York: Ballantine.

Rabkin, Eric S.
     1976   *The Fantastic in Literature*. Princeton:
                              Princeton University Press.

von Rad, Gerhard
     1965   *Old Testament Theology* II. New York:
                              Harper & Row.

Richards, I. A.
1926   *Principles of Literary Criticism*. New
                       York: Harcourt, Brace and Co.

Ricoeur, Paul
1969   *The Symbolism of Evil*. Boston: Beacon
                       Books.

Roszak, Theodore
1975   *Unfinished Animal*. New York: Harper &
                       Row.

Rottensteiner, Franz
1975   *The Science Fiction Book: An Illustrated
                       History*. New York: Seabury.

Rowley, H. H.
1944   *The Relevance of Apocalyptic*. London:
                       Lutterworth.

Russell, D. S.
1969   *The Method and Message of Jewish Apoca-
                       lyptic*. London: SCM Press.

Schaftel, Oscar
1953   "The Social Content of Science Fiction."
                       Science and Society 17:97-118.

Schmithals, Walter
1975   *The Apocalyptic Movement: Introduction
                       and Interpretation*. Nashville: Abingdon.

Scholes, Robert
1974   *Structuralism in Literature*. New Haven:
                       Yale University Press.
1975   *Structural Fabulation*. Notre Dame: Notre
                       Dame University Press.
_____ and Eric S. Rabkin
1977   *Science Fiction: History, Science, Vision*.
                       New York: Oxford University Press.

Scott, Nathan
1973   "'New Heav'ns, New Earth'--The Landscape
                       of Contemporary Apocalypse." *Journal of
                       Religion* 53:1-35.

Sisk, John P.
1971   "The Future of Prediction," *Science
                       Fiction: The Future*. Dick Allen, ed.
                       New York: Harcourt, Brace, Jovanovich.

Skinner, B. F.
1946   *Walden Two*. Toronto: Macmillan.

Smith, Huston
1976   *Forgotten Truth: The Primordial
                       Tradition*. New York: Harper.

Snyder, Graydon F.
1969   "The Literalization of the Apocalyptic Form in the New Testament Church." *Biblical Research* XIV:5-18.

Spinrad, Norman, ed.
1974   *Modern Science Fiction.* New York: Anchor.

Suvin, Darko
1976   "On the Poetics of the Science Fiction Genre," *Science Fiction: A Collection of Critical Essays.* Mark Rose, ed. Englewood Cliffs: Spectrum.

Thrupp, Sylvia, ed.
1970   *Millennial Dreams in Action.* Schocken.

Toffler, Alvin
1975   "Forword," *Cultures Beyond the Earth: The Role of Anthropology in Outer Space.* M. Marayama and A. Haskins, eds. New York: Vintage.

Tolkien, J. R. R.
1965   *Tree and Leaf.* Boston: Houghton Mifflin.

Tracy, David
1975   *Blessed Rage for Order.* New York: Seabury.

Urang, Gunnar
1969   "Tolkien's Fantasy: The Phenomenology of Hope," *Shadows of the Imagination.* Mark R. Hillegas, ed. Carbondale: University of Southern Illinois Press.

Vielhauer, P.
1965   "Apocalypses and Related Subjects," *New Testament Apocrypha* II. Hennecke and Schneemelcher, eds. Philadelphia: Westminster.

Warner, Harry
1969   *All Our Yesterdays.* Chicago: Advent.

Wilder, Amos
1931   "The Nature of Jewish Eschatology." *Journal of Biblical Literature* 50: 210-16.

Wollheim, Donald
1971   *The Universe Makers.* New York: Harper & Row.

INDEX

Italicized page numbers indicate critical discussion
of author's work and ideas.

245